Senator Alan Bible

and the Politics of the New West

To my Good Friend Diana. Sorry there was no parade

Best wishes, Happy Reading, and all of that. Your great =

Paul

United States Senator Alan Bible. (Bible family collection)

GARY E. ELLIOTT

Senator Alan Bible and the Politics of the New West

University of Nevada Press Reno Las Vegas London

Winner of the Wilbur S. Shepperson Humanities Book Award for 1994

This book is the recipient of the Wilbur S. Shepperson Humanities Book Award, which is given annually in his memory by the Nevada Humanities Committee and the University of Nevada Press. One of Nevada's most distinguished historians, Wilbur S. Shepperson was a founding board member and long-time supporter of both organizations.

Wilbur S. Shepperson Series in History and Humanities No. 36
Series Editor: Jerome E. Edwards
A list of books in the series follows the index.

University of Nevada Press
Reno, Nevada 89557 USA

Cover design by Heather Goulding

The paper used in this book meets the requirements of American National Standard for Information Sciences—Permanence of Paper for Printed Library Materials, ANSI Z 39.48-1984. Binding materials were selected for strength and durability.

Photographs from the Alan Bible Collection, the Bible family collection, and the Eva Adams Collection are all housed in the Special Collections Department, Getchell Library, University of Nevada, Reno.

CIP data at end of book

9 8 7 6 5 4 3 2 1

To the memory of Wilda and David "Shorty" Elliott

Rest in peace

Contents

Foreword

Serving with Alan Bible in the U.S. Senate, I gained great respect for his knowledge and his integrity.

As a senior senator when I arrived in Washington in 1968, Alan Bible gave me much more help than many senators in my own party.

He was, I believe, the consummate senator. Dignified and efficient, with a lively sense of humor, he worked without seeking public recognition. Alan was attentive to his constituents, but never forgot the needs of our nation as a whole.

Working with Alan Bible was a pleasure. Fair-minded, and a skilled public servant, he studied the issues carefully, paid close attention to arguments on both sides, and tried to do what was right for America.

During the long consideration of the Alaska pipeline, Alan Bible listened to every word of debate on the Senate floor. He made up his mind on the basis of that debate. Few senators ever do that. Alan questioned me carefully and at length, seeking clarification on many details before he voted in favor of Alaska's great project. The vote was 49 to grant right-of-way for our pipeline and 48 against. Alan Bible truly made the difference to me on the critical vote of my Senate career.

I served with him on the Senate Interior Committee and the Appropriations Committee and admired his pioneering efforts in guiding the National Park Service through its greatest period of growth.

We also worked together, with Nancy Hanks, to begin the concept of challenge grants to restore our national arts efforts.

He was responsible for countless bills which led to the development and preservation of our national heritage. I served in the Interior Department during the Eisenhower Administration and worked with Conrad Wirth to plan Mission 66, President Eisenhower's dream to upgrade our parks in a ten-year period of renewal. Americans who visit our national parks and take pleasure in their scenic and recreational facilities will always owe a debt of gratitude to Senator Bible for what he did to make Mission 66 a successful crusade.

Alan Bible was essential to the economic development of our western states in the 1960s and 1970s. He worked tirelessly on water projects, min-

ing legislation, and federal highway construction programs for the West and
Northwest.

As a senator from the West, Alan had a special feeling for the land and for
westerners who knew how to use it. He personally understood the diverse
land-use issues that came before our Interior Committee. And, as chairman
of the Interior Appropriations Subcommittee, Senator Bible made sure that
Congress funded the commitments it made to the Park Service, Bureau of
Mines, Forest Service, and other land and recreation programs.

As an Alaskan, I am especially grateful to Alan Bible for being a champion
of our statehood effort when it wasn't popular to be in favor of a forty-ninth
star on our flag. After my state was devastated by the 1964 Good Friday
Earthquake—the worst ever to hit our nation—he worked hard to help us
recover quickly. A few years later he joined me in the fight in a Senate conference committee to approve the Alaska Native Claims Settlement Act, which
brought to an end a battle which had lasted over a hundred years.

When Alan resigned, he terminated his Senate service before the end of
the 93rd Congress so that his successor—Senator Paul Laxalt, who would sit
on the other side of the Senate aisle—could be sworn in early so that Nevada
would gain a measure of seniority in the 94th Congress.

Alan Bible gave much to our nation without asking for applause. He made
sure his people in Nevada were not forgotten. He commanded the respect of
our whole national government through his gentle manner, his hard work,
and his fairness. He left a great heritage, but he never asked to be recognized
for his accomplishments.

This volume will go a long way toward ensuring that Alan Bible's contributions to Nevada and Nevadans and to all Americans won't be forgotten.
My friend deserves an honored place in the history of our nation. These
chapters put the spotlight on his achievements, giving him recognition that
he avoided during his years of public service.

As you read this, it is my hope that you will come to know Alan Bible as
we in the Senate did; if you do, you will realize he was a true statesman.

Those of us who knew him and worked by his side had a valued friend in
Nevada's senior senator.

Ted Stevens
U.S. Senator
State of Alaska

Acknowledgments

This book is largely the product of two related events. Early in 1985, while I was teaching American history at the Community College of Southern Nevada, Professor Candace Kant persuaded me to develop a course in Nevada history. Later, while preparing for the course, I read Professor Jerome Edwards's book, *Pat McCarran: Political Boss of Nevada*. Aside from being interested in McCarran's colorful, and often outrageous, public statements, I was struck by the many references to his successor—Alan Bible. A year later I found myself pursuing a Ph.D. degree at Northern Arizona University. My committee chairman, Professor Monte Poen, is a no-nonsense academician who immediately pressed me for a dissertation topic. After some indecision and preliminary research, I discovered that Senator Bible's papers were readily available and that he was living in nearby California. Thus began a seven-year trek through more cartons of documents and papers than I care to recall.

Alan Harvey Bible served Nevada for twenty years in the United States Senate, from 1954 to 1974. During that time he unashamedly sought federal dollars for every conceivable project and plan that would bolster Nevada's economy. Every section of the state bears the imprint of his effectiveness, from Lake Tahoe in the North to Lake Mead in the South. He was the author and moving force behind legislation that brought millions of dollars to Nevada for water projects, recreational facilities, improved roadways and airports, flood control, waste treatment plants, electrical power, and advanced mining facilities, which improved the living conditions of thousands of Nevadans. In 1974, when he was at the peak of his power in the Senate, ill health forced his retirement. He died on September 12, 1988, fourteen years after leaving the Senate.

While Bible concerned himself primarily with Nevada's welfare and often considered himself an ambassador for the Silver State, he had a profound impact on land-use policy, particularly in the West. As he evolved into a leading advocate for recreationists in the post–World War II period, he shepherded the development and expansion of the national park system. Late in his career Bible played a key role in the preservation of millions of acres of pristine land in Alaska, his greatest legislative triumph affecting the national interest.

Constraints of space and length prohibited an in-depth treatment of all areas of Bible's legislative career. His chairmanship of the Committee on the District of Columbia is worthy of a separate book. For historians concerned with the civil rights movement and urban development in the 1960s—and with the nation's capital, which heretofore has received only limited coverage—that committee's papers provide a rich source of primary material. Other omissions include the Senate Select Committee on Small Business Administration and the Joint Congressional Committee on Atomic Energy, neither of which formed the focus of his legislative agenda. Land, water, and mining issues were his primary concerns for the better part of his twenty years in the Senate, and they are the focus of this study.

This book has taken many forms over the years, and I have been assisted by many helpful hands. Between 1986 and 1988 I spent more than forty hours interviewing Senator Bible, who was always cheerful and pleasant, despite his poor health. His wife, Loucile Bible, assisted me in many ways. I am grateful for the materials she provided and for her kindness. More importantly, she never tried to influence my opinions of the senator's career. Additionally, Bob McDonald and Jack Carpenter, longtime aides and associates of Senator Bible, provided valuable insights which prevented me from stumbling into grievous errors of fact and interpretation. Whatever errors remain are entirely my own responsibility.

I wish to single out for special thanks several people who helped me in the formulation of the final draft of the book. Senator Ted Stevens found the time to write the foreword despite his enormous legislative agenda, and Dwight Dyer assisted in that effort. Governor Mike O'Callaghan, Governor Grant Sawyer, and Senator Howard Cannon gave their time and support in many ways. Dr. Fred Anderson, George Hartzog, Jr., and Gordon Rice provided insight into the complex personality of Senator Bible.

Professor Robert Dallek, University of California at Los Angeles, found the time and willingness to help in the final hectic days of editing. Professor Jerome Edwards, University of Nevada, Reno, provided helpful suggestions since our first meeting in 1986 and continued to be the single most important inspiration for the publication of this book.

Chester Smith spent many hours of his time and energy providing materials and facts to ensure that the manuscript was as historically accurate as possible. I will always be grateful.

To my colleagues and friends I owe a special debt of gratitude. Professors Monte Poen, David Strate, George Lubick, Leonard Ritt, and William Burke of Northern Arizona University provided great encouragement and support over the years. Michael Green read this manuscript in many forms and offered criticisms and suggestions that greatly enhanced the final product. This book would not have been possible without his advice, judgment, and vast knowledge of Nevada history. He has been a valued and trusted friend in more ways than I deserve or had a right to expect. Lastly, Carol Cox's good humor and kindness made this task much easier than it would have been otherwise.

Many others have contributed in different but nonetheless important ways. I especially want to thank Robert E. Blesse and his staff at Special Collections, Getchell Library of the University of Nevada, Reno, for their courtesy and thoughtfulness. Without their assistance, my job would have been much more difficult. Thomas R. Radko, Nicholas M. Cady, Sandy J. Crooms, and Sara Vélez Mallea made it a pleasure to be associated with the University of Nevada Press. They were all so helpful that I cannot begin to thank them. To those I have failed to mention, my sincere thanks and apologies. Finally, my wife, Debbie, and my daughter, Kimberly, have exercised more patience and understanding than I would have done—thank you.

Introduction

In 1982 Peter Wiley and Robert Gottlieb made a major contribution to the scholarship and historiography of the West in *Empires in the Sun: The Rise of the New American West*. In their introduction they borrow a line from *All the President's Men*, when Deep Throat tells Bob Woodward to "follow the money." The phrase is also applicable to the West in the post–World War II era: follow the money trail from Washington, D.C., to the western rivers and waterways and behold the transformation from colonial outpost to empire. The Southwest has made impressive gains since the end of World War II. It is now, in many ways, the predominant region of the United States. With one-eighth of the members of the House of Representatives, California has become the nation's most important state. The whole region has been built on federal water and power projects that are following the water, the resources, and the migratory trails. An examination of the index to *Empires in the Sun* shows no reference to Alan Bible. Bible might not have minded this, for he craved anonymity outside the Senate. Yet he played a critical (if usually behind-the-scenes) role in developing the postwar empire that is the American Southwest.

By constitutional design and institutional evolution, the U.S. Senate has become the guardian of states' rights. While this process began well before the distribution of New Deal funds in the 1930s, it accelerated in the 1950s, when a large number of senators came to Washington, D.C., with backgrounds as governors and state legislators. Acutely aware of the economic problems their states faced in the post–World War II era, they were determined to use the federal treasury to relieve the distress. Less-populous states like Nevada probably benefited the most from these pork-barrel projects. Their representation in the Senate was the same as that of the large states, but they accumulated power and rewards for their constituents through seniority, committee chairmanships, and old-fashioned horse-trading. This enhanced their special economic interests beyond their overall importance to the nation's economy as a whole, just as it enhanced the power of their senators.

Alan Harvey Bible was a typical western senator of his era. He grew up amid the sandy sagebrush of the Great Basin, which molded his character and formed the basis of his political beliefs. Shortly after graduating from the University of Nevada in 1930, Bible struck out for Georgetown Law School in Washington, D.C. Here, in 1933, he enountered newly elected Democratic senator Patrick A. McCarran, destined to become Nevada's political boss. McCarran helped the young Nevadan obtain a part-time job as a Senate elevator operator, and so began a relationship that lasted two decades, until McCarran's death in 1954. As his successor, Bible emerged briefly from McCarran's long shadow, only to be obscured again by the conformity demanded by the Senate and its Democratic leader—Lyndon Baines Johnson.

Bible's political career began with his appointment as the district attorney of Storey County and his subsequent election to that office in 1936. He was appointed deputy attorney general in 1938, then elected attorney general in 1942 and again in 1946. Like so many of his future Senate colleagues, Bible came of age as a state official when the western states confronted a perplexing variety of postwar economic problems. Moreover, Bible's political tutelage under McCarran and his own experience in the attorney general's office reinforced his belief that "all politics is local." He accepted the political wisdom of his mentor that Nevada, and the needs of its constituents, superseded all other political or economic considerations. He learned the arts of horse-trading and compromise long before he succeeded McCarran as a U.S. senator.

When Bible entered the Senate in 1955, an institutional revolution was in the making. The states of the semiarid West were poised to take advantage of their overrepresentation to legislate economic expansion through a vast and expensive system of reclamation projects, and Bible readily joined in the pork-barreling. His Senate career is largely the story of water projects, mining legislation, land and resource development, parks and recreation expansion, wilderness protection, and the fight to preserve a state veto against perceived encroachment by the federal government. For Bible and many other western political leaders and policymakers, federalism was simple and straightforward: the federal government would provide financial support for economic expansion in the western states with no strings attached. A dispute was inevitable, and the battleground was state versus federal water rights. For twenty years Bible labored in support of state water rights as articulated in the 1902 Reclamation Act, the top legislative achievement of another Nevadan, Francis G. Newlands.

Indeed, Bible built his political career on water development issues, the area in which he scored his most impressive victories. In his eight years as Nevada's attorney general, Bible became the state's leading expert in the complicated legal field of western water rights. He represented Nevada's Colorado River Commission and later the state's vital interest in the landmark Supreme Court case of *Arizona* v. *California* (1963), which clarified the question of state water rights to the Colorado River. Bible wasted no time in staking out Nevada's water interest during his freshman year in the Senate. He took advantage of the Upper Colorado River Storage Act—the brainchild of another western Democratic senator, Clinton Anderson of New Mexico—to advance power development in southern Nevada. Later, he shepherded the Washoe Project through Congress to develop northern Nevada's water resources for agricultural, municipal, and recreational use.

But his greatest triumph was the Southern Nevada Water Project, which allowed Nevada to develop its 300,000 acre-feet of water from the annual flow of the Colorado River. The project's success is a tribute to his personal and political skills, which were sorely tested over the nearly ten years it took to design the project and pass the legislation. As the primary force behind Clark County's emergence as Nevada's dominant political entity, the project triggered the phenomenal economic and population explosion in southern Nevada.

The development of western mining and water resources formed the twin pillars of Bible's political life. In contrast to his record in water development, however, he encountered far less success in his legislative agenda for mining. He became a spokesman for western mining interests and tried unsuccessfully to enact a national minerals policy that would curtail imports while underwriting exploration and development with federal dollars. Still, he achieved modest gains in helping western mining interests as a member of the Public Land Law Review Commission and through modifications of the 1964 Wilderness Act. Bible also used his political clout as a member of the Senate Appropriations Committee to aid Nevada's slumping mining industry by keeping the research center in Boulder City operating despite annual efforts by the Bureau of Mines to close the operation. But his tremendous expenditure of time and energy brought precious few accomplishments.

Other issues involving natural resource management commanded center stage in the 1950s and 1960s, and Bible was an influential force throughout his career. When ill health diminished the energies of Clinton Anderson, the Senate's acknowledged leader on environmental issues, Henry "Scoop" Jackson (D-Washington) assumed leadership of the Interior and Insular Affairs Committee, and Bible took control of the Parks and Recreation Subcommittee. For a decade Bible's leadership resulted in the greatest expansion of parks, historical monuments, and recreation areas in American history. Through such legislative achievements he left an everlasting imprint on the lives of millions of Americans.

Bible was an important if anonymous player in the "green decade." The environmental movement of the 1960s is poorly defined, with confusing boundaries and conflicting and overlapping constituencies that have been variously described as conservationists, preservationists, and recreationists. Although all three groups were sometimes on the same side of an issue, Bible most often could be found advancing the cause of recreationists, partly because of the economic benefits to local communities and partly because he believed that use and preservation could co-exist. He was convinced that national parks helped local communities by attracting federal dollars, while at the same time preserving America's scenic wonders and vanishing landscape. Yet the proliferation of commercial ventures inside the national parks was disturbing enough for him to try to legislate reforms in the licensing of concessionaires. The park service virtually ignored him. Today the national parks are in danger of destruction by commercial forces, which Bible first helped to advance and then sought to hinder. Still, he is largely the one to thank for a legacy of expansion and improvement of the national park system. It remains for another generation of legislators to preserve what he helped to create nearly three decades ago.

While parks and recreation remained his primary committee focus, Bible also played a key role in preserving millions of acres of pristine land in Alaska. In 1972, when the House Interior and Insular Affairs Committee turned down the Alaska Native Claims Act, Bible took up the challenge in the Senate. After an extensive tour of the state, he introduced section 17(d) (2) of the act, which set aside eighty million acres for parks, wildlife, forest service, and wilderness protection. Moreover, Bible provided for a five-year grace period to study these plans, giving all interest groups a voice in the final disposition of America's last frontier. Some would have preferred greater wilderness protection; others sought a wider use of natural resources to advance the cause of economic expansion. The result was vintage Bible: a compromise which protected the federal government's interest in preservation, use, and exploration and recognized Alaska's property rights and desire to exploit its rich storehouse of natural resources.

Like his approach to natural resource policy, Bible's Senate career as a whole emphasized balance and compromise, lessons learned from McCarran and reinforced by Lyndon Johnson. Bible deeply admired Johnson, and his critics labeled him a rubber stamp for Great Society measures. While he believed in and supported an activist government that would improve the quality of life in America, Bible also realized that "to get along, you go along." To incur Johnson's legendary wrath could be dangerous indeed. Bible's fifteen-year relationship with Johnson as Senate majority leader, as vice-president, and finally as president resulted in enormous economic benefits for Nevada and personal rewards for its senior senator. With Johnson's support, Bible became a member of the Senate's "inner club" and an influential member on the Appropriations Committee. Throughout his career Bible carried the LBJ banner.

For most of his career Bible worked in the shadows of the cloakrooms and committee rooms of the Senate, where tradeoffs, compromises, and bargains were a way of life. He was not a national figure because he never strayed far from the Nevada reservation or broke the rules of the Senate "club"; he quietly supported civil rights legislation and the Vietnam War during the Johnson years. Bible believed that he had been elected to advance the cause of his constituents. He always kept sight of that objective and understood that achieving it would bring support and reelection. He set a course in 1954 and maintained it for twenty years.

Although his actions clearly had a national impact, Bible represented Nevada first and foremost. His unabashed and unwavering support for massive water projects in the West and his battle to restore the western mining industry may justly be criticized. Public policies that lead to environmental deterioration are clearly dangerous, and many of Bible's actions certainly had negative consequences. Still, those who see Bible simply as a spokesman for the growth and development interests in Nevada overlook the more important aspect of his career: he understood the function of the Senate in the political process. In a pluralist society with representative government, compromise and balanced approaches to public policy are inevitable in the political tug-of-war. Bible mastered the give-and-take of politics, and his constituents benefited economically. That was his objective—to improve the economic well-being of Nevadans. In this he was unquestionably effective.

Gary E. Elliott
Las Vegas, Nevada

Chapter One

The Making of a Political Protégé

On February 16, 1974, national and state Democratic Party leaders gathered at the MGM Grand Hotel in Las Vegas to pay tribute to Alan Bible on his retirement after twenty years in the United States Senate and forty years in Nevada political and legal life. Senator Gale McGee (D-Wyoming) delivered the keynote address to an assemblage that included Democratic governor Mike O'Callaghan, former two-term Democratic governor Grant Sawyer, and Bible's Senate colleague from Nevada, Howard Cannon. Nevada Supreme Court justice John Mowbray and a host of civic, business, and union leaders from across the state also attended to honor one of the most important Nevada politicians of their generation.

Bible's senate career stretched from 1954 to 1974, a period of fundamental change in American life and near revolution in the economy, society, and politics of the West. Those who attended the gala retirement dinner came to celebrate Bible's many contributions to the economic development of this new American West and his tireless efforts in behalf of Nevada. He had accomplished at least as much as any senator in the 110-year history of the state, a considerable achievement, considering such notable Nevada political figures as William M. Stewart, Francis G. Newlands, Key Pittman, and Pat McCarran.

The circumstances that propelled Bible into positions of leadership, first in the state and then in national affairs, began with his own social and regional training. His family background, formal education, and exposure to local economic and political concerns foreshadowed many of the issues that would dominate his Senate career and mold his political philosophy.

Alan Harvey Bible was born November 20, 1909, in Lovelock, a small community of 1,400 in northwestern Nevada. As in other parts of the state, the main economic activities in Lovelock were mining and ranching. During Bible's early years farm and ranch life characterized much of Nevada: fully 83 percent of the population was rural. Reno, Nevada's largest town, remained below 20,000 until the 1930s. The state had fewer residents than any other far western state: 82,000, compared with the largest, California, with 2,378,000.[1]

Social life in the small town of Lovelock centered on the family, and by

1

all accounts the Bible household was loving and happy. Bible's father, Jacob "Jake" Harvey Bible, born in Lima, Ohio, came West in the postfrontier era to seek his fortune in gold and silver mining. After failing to strike it rich, he settled in Lovelock and took a job milking cows for a dairy farmer. He continued to prospect and patent mining claims, but eventually found more lucrative employment managing a grocery store and operating a small ranch on the outskirts of town. Like so many others who came West in search of precious metals, Jake Bible remained a miner at heart and continued throughout his life to invest small amounts of money in mining claims—a heritage he passed on to his son.

Bible's mother, Isabel Welch, the second of six children, was born on March 7, 1883, in the declining mining town of Unionville, Nevada. The Welches moved to Lovelock and owned a small cattle ranch near town. Isabel attended the University of Nevada for about two years before returning to Lovelock to become a schoolteacher. There she met Jake; in 1909 they married, a union that lasted nearly fifty years and produced two sons who were to distinguish themselves in public and military service.[2]

Jake Bible was a patient father who taught his sons to appreciate the outdoors by taking them fishing and hunting. He emphasized the need for a formal education, along with household chores and work in the family store. Isabel stressed the importance of reading and being kind to people and animals. She often told her sons, "If you can't say anything good about someone, then don't say anything," a lesson that young Alan found valuable in his adult years. It became a key to his later success in politics. When Isabel caught Alan using a whip on a horse that would not obey his commands, she forbade him to ride the animal to school for a week. The sobering experience of walking nearly five miles back and forth reinforced the virtue of being kind—at least to the family horse while mother was around.[3]

Another event added to this lesson. In 1919 a fire destroyed the Bibles' home. They lost everything, including much of the family history that Isabel had been collecting. The horrifying spectacle and the total devastation remained firmly planted in the mind of the nine-year-old Alan, contributing to his sense of sympathy for people less fortunate than himself.[4] The lives of the Bible family changed in other ways. Rather than rebuild his home in Lovelock, Jake Bible accepted an offer to buy Peoples Brothers Grocery Store in Fallon. The family moved to a new home in the center of Nevada's most impressive agricultural community. The years Bible spent growing up in the desert oasis made a permanent impression that manifested itself later in a staunch conviction that water was the key to economic development in this arid land.

This view was a central part of a Nevada political tradition. One unmistakable physical characteristic of most states west of the hundredth meridian is the semiarid landscape, and no state is more deficient in water resources than Nevada. When mineral production declined late in the nineteenth century, westerners sought to diversify their regional and local economies by freeing themselves from their dependence on mining.[5] They pleaded with the federal government to finance water development projects to irrigate crops.

No state was more persistent in this effort than Nevada. The push began in the 1880s, when Senator William M. Stewart made reclamation a campaign issue and brushed aside planning and geological considerations in his drive to obtain federal dollars for irrigation projects. Stewart's efforts failed; but by the turn of the century reclamation's time had come, spurred on by President Theodore Roosevelt, the Progressive movement, and Nevada's congressman, Francis G. Newlands. The Newlands Reclamation Act of 1902 brought federally financed water reclamation projects to the West. One of the first, in Churchill County, Nevada, gave birth to the town of Fallon. Reclamation advocates expected more than 400,000 acres to be irrigated and Fallon's population to reach about 100,000 by 1920.[6]

The demand for agricultural and livestock products during World War I sent prices soaring, and Nevada's agricultural economy boomed—but only temporarily. With the end of the war came a return to the all-too-familiar cycle of boom and bust that had weakened Nevada's mining-based economy and now did the same in the farming sector. While some sectors of the nation enjoyed the prosperity of the 1920s, Nevada's agricultural producers suffered a severe depression brought on by decreased demands and overproduction.

Still, reclamation projects expanded all over the West, producing cotton in west Texas and alfalfa in Fallon, while the plight of the western farmer grew worse. Now the dream of more water to produce more crops only meant a further glut on the market, with a corresponding decline in the price of commodities. Growing up in the heart of Nevada's alfalfa country, Bible naturally believed, like Stewart and Newlands before him, that reclamation would turn the desert into an agricultural paradise.[7] The desert did bloom, but not as the beneficiaries of the Newlands Irrigation Project imagined. In the years to come Nevada's meal ticket would be not fruits and vegetables, but casinos, hotels, motels, gas stations, fast food stands, off-road races, and other businesses tied to tourism. Bible would be in the forefront of Nevada's drive to obtain more and more water development projects, not only for agriculture, but for urban and industrial expansion.

But in 1919 water development was the furthest thing from nine-year-old Alan Bible's mind. In Fallon he continued his education at Oak Park Grammar School, a step up from the two-room schoolhouse he had attended in Lovelock. An excellent student, he readily accepted academic challenges. In the fifth grade he became a member of the class debating team, and debate remained a passion throughout his formative years. His childhood experiences contributed to his ability to analyze controversial subjects from several perspectives and to seek balance and accommodation rather than confrontation.

Bible entered Churchill County High School in 1923, continuing both his excellent scholastic record and his passion for public debate. In 1926 he won the state oratorical contest. Selected to represent Nevada in the regional finals in Los Angeles, he finished last among eight contestants, but his discouraging performance nonetheless provided what he later remembered as a "lesson in humility" amid a great deal of success.[8] A popular student, Bible twice won election to the school's highest offices: he was president of the freshman and senior classes.[9]

With family encouragement and the support of his high school principal, George McCracken, a college career was never really in doubt. Bible's father wanted him to take over the family business, which had become highly successful. His mother also urged a business career. But after working in the grocery store, often from six in the morning to early evening, Bible, who always had been more bookish than physically active, decided that a career in law was preferable to such demanding labor.[10]

Bible decided to major in economics at the University of Nevada in preparation for law school. During his freshman year he lived at the home of a high school friend, Mel Hancock, who was also a student at the university. Bible took the train home every weekend.[11]

Bible's college career was even more productive and rewarding than his high school years. In his sophomore year he joined the Lambda Chi Alpha Fraternity and took up residence in the fraternity house. Still a member of the varsity debating team, he traveled to other western universities, broadening his exposure to people and places outside Nevada. He also started writing for the school newspaper, the *Sagebrush*. In his junior year he became the paper's assistant editor and was elected class treasurer.

From his vantage point on the *Sagebrush*, Bible came into daily contact with the issues of campus life. None was more controversial than the competence of the university's president, Walter Clark. Throughout 1927 President Clark feuded with the Board of Regents, which charged him with insubordination and failing to monitor the progress of construction work on campus. By February 1929 the *Sagebrush* was demanding an end to the bickering and the completion of all of the construction projects. For good measure, the *Sagebrush* demanded that something be done about the school's losing football team, although it was by no means certain that this was due to President Clark's dereliction of duty.[12]

The controversy continued until the newspaper decided to take a stand. The *Sagebrush* editors and managers chose Bible to deliver a message to Clark—resign or else. On a cold February night Bible knocked at the door of President Clark's home. The school's highest authority shocked Bible by greeting him in a stocking cap and robe. Bible presented Clark with the *Sagebrush's* demands and an editorial calling for an investigation of his handling of campus matters. Clark took the bad news in stride while commending young Bible for doing what he thought was right under the circumstances. The editorial was published, the state legislature looked into the matter, and President Clark was cleared of all alleged wrongdoing, bringing an end to student unrest.[13]

By his senior year Bible was well entrenched in college life. As treasurer of the student body, he served on numerous committees in addition to being a member of the debate team. He continued to achieve high grades, making the honor roll for four consecutive years and earning membership in the national honor society, Phi Kappa Phi.[14] He closed his college career by avenging his high school embarrassment in the regional debating championship in Los Angeles. He defeated Gregson Bautzer, then attending the University of Southern California, in a rematch on the Reno campus by a vote of 2 to 1. Although Bible considered it a hometown decision, it was nonetheless rewarding.[15]

Far more important to Bible's future was the Progressive reform movement that dominated the first decades of the twentieth century. Like the Progressives, Bible considered an activist government working in behalf of the general welfare preferable to private-interest politics. It was entirely natural for him to embrace the principle of activist government because Progressive water legislation such as the Newlands Act had been responsible for Fallon's development and thus for his family's prosperity.

Progressive ideas about prudent land use and scientific management of the West's natural resources made sense to Bible. He shared with Theodore Roosevelt and Gifford Pinchot a belief that the West's resources had to be managed in such a way as to benefit the greatest number of people over the longest period of time. Bible would have agreed with Roosevelt's initial position on the Hetch-Hetchy dispute. The president argued that water was more important to San Francisco's welfare than the preservation of one scenic valley in Yosemite Park. Likewise, he would have supported the decision to side with Los Angeles in its drive to obtain water from the Owens Valley for municipal and agricultural purposes, in spite of the deception and questionable ethics involved. These early battles over resource development in the Progressive Era were a model for Bible's later public policy judgments as a United States senator.[16]

Despite the depression and general hard times in 1930, Bible graduated with honors and high expectations. The family business, renamed Fallon Mercantile, had expanded to include hardware and clothing in addition to groceries and now occupied a prominent position on Main Street in downtown Fallon. Bible bought a car with his savings and had enough money left over to share expenses with Mel Hancock on a tour of the United States. For several months they traveled the country, sightseeing and visiting prospective law schools. By the time they returned to Nevada both had decided to attend Georgetown Law School in Wshington, D.C. Bible resumed his employment in the family business for another eight months to save money to help with the tuition and living expenses of law school. In the fall of 1931 he and Hancock left Nevada to embark on their new careers. Although the deepening depression forced Hancock to leave school after one year, Bible remained.

During this period economic trends were developing in Nevada that Bible would view from the perspective of his childhood training, reinforced by his exposure to the local economic benefits of an activist government policy. Local concerns continued to influence his desire to specialize in mining and water law, although Georgetown offered little formal training in either.[17] But economics of another kind led him unexpectedly into Nevada politics, a subject of little interest to him before 1933.

The worsening depression compelled Bible to work part time to relieve his parents of some of the financial burden associated with his schooling, which had increased after Mel Hancock's departure. His search for employment began in March 1933 with Nevada's congressional delegation. Senator Pat McCarran's Washington office was the first to offer him a job operating an elevator in the capital building, and Bible quickly accepted it. The next day Senator Key Pittman's office offered him an identical job. He explained to Pittman's staff that it would be unfair to reject McCarran's prior offer in favor of Pittman.[18] From this early and accidental association began a friendship and political alignment that spanned two decades. Bible had hitched his political wagon to Pat McCarran. He never looked back and he never regretted it.

Bible decided his political future unaware of the long and bitter feud between McCarran and Pittman. Even more amazingly, he had no political affiliation with either major party, although his father was on friendly terms with Pittman. His interest in politics resulted directly from his association with McCarran. Although his work and studies left little time for social activities, he had enough time to learn the art and science of politics from McCarran, who later emerged as the leader of Nevada's Democratic Party.[19]

McCarran's political philosophy embodied two basic principles that served him well in his rise to power. First, Nevada's interests were primary and all other considerations secondary. He accepted the Senate's institutional role as the protector of state interests, which more often than not meant economic expansion.[20] Second, every constituent's problem, no matter how minor, received immediate and full attention. McCarran's office operation was renowned for its tireless efforts in behalf of Nevadans. Unquestionably, Bible embraced McCarran's philosophy of state and constituent responsibility and his "home style."[21]

That system was effective and all-encompassing. In communicating with his audience, McCarran relied on his senatorial presence, enhanced by his white hair and commanding demeanor. Moreover, he met as many people as possible, including those in the isolated mining and ranching areas of Nevada. He always depicted his work in Washington as benefiting Nevada, even to the point of claiming credit he did not deserve.[22]

Bible patterned his "home style" on the McCarran model and molded it to suit his own personality. He enjoyed the campaign trail less than McCarran, who always warmed to a good fight. Instead, Bible sought consensus and balance rather than strident language likely to provoke conflict at home and in Congress. Shy and private, he relied on small group contacts rather than the large audiences that McCarran enjoyed manipulating and haranguing.[23] Still, both men saw Nevadans as conservative, economically disadvantaged victims of a colonial economy controlled by eastern money interests, dependent on livestock raising and mining for subsistence.

Bible learned a lot of things from his apprenticeship with McCarran; he applied some and rejected others. While Bible liked and admired his mentor, McCarran's confrontational style contrasted sharply with Bible's personality and inclinations. At times McCarran, like Lyndon Johnson, could be cruel and vindictive, particularly when people disagreed with him or refused his requests, which usually took the form of orders. Bible found it an advantage both politically and personally to be more congenial, although he could be tough when Nevada's interests were threatened.

Eventually, Bible learned that other senators could also act as if everyone should obey their every command. Soon after starting his job as an elevator operator in the capitol building, an incident occurred that Bible never forgot. If the elevator bell rang three times, he was supposed to respond immediately to the call because a senator was in a hurry. Bible was taking an employee from the basement to the top floor when the bell rang three times.

Senator Patrick McCarran. (Eva Adams Collection)

As he passed the waiting senator, he cheerfully waved through the open elevator gate and told him that he would be back as soon as he dropped off the other passenger. He returned and delivered the senator to his destination. The following day he learned that an outraged Senator Frederick Hale of Maine had reported him for insubordination and demanded his firing. After explaining his side of the story, Bible received a mild reprimand but no pink slip.[24] The experience taught Bible a lesson about the treatment of others that he carried with him throughout his political life. As a senator, Bible developed a reputation for kindness, not only to colleagues and employees, but to all who came before him as witnesses representing government and private industry.[25]

In the spring of 1934, as Bible prepared to graduate from law school, McCarran offered him a job in his Reno law firm. The senator's practice had declined considerably since his election had taken him away from home, and Bible's outstanding scholastic record at Georgetown was impressive. McCarran thought that his legal business might improve with the addition of Bible, who could serve as his eyes and ears while gaining insight into the workings of Nevada politics. In 1934 McCarran had only just begun laying the foundation for the machine that ultimately dominated Nevada politics. Bible became an integral part of its operation—the first in a long line of aspiring young Nevadans to go to Washington, work in McCarran's office, and return to Nevada as a "McCarran boy." When these young men rose to positions of prominence in the state, their allegiance to the senator translated into increased influence and control over Nevada affairs.[26]

Bible accepted McCarran's offer to join the reorganized law firm of McCarran, Rice, and Bible, but his interest clearly lay in politics, not law. His ambition to become a United States senator would be unfulfilled for another twenty years.[27] In the meantime he had to earn a living. In 1934 McCarran's law firm seemed a good place to begin.

After passing the Nevada bar examination in 1935, Bible and partner Gordon Rice set out to reestablish the preeminence of McCarran's law firm. This proved difficult, despite McCarran's reputation as a superb lawyer. Without the senator's presence in the courtroom, few clients were attracted to a firm that featured two young and inexperienced lawyers, and clients drawn by political considerations were too few to make it a thriving practice. After six months Bible was offered an appointment as district attorney of Storey County, which he quickly accepted. The firm continued to operate under the name McCarran, Rice, and Bible until 1939, with Gordon Rice doing most, if not all, of the legal work.

The vacancy in Storey County resulted from the resignation of W. Howard Gray, who had accepted an offer to become deputy attorney general of Nevada. With Senator McCarran's support, the Storey County Board of Supervisors chose Bible to fill Gray's unexpired term. Located in Virginia City, the district attorney's office was a one-man operation with low pay, no clerical help, and little to do except attend to minor crimes. But unlike his mentor, who had disliked his tour as district attorney of Nye County two decades earlier, Bible enjoyed his duties and used his spare time to learn the art of grass-roots politics.

Once Nevada's premier mining town, Virginia City offered a nostalgic interlude for a native Nevadan. More than half a century after the glory days of the Comstock Virginia City residents still entertained hopes for a new bonanza. But it was a dying town that looked more to the past and the revenue from a thriving divorce trade than it did to new mineral discoveries.[28]

While new mining activity was scarce, the numerous legal problems associated with old and new claims required Bible's attention. As district attorney, he assisted the county and his friends in unraveling the complexities of mining law. In the process, he learned a great deal about this little-known field. The experience strengthened his earlier ties to the postfrontier mining West, which provided the basis for his unflinching support of the mining industry in his later years.[29]

With their hard work and good humor, the people of Virginia City influenced Bible and his future. Politics on the mining frontier had been practiced in social clubs, and no meeting place was more important than fraternal lodges such as the Eagles, Odd Fellows, Masons, and Elks, where the politics and news of the day were discussed.[30] Nor did the passage of time diminish the importance of these fraternal orders. The Eagle Lodge remained the dominant fraternal order in Virginia City in the 1930s. Bible quickly joined, brining him into daily contact with influential community leaders. From this solid political and social base, he learned more about the problems of ordinary people who worked and lived in Nevada's small towns. More importantly, he became known as a McCarran Democrat as well as a friend and a supporter of mining causes. He later expanded his fraternal contacts by joining the Masons, Elks, and Moose, so that he had friends and connections in nearly every town that he visited.

Virginia City was a training ground where Bible honed his political skills. He helped organize and became a charter member of the Young Democrats Club. He participated in the selection of local delegates to the state Democratic Committee, which gave him firsthand experience in the operation of local party affairs and precinct politics. These contacts at the grass-roots level paid handsome political dividends later in the form of experience and supporters. In 1936 Bible ran unopposed for a full term as district attorney. He was popular with both local politicians and voters.

Bible met his future wife, Loucile Shields, at a bridge game in Virginia City. They went out together the following night and shortly afterward he proposed marriage. Even then he was self-confident: he asked Loucile to wait about five years until he was established and had the financial resources to raise a family. In Bible's mind, his life was mapped out. He would become a United States senator and Loucile would join him in Washington.

Virginia City suited Bible's temperament better than any other place he had lived. He felt at home among the small groups, whether helping to organize a volunteer fire department, playing cards after work, or sitting with county commissioners as they disposed of routine business. Being district attorney was, he mused, "the best job I ever had."[31] He never lost his sense of closeness to western miners. Indeed, his politics were rooted in the mines and the bleak and struggling agricultural hamlets that dotted the Nevada landscape. He also developed self-assurance, which, coupled with his ambition, guaranteed that he would soon move beyond the confines of Virginia City.

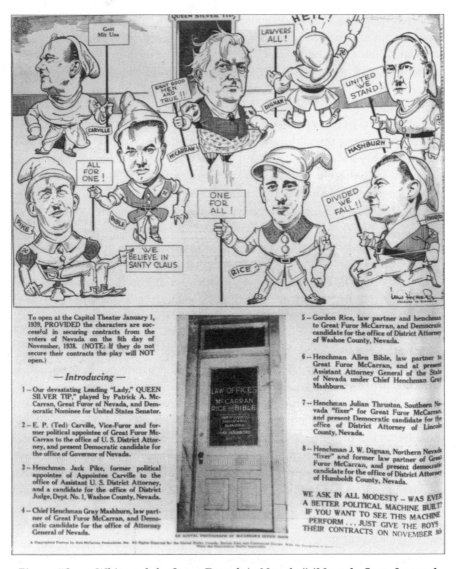

Fig. 1. "Snow White and the Seven Dwarfs in Nevada." (Nevada State Journal, October 22, 1938)

The move came quickly. In 1938 Gray, whom Bible had replaced as district attorney, resigned as the state's deputy attorney general to accept a position with the Kennecott Copper Company in Ely, Nevada. Gray recommended Bible to the attorney general, Gray Mashburn, a longtime McCarran ally. Mashburn agreed that Bible would make an ideal replacement.

The relationship between Gray and Bible deepened over time. As an expert in mining law, Gray often spoke in behalf of the American Mining Congress in its lobbying efforts in Nevada and in Washington, D.C. On many occasions Bible consulted with Gray, who impressed upon him the position of the western mining industry, which Bible already considered important. Most of the time Bible was receptive and could be counted among mining's staunchest supporters. Their friendship and mutual respect spanned four decades. They knew and understood the dying mining towns and the expanding mining operations in such base metals as copper, which would become so important to eastern Nevada's economy.[32]

Bible was dedicated to the cause of western mining, a progressive and activist government, and federally financed water projects to make the desert bloom. He was a product of Nevada's economic roots, which found expression in the policies of Senators William M. Stewart and Key Pittman on mining and in the leadership of Francis G. Newlands on water development. Bible's twelve years in the state attorney general's office, spanning the New Deal, World War II, and the postwar years, exposed him to larger policy considerations within Nevada and the intermountain region. Finally, he had a well-developed sense of local politics, rooted in the oft-quoted phrase, "All politics is local."[33]

Bible also retained close ties to the increasingly well-oiled McCarran machine, which gained considerable strength during the 1930s. Key Pittman's drinking problem had worsened, and his duties as chairman of the Senate Foreign Relations Committee left him less time for state politics.[34] By 1938 McCarran had gained a reputation as Nevada's political boss, making him the target of biting satire. Just before his 1938 bid for reelection the *Nevada State Journal* ran a full-page cartoon depicting the McCarran machine as "Snow White and the Seven Dwarfs" (fig. 1), likening McCarran's political methods to those of Hitler's Nazi "henchmen," replete with swastikas. McCarran was outraged. His close friends could recall no time when his volatile temper exploded as it did in 1938. To compound his troubles, McCarran had alienated Roosevelt by opposing the president's plan to "pack" the Supreme Court with justices favorable to his New Deal reform legislation. Nonetheless, it was a good year for the senator and his machine. McCarran won reelection, and Bible moved into Nevada's attorney general's office, perhaps never reflecting on the inherent conflict between his own Progressive ideals and his pragmatic support for bossism.[35] This combination of Progressivism and pragmatism, reinforced in his early years in politics, would prove to be the hallmark of Bible's career.

Chapter Two

Defining the New Empire:

The Attorney General Years, 1938–1950

Beginning in the 1930s, the American West was transformed from an economy rooted in mining, agriculture, and livestock raising to a national economic power based on government spending during the New Deal and World War II. For more than a decade Alan Bible stood on the cutting edge of this change. As attorney general, he followed the course McCarran had charted to expand the federal government's role in the lives of Nevadans.

The change in course was necessary to reduce the heavy reliance on mining in the intermountain West, which had created an economic imbalance. Absentee ownership in both mining and railroads exerted an all-too-pervasive influence on the region. As Richard Lillard observed in 1942, "Railroads sucked Nevada like an orange."[1] Unlike their neighbors along the Pacific Coast, the intermountain states lacked not only capital investment, but a diversity of natural resources. Once the mines were played out, few owners, investors, and workers stayed behind; they sought more lucrative ventures in California, Oregon, and Washington.[2]

But President Franklin D. Roosevelt's New Deal changed the economic balance in the West by developing water projects for agriculture and hydroelectric power for expanded municipal and industrial use. Thus, the prevailing attitude of "rip, rape, and run" gave way to a philosophy of permanence. Great engineering accomplishments such as the Grand Coulee and Bonneville dams were symbolic of the New Deal. The power of the federal government and the Bureau of Reclamation was evident everywhere, changing and revitalizing the western economy. Less spectacular New Deal programs—the Civilian Conservation Corps, National Youth Administration, Rural Electrification Administration, Soil Conservation Service, and Forest Service Revitalization—also aided distressed sectors in the economy and expanded the government's role in the West.

Indeed, New Deal per capita expenditures benefited the West more than any other region, and Nevada set the pace in the rush for federal dollars.[3] Per capita, Nevada ranked among the top ten states in federal expenditures on New Deal programs between 1933 and 1939, receiving money in twenty categories. The reason for the New Deal's generosity in Nevada is unclear, although the influence of Pittman and McCarran was undoubtedly a factor.[4]

Two other pieces of legislation passed in 1934 had a dramatic effect on western states by increasing the yield of land-based industries. First, the Pittman Silver Purchase Act provided a federal subsidy to western miners by guaranteeing government purchases of silver until the price reached $1.29 an ounce or until silver accounted for a quarter of the federal reserve. Not only did this boost silver mining, but it also aided copper, since silver is a by-product of copper extraction. The effects were immediate and impressive. Mineral production in Nevada nearly tripled between 1934 and 1936, and mineral wealth increased every year in the 1930s with the exception of 1938.[5]

While the Pittman act subsidized western miners, the Taylor Grazing Act solidified the hegemony of large livestock interests. The law guaranteed the largest operators a strong voice in local range management through advisory boards, while federal dollars flowed westward to revitalize and enhance the public domain. Still, grazing continued to decimate the public domain, to the detriment of the ranchers suffering from the depression. Unlike the silver measure, the Taylor Grazing Act proved to be a nightmare, both in its failure to improve western lands and in its enforcement. When the Grazing Service, and later the Bureau of Land Management, tried to police and enforce the range codes, western representatives and senators descended upon them with a vengeance seldom seen anywhere on Capitol Hill.[6] Cattle interests profited, but the public lost control over its own domain and was unable to recapture the initiative until the 1960s.

While the New Deal expanded Nevada's economic foundation in mining and stock raising, state leaders also moved to open new areas of economic opportunity. In 1931 Nevada legalized gambling and liberalized the divorce laws by reducing the residency requirements from three months to six weeks. The depression limited their immediate effects, but in the long run gambling and divorce proved to be far more permanent and reliable sources for economic growth than temporary New Deal programs.

In 1939, as Bible settled into his job as deputy attorney general, the New Deal had ground to a halt and war hysteria consumed Europe. While the pace and complexity of legal affairs had certainly quickened from Virginia City days, Bible still had to be content with mundane legal questions of purely state interest. The state's legal staff consisted of an attorney general and two deputies, who mainly wrote legal opinions for the governor and heads of state agencies on a wide range of topics from state taxing power to social security eligibility, from marriage laws to minority rights, and from government powers to unemployment compensation. Extradition proceedings also required many hours of legal work, particularly in the prewar years.[7]

Between 1936 and 1942, while tending to these details, Bible capitalized on his political opportunities and laid the foundation for his postwar involvement in Nevada's development. He realized that his political future depended on economic trends, not on simple allegiance to a political party.[8] Accordingly, he moved quickly to identify himself as a politician dedicated above all to the state's economic betterment—a position he maintained throughout his political life.

When the United States entered the war Bible tried to enlist, but the army denied him induction because of poor eyesight, which became worse in later life. McCarran was no help to him in obtaining a commission. With military service excluded, Bible had the opportunity to further his political ambitions when Gray Mashburn announced that he would retire when his term as attorney general expired in 1942. Bible surprised everyone when he decided to enter the Democratic primary against his colleague, William T. Mathews. The race proved little more than a beauty contest, with Bible showing his superior personal appeal against his much older rival, who campaigned largely among his small circle of friends. Bible outhustled him and won by a comfortable margin of 2,800 votes. In the general election, he swamped Republican John Ross by more than 7,000 votes.[9]

Bible's first official act was to name Mathews his chief deputy. Still, Mathews remained bitter; he did not attain the state's top legal office until 1950, when Bible retired. The two men apparently established a working relationship based on their consistent view of the issues. Of these, none was more important at the time than Clark County's contention that the federal payment it received "in lieu of taxes" from the construction of Hoover Dam belonged not to the state, but to the county.

The controversy centered on the amount of money the county should receive under the provisions of the Boulder Canyon Project Adjustment Act. The legislation specified that the federal government would compensate Nevada for the loss of tax revenue it would have received if private utilities had built Hoover Dam. The agreed-upon compensation was $300,000 annually, and the state soon passed legislation authorizing the treasurer to receive payment and transmit 20 percent (or $60,000) to the Clark County treasurer.[10]

Clark County felt cheated by receiving only 20 percent and threatened to sue the state. At issue was the constitutionality of the Nevada statute that awarded the money to the county. Clark County was in a tenuous position. The state could abolish it as a legal entity, meaning that it would lose any

William T. Mathews (left), Alan Bible, and Bill Kane (right), in the 1940s.
(Bible family collection)

right to part of the $300,000. Still, the county where the dam was located un-
deniably received meager compensation, as compared with the state, which
kept 80 percent of the revenue. The attorney general—first Mashburn, then
Bible—took the position that the money for Clark County was a matter of
legislative prerogative, not a right.[11]

Before retiring in 1942, Mashburn urged Clark County leaders to think
carefully before pursuing the matter either in the press or through the courts.
But the state moved before the county could take action. The 1943 legislature
considered legislation to prohibit Clark County from receiving any money
from the Boulder Canyon Adjustment Act. Bible agreed that the legislature had the right to distribute state money in any way it saw fit, whatever
the real or perceived inequities.[12] County officials grumbled, but in time
they accepted the state's supremacy and the original distribution of federal
money.

While this controversy consumed much of Bible's time, he spent a far
greater percentage of the war years representing Nevada at regional meetings concerned with postwar economic stabilization. He served as chair-

man of the state Committee on Interstate Cooperation, formed to discuss matters of postwar conversion, public works, and planning. He was also a member of the California Commission on Cooperation and the Reclamation Advisory Committee.[13] Bible believed that reclamation would continue to play a vital role in the development of the western states. By 1946 he had established himself not only as a rising political figure, but as an attorney general thoroughly familiar with the issues facing Nevada and the West.

Bible understood that World War II defense spending had radically altered the West.[14] New Deal spending on hydroelectric power dams enabled the Pacific states to become primary contractors in ship building and aircraft manufacturing. National defense priorities and the military considerations inherent in fighting a two-ocean war prompted the building of important defense installations along the West Coast and in the intermountain states, both for staging operations and for research. The tremendous increases attributable to government payrolls stimulated support industries such as agriculture, livestock raising, and mining—all important to the far western economy.

Western-based defense jobs drew people to the region like a magnet. Eight million Americans relocated to the West during the war years, creating a population shift that continued into the 1980s. Nor did the trend slow after the fighting ended. The continued fear of foreign military aggression stimulated the Cold War and atomic energy research and development. Later concerns about Chinese Communists, Korea, and Vietnam poured a continuing stream, then a flood, of federal dollars into the West for defense. With tax dollars came more jobs and people, fostering a greater reliance on the federal government for the region's continued prosperity.[15] The expanding role of the federal government transformed Nevada's economy. Gone were the days when the state depended solely upon the mining and railroad industries to generate revenue. Yet while the Silver State was liberated from its older colonial economic status, newer forces proved equally domineering—the federal government and, eventually, tourism.

These factors created an interlocking regional economy that made Nevada an appendage to California's growing economic empire.[16] The reliance on money flowing from California was not unique in the history of Nevada, for California banking interests, especially William Sharon and the Bank of California's branch in Virginia City, had financed many mines and railroads in the nineteenth century. But unlike earlier investments that had siphoned Nevada's riches off to California, casino gambling drew California money to Nevada, where it fueled further growth. With 10 percent of wartime federal expenditures, California had both the population and the money for recreation and leisure activities. Thus, Reno and Las Vegas depended upon people and dollars from the larger metropolitan centers of San Francisco and Los Angeles.

Only the influence of the federal government could match California's impact on the Nevada economy. The government's expanded role in Nevada's economic life that began during the New Deal continued in 1941 with the construction of the $150 million Basic Magnesium plant near Las Vegas. Magnesium production, essential to the nation's growing defense needs, stimulated southern Nevada's economy. The Las Vegas area boomed in jobs, housing construction, and a host of service-related businesses. Before the plant closed in 1944 (when stockpiles had become sufficient to meet war demands), the new town of Henderson had been created and the outline for future industrial development had been established.

The war years also brought the creation and expansion of permanent military facilities. The Las Vegas Army Air Corps Gunnery School, later Nellis Air Force Base, opened near Las Vegas in 1941. The Stead facility outside Reno followed in 1942, and lesser installations in Fallon, Tonopah, and Hawthorne expanded.[17] By the end of the war, profits from defense spending and tourism had financed additional casino construction, the mainstay of Nevada's nongovernment-based postwar economy.[18]

With these changes in economic patterns came changes in political alignments. The popularity of Franklin D. Roosevelt and the New Deal propelled the Democratic Party to an easy sweep in all four presidential contests in the West between 1932 and 1944. But western Democrats again lost ground to Republicans as a new wave of conservatism swept the country after the war. Western voters often exhibited little attachment to political parties, creating wide swings in voting patterns from one election to another. Those who came west found weak political parties, less partisanship, and more voter independence than elsewhere. The postwar electorate responded more to short-term influences, regional self-interest, and personalities than to more national agendas and loyalties.[19] Issues like reclamation, water, power, colonialism, and the continued federal financing of western prosperity dominated the political agenda.

No one more persistently supported this agenda than Senator Pat McCarran, and few believed more in his policies than did Alan Bible. McCarran took the lead in denouncing eastern money that had for so long strangled western prosperity by squeezing every dollar of profit without reinvestment. The prime mover in developing a sense of regional solidarity to further the cause of western economic expansion, McCarran demanded economic equity for the West.

In February 1944, at a meeting of the Interstate Cooperation Commission in Carson City, Nevada, McCarran electrified the delegates by demanding an end to "colonialism" and urging a planned response to the problems confronting western states. Bible and California's attorney general, Robert W. Kenny, echoed the same message to the assemblage of dedicated developers. They called for coordinated government planning, transfer of war plants to private enterprise, continued power development, road construction, new airports, and further mineral development—in short, industrial self-determination financed by the federal government.[20] McCarran followed through on his demands by organizing the Western Conference of Senators in 1947 to push for more federal dollars. Bible later played an active role in the organization as its vice-chairman and a stalwart supporter of an expanded federal presence in Nevada. Like McCarran, he staked out a truly western position on the national government's role: give the West its pork and then leave it alone.

While McCarran thereby helped the state economically on one front, he destroyed the harmony of the Democratic Party. Between 1942 and 1946 Nevada had been solidly under Democratic control: both U.S. senators and the governor were Democrats. But the party's continued success depended on reconciling the various factions uncomfortable with McCarran's heavy-handed domination; some of them refused to submit. In 1944 Vail Pittman, the lieutenant governor and Key Pittman's younger brother, challenged the "boss" in the Democratic Senate primary. He lost in a close election that left a residue of bitterness and distrust for years. In the general election, McCarran swamped his Republican rival, George Malone, but hostility lingered. When the state's other Democratic senator, James Scrugham, died the following year, Governor E. P. Carvill (whom McCarran had backed in his two successful campaigns for office) resigned to seek the Senate seat. McCarran's arch-enemy, Vail Pittman, became governor and promptly appointed Carville to succeed Scrugham.

McCarran saw a conspiracy against him, yet another low point in his deteriorating relationship with Carville. From Carville's perspective, McCarran's desire to control every facet of Nevada politics, including the governor's political appointments, had become insatiable. Carville not only resisted and resented McCarran, but pointedly ignored him. Although Bible privately considered McCarran's meddling in state affairs divisive, he stayed out of the feud. His actions were predictable as well as practical. Dominated by McCarran, he would never have broken with him on a party squabble. Seeing no need to take either side, in effect, he adopted a pro-McCarran position.[21]

Although a possible challenger to Pittman in the party primary in 1946, Bible had no desire to run against the governor. That May Pittman announced his intention to seek a full term in the executive mansion. Powerful Clark County Democrats, wanting to avoid a party war, counseled Bible not to run against him. Although McCarran preferred almost any candidate to Pittman, he reluctantly supported the acting governor because he felt that Bible lacked the voter appeal necessary to defeat a popular veteran politician. Bible declared his candidacy for a second term as attorney general and ran unopposed in the primary and general elections.[22] In his second term he gained more respect and experience. He was elected president of the National Association of Attorney Generals, reflecting his popularity with powerful western leaders.

It is unlikely that Bible ever seriously considered running for governor. From McCarran's perspective, he would have been ideal. With Bible in the governor's mansion instead of the independent Carville or the distasteful Pittman, McCarran would have had absolute control over Nevada's internal affairs. Maybe Bible sensed the unpleasantness this would have caused. He was uncomfortable taking the lead or moving forward in a new and bold way. Moreover, he detested acrimony and confrontation and hated to tell people no. Bible preferred to confine his political future to the United States Senate, where his personality and temperament proved more beneficial to his constituents.[23]

Despite Bible's wise course, the state Democratic Party in 1946 engaged in yet another round of self-flagellation. Senator Carville found himself in a bitter primary struggle with Representative Berkeley Bunker, whom Carville had appointed to succeed Key Pittman upon his death in 1940. Angered that Carville had failed to consult him about the appointment and resenting Bunker's independence, McCarran had induced Representative Scrugham to run against Bunker in 1942. But this time McCarran supported Bunker, which probably turned the tide against Carville. In the general election, Carville and Pittman Democrats deserted Bunker and the party to vote for Republican George Malone, who won by a comfortable margin. At the same time, Republican Charles Russell won Nevada's lone congressional seat, which McCarran had encouraged Bunker to vacate, although his reelection was likely. This gave the Republicans a majority of the congressional delegation for the first time in more than a decade. McCarran's dislike for Carville and hatred for Pittman caused the break in party unity. His constant meddling in state business and efforts to dominate every aspect of Nevada political life forced Carville, Pittman, and others to submit to his dictates or suffer retaliation.[24]

The bitter party battles of the 1940s made a lasting impression on Bible. McCarran gained satisfaction from Carville's loss in the 1946 primary, but it cost the Democrats a Senate seat; a united Democratic Party probably would

have defeated Malone. Moreover, the bruising battles and intraparty squab-
bling left a residue of bitterness that lingered, and sometimes exploded,
until McCarran's death in 1954.[25] Unlike McCarran, Bible never supported
a Democratic candidate in a primary or even hinted at his preference. This
refusal to endorse primary candidates, though hardly novel in party affairs,
represented a break with McCarran's heavy-handed methods and proved
both prudent and necessary, if at times personally painful.[26]

Between 1946 and 1950, while Bible continued to toil as attorney general
and to dream of the Senate, Nevada, like most western states, was concerned mainly with expanding its economy and raising revenues to meet
the ever-increasing demand for services that the postwar population boom
had created. Governor Pittman concentrated on efforts to buy the Basic Magnesium plant in Henderson from the federal government, and McCarran
continued his drive to improve transportation through airport expansions
and appropriations for highway construction, both important to Nevada's
blossoming tourist trade. Tourism—or, more precisely, gaming—exploded
on the scene in the late 1940s, becoming Nevada's leading industry in 1957.

As attorney general, Bible became an early architect of gaming regulation.
The Gambling Act of 1931 had left the licensing of gaming establishments
entirely to the discretion of county commissioners, while the state simply
collected its share of the tax revenue. Gaming taxes mainly benefited the
counties, which kept 75 percent while the state collected the rest. Because
profits far outpaced taxes, Nevada sought new revenue sources to support
schools, sewers, roads, and a host of other civic improvements for its bur-
geoning population.[27]

These concerns prompted the state's first steps toward gaming control and
the first restructuring of the gambling law. The 1945 legislature amended the
taxing provisions of the gambling act to provide for a 1 percent across-the-
board tax on all net gaming revenues. Operating gaming establishments now
would require both county and state approval. Significantly, the state also
tried to control the industry by placing the power over licensing and taxing
in the hands of one agency, the Nevada Tax Commission.[28] But the state's
interest was primarily in revenue, not in control or regulation.

That soon changed. Rumors began to circulate about underworld involvement in casino ownership, particularly in Las Vegas, where Benjamin
"Bugsy" Siegel built the lavish new Flamingo Hotel in 1946. Siegel's mur-
der a year later made Nevada the center of national attention. The uproar
continued when another shady underworld figure, "Russian Louie" Strauss,
was arrested in Reno for killing another gambler of equally unsavory reputation.[29] In response to these shocking incidents of mobsters killing one
another in or over Nevada's gambling centers, Robbins Cahill, secretary of

the Nevada Tax Commission, wrote to Bible on September 27, 1947, to request a legal opinion on the extent of the tax commission's powers to control persons connected with the gaming business.

Bible's opinion not only clarified the gambling law, but strengthened the state's power to regulate the industry. Specifically, he declared county operating permits invalid without a state license from the Tax Commission: gaming applicants needed state permission before getting county approval. Bible also held that the Tax Commission could deny an applicant permission to operate a gambling establishment for "just cause, unsavory reputation, or other reasons of public interest."[30] Previously, the Nevada Supreme Court had upheld the denial of a liquor license on grounds of overriding public interest in the regulation of liquor sales. Accepting the court's reasoning, Bible told the Tax Commission that it had the same obligation to protect the public welfare. And he went further, ascribing to the commission broad powers of inquiry into an applicant's character, reputation, and associates. Based on Bible's opinion, the Tax Commission took only a month to announce new and tighter licensing regulations along the lines he had advocated, and gaming regulation since has evolved largely as Bible sketched it out.

In 1948 Bible also moved to strengthen Governor Pittman's hand in firing state employees engaged in unlawful gambling. The case involved the questionable activities of the superintendent of the State Police, Lester L. Moody, allegedly a participant in unlicensed games of chance at highway stopping points known as "roadside zoos." After reviewing the matter, Bible told Pittman that he had the power to remove the superintendent without notice or review, establishing the precedent of executive control over state employees involved in gambling activities.[31] Similarly, the Tax Commission received an additional boost when Bible ruled that gaming licenses were not automatically transferable to new owners.[32]

In 1947 and again in 1948, when the legislature was out of session, Bible's opinions strengthened the state's infant gaming control machinery. In 1949 the legislature followed up on Bible's rulings by giving tax commissioners the status of peace officers and the right to make such rules and regulations as they considered in the public interest. Nonetheless, by the end of the decade organized crime had established a presence in Las Vegas that would take decades to eradicate, and the Tax Commission proved inadequate and ill-equipped to cope with the many problems associated with licensing and controlling gambling activities. In the late 1950s and again in the 1960s the state moved to institute stronger control machinery that remains the basis for executive power over the industry.

Beyond doubt, organized crime moved easily into Nevada and became a fixture in Las Vegas casino operations during Bible's years as attorney general. The city established an image as a haven for shadowy underworld figures. Implicit in the ever-expanding picture of Nevada as the sin state was the notion that criminal elements controlled the state—a perception that raises the important question of why this view of Nevada developed and persisted in the postwar period.

Nationally, the interrelationship of politics and ideology played a crucial role immediately after the war. Republicans led by U.S. Senator Robert Taft of Ohio launched a conservative counteroffensive against the New Deal and pro-welfare Democrats. Taking advantage of a change in American attitudes from the preceding two decades, Taft decried an erosion of national principles and the threat of foreign-bred communism, hitting at the core of American uneasiness about Soviet subversion, the bomb, inflation, civil rights, labor strife, and, in general, the chaotic nature of the world in the war's aftermath.[33]

This resulted in a persistent drive toward conformity and consensus in American values and an effort to silence the dangerous ideas of those who always seemed to find the United States wanting. Leaders of the public and private sectors began purging leftist influence from such institutions as trade unions and schools, firing more than 600 teachers. Professional organizations such as the American Medical Association, American Bar Association, and National Education Association established tests designed to admit only those with orthodox political views.[34] Then came 1949, the year of shocks, with the "loss of China" to communism, the Soviet detonation of an atomic bomb, and the startling revelations of alleged espionage involving Alger Hiss, Klaus Fuchs, and Julius and Ethel Rosenberg the following year. Traitors lurked everywhere, or so many people believed. In 1950 North Korean troops swarmed over the 38th Parallel, and U.S. soldiers returned to battle, ostensibly to defend the "American way of life."

As the Korean War heated up, so did the crusade against "un-American activity." Senator Joseph McCarthy (R-Wisconsin) led the way with sensational charges of conspiracy and duplicity among high-ranking government officials. Senator McCarran joined him and often led the fight. The McCarthyite message was always the same: morally weak Americans had sold out their country by failing to act or by gross stupidity. Between 1950 and 1954 few were safe from government probes and industry regulators that institutionalized blacklisting, loyalty oaths, censorship, and the firing of persons suspected of subscribing to differing viewpoints.[35]

Nor were suspected Communists the only targets. The federal government had long known about the link between organized crime and political figures who allowed vice to flourish in exchange for money, gifts, and political support. On March 12, 1950, Estes Kefauver (D-Tennessee), the ambitious chairman of a Senate Select Committee to investigate organized crime in interstate commerce, touched off his probe in New York. Thus began the nation's first sensational daytime television news event, watched by more than thirty million Americans. For those who watched the extraordinary spectacle, which included testimony by reputed mobster Frank Costello and money courier Virginia Hauser, the conclusion was inescapable:

> The endless shadowy figures that obviously controlled so much catalyzed the whole vague feeling that corruption was moving through all American life like a swarm of maggots. Out of many pictures has come a broader picture of the sordid intermingling of crime and politics, of dishonor in public life.[36]

By the time the hearing rolled into Las Vegas, the central question on the minds of committee members and the public was, what had happened to American standards of morality?

Clearly, Nevadans were unprepared for the onslaught of organized crime figures in their state, just as they were surprised that gambling was fast becoming the basis of their economy. Nor did they expect that a mushroom cloud hovering over the Nevada Atomic Test Site would attract thousands of visitors to the desert, inspiring cocktail mixes, hairstyles, songs, and science fiction movies. The popularity of Nevada's peculiar institution, gambling, shocked state and congressional leaders like McCarran, who saw industry— the Basic Magnesium plant in Henderson, for example—as the wave of the future.[37]

When gangsters, hoodlums, and racketeers came from other states, Nevada authorities took no action against them. There was little evidence of wrongdoing beyond rumor, innuendo, and hearsay to support prosecutions in local courts.[38] With these new arrivals building up Nevada's historically shaky economy, state officials were understandably loath to turn away a new source of revenue.

But the Kefauver committee criticized Nevada for failing to accomplish what no other state or city had been able to do for many years—control organized crime. Implicit in the committee's findings was the condemnation of gambling, prostitution, and easy divorce in the desert oasis.[39] Even so, the committee recognized that Nevada could not be held solely responsible for the lack of prosecutions. Therefore, it recommended federal assistance for state authorities in fighting crime, a request ignored for more than a decade.

Had Nevada's attorney general, Alan Bible, wanted to conduct an independent investigation of organized crime (and there is no evidence that he did), he would have been severely hampered. His meager staff could

barely keep pace with the growing workload in its usual fields of expertise. In fact, while the state's population rapidly increased, and gambling
mushroomed from a small-time operation to big business between 1938 and
1950, the attorney general's office added only two lawyers to its staff. A further hindrance was the need for federal, state, and local law enforcement
cooperation, which was virtually nonexistent in the 1940s and remains a
major problem in Nevada today.[40] Although the Kefauver committee recommended closer ties, the FBI refused to take other law enforcement agencies
into its confidence or to participate in joint investigations.

Furthermore, the Kefauver committee ignored the nature of Nevada's
government. The state legislature consisted of part-time lawmakers with
small support staffs, limited travel budgets, and no built-in mechanism for
extensive public hearings. The state government machinery already was inadequate to cope with gambling's expanding role in Nevada life. Like other
western state governments, Nevada proved incapable of dealing with the
demands of a postwar economy.

Similarly, the critics never considered the limitations of local law enforcement, due to the nature of Las Vegas's fragmented government. Downtown
gambling, clustered in and around Fremont Street, came under the jurisdiction of city police officials. Located in the county, strip casinos lay beyond
the reach of city police, who were forced to fall back on the goodwill and
cooperation of the county sheriff's office. Routine administrative tasks, such
as fingerprinting and registering casino employees, strained the limited resources of both agencies to the breaking point. The construction of new
and larger casinos exacerbated the problem: city and county police failed to
keep pace, partly because voters opposed the tax hikes needed to finance
expanded police operations. Consequently, police service deteriorated just
as organized crime made its move into Nevada.[41]

Another major problem was the lack of adequate federal statutes to prose-
cute entrenched organized crime operations. Not until years later did Congress pass racketeering laws, money laundering statutes, and related measures that allowed the newly organized and well-trained prosecutors in the
Department of Justice's Strike Force units to conduct successful prosecutions. In the late 1940s the problem appeared too small to merit so drastic a
solution, and the federal government was unprepared to act.

It was also too much to expect Nevada leaders to begin attacking what they
had only recently become accustomed to defending. Many prominent Nevadans, including Governor Pittman, grew more vocal in their support for legal
gambling when they realized that the industry would become the state's
chief enterprise. This offended many, both inside and outside of Nevada,
including community leaders, church officials, and parents who considered

gamblers and casino owners poor role models for their children. But defending gambling as a legitimate business was different than supporting racketeers and gangsters. Bible and other state officials encouraged the business of gaming in the 1940s and later welcomed a new era in casino ownership, beginning with billionaire Howard Hughes's entry into Las Vegas in 1967 and continuing with the corporate Gambling Act of 1969.[42]

Bible probably would not have initiated bold and forceful measures to curb organized crime activity in Nevada even if he had been aware of the problem (and there is no evidence that he was). Neither a risk taker nor a strong leader who could inspire the public or move the legislature to action, Bible often had to be forced into action himself. Reform in gaming control required executive leadership from the governor's office, not from the attorney general. That kind of energy and dedication was a decade away, when a young, energetic governor—Grant Sawyer, Bible's fellow McCarran protégé—would lead in the establishment of new safeguards and detection of corruption in gaming.

While southern Nevada was reaping its questionable harvest, economic development on another level helped stimulate northern Nevada's economy, and Bible was deeply involved in this attempt at diversification. During the war warehouse storage businesses had thrived on government leases of space to house war supplies. Peace had virtually ended the business, since available warehouse space far outran the supply of goods requiring storage. Stored goods were taxable under Nevada law, which further depressed the industry. After the war Edwin Bender, a Reno warehouse owner, set out to change the law, enlisting the support of longtime McCarran and Bible ally Joseph F. McDonald, Sr., who edited the *Nevada State Journal* and whose son, Bob McDonald, was Bible's deputy attorney general and close friend.

Bible immediately saw the possibilities of additional business if Nevada let goods stored in the state go untaxed. The prospect of increased construction, building maintenance, employment, gasoline taxes, and a host of business sales related to the trucking industry—all of which the state would tax— was also attractive. He enthusiastically agreed to help Bender and Joseph McDonald by writing the legislation that eventually became known as the Freeport Law. The bill provided that goods in transit through Nevada could be stored without being subject to personal property taxes.

The 1949 legislature passed the Freeport Law, and its beneficial effects became apparent almost immediately. Warehouse construction expanded, and light manufacturing firms relocated to the state for its favorable tax climate. The legislature later amended the law by extending the provisions to include goods not only stored, but processed, repackaged, and relabeled, attracting additional businesses. The success of this Freeport doctrine, in Nevada and elsewhere, was unmistakable: twenty-seven other states have enacted similar legislation since 1957.[43]

The Freeport doctrine's author faced a less certain future. In 1950 Democrats expected Vail Pittman to challenge McCarran again for the Senate. But at the state Democratic Convention Pittman surprised everyone by announcing that he would seek another term as governor. Bible, otherwise silent, declined to seek a third term as attorney general.[44] He no doubt had his eye on 1952, when he could challenge Republican U.S. senator George "Molly" Malone, whom most Democrats (and many Republicans) considered a weak candidate for reelection.

Meanwhile, McCarran encouraged Republican Charles Russell's candidacy for governor. Russell spoke with McCarran about his plans even before the Democratic Party met in Tonopah. As events unfolded, the "boss" went to considerable lengths to help the Republican defeat Pittman.[45] From McCarran's standpoint, a friendly Republican in the governor's chair seemed preferable to Pittman. Russell defeated Pittman, temporarily eliminating McCarran's old nemesis from the political scene, although Russell proved anything but a pliant tool for McCarran.

In the game of politics, Bible was the odd man out in 1950. A politician without an office, he had limited influence in the councils of government as a private citizen. Still, he retained the support of McCarran and his political machine, which would later prove invaluable. In early 1951 he left Carson City for Reno to open a law firm with his friend Bob McDonald. Tremendous changes had taken place in his life and in Nevada's in the dozen years since he came to Carson City.

True to his word, he had married Loucile on November 17, 1939, almost five years after they met in Virginia City. Loucile had a daughter (Debra) from a previous marriage, and three sons (Paul, Bill, and David) were born during their years in Carson City. In his family relationship Bible exhibited many of the personality traits of his mother. He kept his innermost thoughts to himself and rarely discussed office business or troubles at home. For Bible, his home was a place to relax and enjoy his family—not a place to discuss business or political affairs.

Nevada had been transformed during this period, first by the New Deal, then by World War II. By 1950 Nevada and Arizona were the West's fastest-growing states—a dramatic turnabout from the pre–New Deal years. In two out of three decades from 1890 through 1920 Nevada's population decreased, due to the decline in mining production and the depression in agriculture and livestock raising after World War I (see table 1). Nevada gained a startling 45 percent in population during the New Deal and World War II (see table 2).

TABLE 1

Population and Growth Rates of States, 1890–1920

	Population (thousands)				% Increase		
	1890	1900	1910	1920	1890–1900	1900–1910	1910–1920
Arizona	88	123	204	334	40	66	64
Colorado	413	540	799	940	31	48	18
Idaho	89	162	326	432	82	101	33
Montana	143	243	376	549	70	55	46
Nevada	47	42	82	77	−11	95	−6
New Mexico	160	195	327	360	22	68	10
Utah	211	277	373	449	31	35	20
Wyoming	63	93	146	194	48	57	33
California	1213	1485	2378	3427	22	60	44
Oregon	318	414	673	783	30	63	16
Washington	357	518	1142	1357	45	120	19

Source: Hist. Stat. U.S., 1975, series A195–A209.

Above all, federal expenditures spearheaded the population boom. Western politicians understood the impact of federal dollars in maintaining prosperity and were determined to keep the money flowing. Within four years Bible, too, joined the congressional scramble for federal subsidies to bolster the region's and Nevada's economy. In political terms, Bible remained a New Dealer because economic concerns played a central role in the West's political life.

But military installations and mining subsidies, although helpful, were incapable of creating a base for Nevada's economic growth. Gambling was the bedrock of the state's economic future. Postwar gambling profits rose steadily, sometimes dramatically, reflecting not only the industry's growth, but also the state's increasing dependence on it as a revenue source.[46]

After 1950 gambling's survival and Nevada's future prosperity depended on two factors that are more intertwined than they may seem at first glance. First, protecting gambling from federal regulation, which could destroy it by taxation or by simply declaring it illegal, was a necessity. McCarran and Bible used the rules and procedures of the Senate to ensure that no federal legislation detrimental to gambling would be enacted. Second, southern

TABLE 2

Population and Growth Rates of States, 1920–1950

	Population (thousands)				% Increase		
	1920	1930	1940	1950	1920–1930	1930–1940	1940–1950
Arizona	334	436	499	750	31	14	50
Colorado	940	1036	1123	1325	10	8	18
Idaho	432	445	525	589	3	18	12
Montana	549	538	559	591	−2	4	6
Nevada	77	91	110	160	18	21	45
New Mexico	360	423	532	681	18	26	28
Utah	449	508	550	689	13	8	25
Wyoming	194	226	251	291	16	11	16
California	3427	5677	6907	10586	66	22	53
Oregon	783	954	1090	1521	22	14	40
Washington	1357	1563	1736	2379	15	11	37

Source: Hist. Stat. U.S., series A195–A209.

California and the West had to prosper to assure a steady flow of tourists to Nevada. The key to prosperity was water and power development. Again, McCarran provided the leadership with his emphasis on regionalism and cooperation in problem solving. In the postwar years western senators and congressmen of both parties united in their drive to develop every conceivable water source to promote economic development. No one was more devoted to the cause than Alan Bible, who spent the next quarter of a century promoting Nevada and western water development. First, however, he had to put himself in a position to wield influence. That proved to be harder than he expected.

Chapter Three

Twists and Turns, 1951–1954

When Bible left the attorney general's office in 1951 to establish a private practice, no one who followed Nevada politics expected the move to be permanent. Although his successful practice included representing Nevada in *Arizona* v. *California*, the most important legal battle involving distribution of Colorado River water, even Bible saw it as only a brief interlude between political offices. In keeping with his ultimate ambition for two decades, he had set his sights on Republican George Malone's U.S. Senate seat. Anticipating no difficulty in winning the Democratic nomination in 1952, he felt certain that he could defeat the vulnerable Malone in the general election.

But Bible and the political experts thoroughly miscalculated. In losing the primary to Thomas Mechling, his Democratic rival and a virtual newcomer to Nevada, Bible fell victim to the increasing animosity toward McCarran's machine. The defeat was easily the most heartbreaking experience of Bible's political life. Not only had he expected to win, but he believed—correctly— that if he had worked harder, the outcome would have been different.

From his earliest days in the attorney general's office, Bible benefited from many personal and political connections, and one in particular: Joseph F. McDonald, Sr., editor of Reno's influential *Nevada State Journal*. Like Bible, McDonald was a tireless advocate of economic development, and he worked with Bible to secure passage of the Freeport Law to encourage expansion of the warehousing industry in the Reno/Sparks area. Moreover, with Key Pittman's death, McDonald's Democratic daily became a crucial part in McCarran's machine. When McDonald's son Bob returned from World War II, Bible put him to work in the attorney general's office. Bob McDonald and Bible remained close personal friends, law partners, and political allies until Bible's death in 1988.

McDonald, like Bible, was warm and outgoing. But, unlike Bible, McDonald had a colorful personality and was physically active. He claims never to have seen anyone as physically lazy as Bible. On a fishing trip together in Mexico, Bible hooked a marlin; instead of reeling in the catch himself, he gave his pole to one of the crew, who brought the fish aboard. Afterward Bible had his photograph taken with his prize fish, explaining to the stunned crew that "he had a bad back." Once, while bird hunting, Bible was supposed to take a position a few hundred yards down the road and flush the prey toward the other hunters. McDonald was shocked when he returned to the meeting area and found Bible seated in the car, listening to the World Series on the radio. When pressed for an explanation, Bible said he could do as good a job in the car as walking all that way down the road.[1]

Moreover, Bible was, to use the fun-loving McDonald's phrase, "a square's square." The remark about another politician, Speaker of the House John McCormack, applied to Bible, too: "He was so conservative he didn't even burn the candle at one end."[2] Still, McDonald and Bible made an ideal team—Bible handled the political affairs and the complicated litigation involving water issues, while McDonald concentrated on the general practice of law.[3] With their political connections and personal appeal, Bible and McDonald were in a good position to capture a fair share of the legal work in the Reno area.

Initially, the firm relied heavily on Bible's knowledge of water law and the workings of state government to obtain legal work. Nevada had established the Colorado River Commission to act in its behalf in dealing with the federal government in matters involving water and power flowing from the Colorado River (for example, the Colorado River Commission and the Department of the Interior had negotiated the "in lieu of tax issue" that created the controversy between Clark County and the state discussed in chapter 2). In 1951 no one in the attorney general's office had the expertise to represent the state in water rights litigation. They naturally turned for assistance to Bible, who was also the Colorado River Commission's legal adviser. From 1951 to 1954 Nevada provided the Bible-McDonald law firm with a steady source of income. Bible also received help from Senator McCarran, who directed the Stauffer Chemical Company's legal business to the Reno firm, thereby increasing its revenue and reputation.[4]

But for Bible, politics, not law, was the key to his future. In 1952 his quest for the Senate began. Although likable, Malone commanded neither great respect nor a committed following, which guaranteed a strong Democratic challenge to unseat him. Malone's victory in 1946 had been due to bitter divisions in the Democratic Party, not to personal popularity or political acumen. If the Democratic Party could achieve a semblance of unity—an elusive goal indeed—it would have little trouble electing one of its own to join McCarran in the Senate.

The nation and Nevada remained preoccupied with the threat of communism and Senator Joseph McCarthy's charges of infiltration and treason, however. Not even Republican presidential candidate Dwight Eisenhower would challenge the increasingly reckless McCarthy and his followers, including McCarran.[5] Only a few voices cried out for reason amid the prevailing atmosphere of fear, intimidation, and hearsay. One of the most courageous was New Yorker–turned–Nevadan Hank Greenspun, owner and publisher of the *Las Vegas Sun*.

Almost immediately after buying his paper in 1950, Greenspun emerged as an independent, iconoclastic force in Nevada politics and journalism. Greenspun attacked first McCarran, then McCarthy, and later both, seeing little difference between the two. He continued to wage his campaign nearly single-handed and had won considerable local and nationwide attention by 1952.[6] Then he began to receive warnings from business and gaming leaders in Las Vegas to lay off McCarran. Greenspun refused, even stepping up his assault on the "boss." The crisis came in March 1952, when Greenspun endorsed political newcomer Thomas Mechling in the Democratic Senate primary over McCarran's choice: Alan Bible. The major hotels and casinos suddenly withdrew all of their advertising from the *Sun*. Greenspun sued McCarran and forty hotel executives for $225,000, accusing them of conspiracy to drive him out of business by violating federal antitrust laws.[7]

The case had an immediate impact. The out-of-court settlement—the defendants agreed to pay $80,500—demonstrated Greenspun's perseverance and his growing strength. Although technically not charged with wrongdoing, McCarran had played a key role in inspiring the mass exodus of advertisers to silence the newspaper.[8] McCarran continued to bristle at Greenspun's crusade against machine politics, red-baiting, and McCarthyism, but he could do little to stop Greenspun, whose influence in postwar Nevada politics became increasingly important. Bible obviously suffered more from the fallout than did McCarran.

The primary agent of Bible's suffering was Thomas Mechling, a youthful, good-looking newcomer to Nevada and to Democratic politics. He came from Washington, D.C., where he had worked as a newspaperman and married Margaret DiGrazia, whose family was well known in Nevada. Without any direct evidence, many well-connected Democratic Party insiders believed that columnist Drew Pearson and the liberal, Washington, D.C.–based Americans for Democratic Action, opponents of both McCarthy and McCarran, encouraged Mechling's political ambitions.[9] For whatever reason, Mechling entered the Democratic primary in January 1952 and waged the most effective door-to-door campaign in the history of Nevada politics. His message was always the same—"Bible is a McCarran stooge." [10]

The campaign focused less on the two main candidates than on what they represented. Mechling concentrated his assault on McCarran. Only indirectly did he mention Bible, because in the public's mind the two men were inseparable, politically and ideologically. Meanwhile, Bible's strategy was to ignore Mechling, except for the occasional charge of being a carpetbagger, and to concentrate on Malone. It was a fatal error. Bible drastically under-estimated his opponent and perhaps his audience, many of whom were also new arrivals in Nevada. Most importantly, by refusing to take Mechling seri-ously, Bible demonstrated an uncharacteristic overconfidence that bordered on arrogance.[11]

Shrewd and confident, Mechling successfully portrayed himself as a lone crusader against the evils of machine politics, a modern-day David versus Goliath. The longer the campaign dragged on, the more effective Mechling's message became, particularly when McCarran sought revenge on Mech-ling's lone newspaper supporter, Hank Greenspun. Meanwhile, the *Las Vegas Review-Journal*, a longtime supporter of McCarran, steadfastly endorsed Bible against what its editor called an "unknown carpetbagger who came to the state of Nevada as a snake oil salesman."[12]

On election day the returns showed one of the closest votes and biggest surprises in Nevada history. Mechling upset his better-known opponent, 15,914 to 15,439—a 475-vote margin. Mechling's victory was due mainly to his extraordinarily strong showing in Clark County, then on its way to be-coming the state's most populous county. Bible ran well in all counties except the strongly Democratic Clark County in the south and White Pine County in the north, where he received a meager 37.7 and 36.1 percent of the vote, respectively.[13] Clearly, Bible needed a strong showing not in the sparsely populated counties, but in Clark County—particularly Las Vegas, where Mechling appealed to a larger cross-section of Democrats than did Bible: 7,080 to 4,223. Additionally, Pittman Democrats, seeking revenge against McCarran for his battles with Key in the 1930s and Vail in the 1940s, may have deserted Bible in sufficient numbers to turn the tide in Clark County.

Mechling's strong showing in southern Nevada also may be attributed to the large number of new residents in the 1940s who showed no desire to follow McCarran's lead. In 1940 Clark County's population was 16,414; a decade later 48,289 lived in the county, mostly in the Las Vegas area. A majority of those new arrivals were Democrats with no ties to the state's political heritage.[14] Mechling was as well-known to most southern Nevada voters as Bible; to many of the better-informed members of the electorate, Bible seemed little more than a McCarran appendage. Greenspun, a postwar settler in southern Nevada, had a decisive impact. Day after day, for months, the *Las Vegas Sun* blasted the McCarran machine, while Mechling and his wife went door-to-door in county after county, appealing for votes. In many ways, the vote was a referendum on McCarran's way of doing things. Having lived by that sword, Bible—or, more accurately, his Senate hopes, at least for the moment—died by it.

Bible was heartbroken by his loss. Feeling disgraced and somewhat bitter at the voters who had rejected him, he thought about leaving Nevada. But he soon realized that he was to blame for taking his opponent lightly and failing to campaign hard enough.[15] Bible quickly recovered from his pain and humiliation and returned to his legal practice a much wiser politician, having learned the need to line up his support and campaign hard and the importance of southern Nevada's growing population to the state's political life.

Meanwhile, the general election between Mechling and Malone proved to be one of the strangest in memory. After disposing of Bible, Mechling continued to assault McCarran mercilessly and needlessly, alleging that two of his henchmen had approached him with a deal: McCarran would support him in exchange for his votes on key issues and his patronage appointments. Certainly, McCarran was capable of such bargaining, but not with someone he detested so much—he hated Mechling as strongly as he loathed Greenspun and the Pittmans. Pressed to name the two McCarran operatives, Mechling later identified Thomas Norman Biltz and John Mueller.[16]

Biltz and Mueller—two Republican businessmen who were well-known McCarran supporters and fund-raisers—probably told the truth about the meeting.[17] They met with Mechling, but long before the date on which he charged that they offered him the deal. Surprisingly, Biltz secretly tape-recorded the meeting; when he released the tape to the press, it showed no evidence that he and Mueller had suggested a meeting. Indeed, the tape made Mechling's account seem less than candid. Mechling alleged that Biltz had doctored the tape, which suggested that Mechling had requested the conference to gain McCarran's support in the general election.[18]

If that was Mechling's goal, he failed. McCarran denied the charges in a statewide radio broadcast, informing his audience that he chose not to vote for Mechling. Although he neither mentioned nor openly endorsed Malone, the implication was clear: vote for Malone or do not vote. Thus, McCarran opposed a Democrat who could give his party control of the Senate while favoring a Republican for personal reasons, demonstrating again the highly personal nature of the McCarran machine.[19]

While McCarran may have cost the upstart some votes, Mechling's apparent deception in describing his version of the "corrupt bargain" proved decisive. Once again, Malone benefited from divisions in the Democratic Party, this time defeating his rival, 41,906 to 39,184. After losing to Malone, Mechling entered the Democratic primary for governor in 1954. When Vail Pittman soundly defeated him, Mechling left the state.[20]

Ironically, at a time when southern Nevada voters had rejected Bible, the state employed him to defend their future growth and prosperity. On

August 13, 1952, Arizona filed suit against California, claiming that the state exceeded its share of Colorado River water, to the detriment of Arizona. When the Supreme Court agreed to hear the matter, Nevada's attorney general, William T. Mathews, assigned the case to Bible, who recognized that the high court could rewrite the whole structure of western water law. If that happened, Nevada's share of Colorado River water could be lost.

Bible presented Nevada's case before the Supreme Court in October 1953. He urged the high court to settle once and for all how much water each state should receive from the Colorado River. Bible knew that such a determination would be in Nevada's best interest because the rapid population growth in California and Arizona would appropriate a larger share of Colorado River water in the future, unless allotments were fixed soon. Moreover, as southern Nevada's population growth depleted groundwater sources, the Las Vegas area's continued development increasingly would depend on an assured supply of Colorado River water.[21]

Bible stressed that southern Nevada's growth had been due largely to federal projects. Beginning with Hoover Dam in the 1930s, Clark County enjoyed a population explosion. The workers needed to construct the massive project created a whole new town, and with Boulder City came additional demands on the state's limited resources. In the 1940s the government built other facilities in southern Nevada to bolster the nation's defenses. Both the Basic Magnesium project and Nellis Air Force Base attracted further influxes of population. Furthermore, Bible argued, the emergence of western states as major government contractors created population shifts that would deplete the available water supply by the year 2000. He also emphasized that the tourist business, spurred on by live entertainment and recreation, would continue to draw thousands of people to Nevada each year.

In his arguments, Bible avoided referring to the gaming industry. Appeals based on protecting a business allegedly honeycombed with hoodlums and gangsters would win little sympathy from the Supreme Court, especially in the wake of the Kefauver hearings. Bible saw no need to remind the court of the state's growing reputation for organized crime activities. Instead, Bible preferred the phrase "live entertainment" to "gambling."[22]

Bible tried another tack to play down the present and emphasize the future. In 1953 southern Nevada had enough water to satisfy its needs. As with California and Arizona, the problem was future demand. With the aid of his close friend Hugh Shamberger, the state engineer, Bible argued that by 2000 southern Nevada would need more than 500,000 acre-feet per year, roughly 200,000 more than the whole state received under the 1953 contract with the secretary of the interior (see table 3).[23] Bible and other state officials later expressed satisfaction with an award of much less than 500,000

TABLE 3

Estimated Water Use: Colorado River and Tributaries

Designation of Area	Water Use in Acre-Feet		
	Present Use (1953)	Estimated Additional One-Year 2000	Total Estimated One-Year 2000
Colorado River Direct			
Las Vegas Valley	12,340	220,060	232,400
Big Bend	0	2,700	2,700
Fort Mohave	0	20,300	20,300
Dry Lake	0	115,800	115,800
Boulder City	2,600	2,400	5,000
Subtotal	14,940	361,260	376,200
Virgin River			
Mesquite and Bunkerville	12,020	3,080	15,100
Below Riverside Bridge	1,700	8,300	10,000
Mormon Mesa	0	46,400	46,400
Toquop Wash	0	15,700	15,700
Subtotal	13,720	73,480	87,200
Muddy River			
Upper Moapa Valley	9,480	9,320	18,800
Lower Moapa Valley	14,890	6,110	21,000
Subtotal	24,370	15,430	39,800
Meadow Valley Wash			
Lower Meadow Valley Wash	0	15,500	15,500
Upper Meadow Valley Wash	10,700	9,700	20,400
Subtotal	10,700	25,200	35,900
Nevada total	63,730	475,370	539,100

Source: Arizona v. *California*, motion on behalf of the State of Nevada for leave to intervene, October 1953, 12.

acre-feet, leaving the impression that they greatly inflated their forecast to influence how the court would allocate Colorado River water to each state.

On June 1, 1954, Bible and Nevada won a significant victory when the high court granted Nevada's petition to intervene in the case. The state's position, as Bible first articulated it, had changed little over the years. Nevada wanted Colorado River water allocated on what it considered an equitable basis, while California maintained that its population explosion entitled it to a greater share. Since California's growth outpaced that of the other six states using the river's water, the others feared that their larger partner eventually would acquire the rights to most of the water. Also concerned about Gila River and Mexican water rights, Arizona shared Nevada's fear that California would someday gain control of all Colorado River water.

While the high court moved at a glacial pace in sorting and sifting through the complex world of western water rights, events in Nevada moved more swiftly. In the fall of 1954 the political atmosphere underwent a dramatic change: on September 28, 1954, McCarran died of a heart attack in Hawthorne. While his death surprised most Nevadans, his health had been declining for years. He had become subject to embarrassing public outbursts, calling Adlai Stevenson a "damn fool," Harry Truman a "pissant in human form," and Mechling a "commie plant."[24]

McCarran's death provoked reactions similar to those most Nevadans had while he was alive. A Reno newspaperman commented, "He was a son of a bitch alive and a son of a bitch dead." But FBI director J. Edgar Hoover said, "His work will remain a living inspiration to those dedicated to preserving the American way of life." Still, the most balanced assessment came from his arch-enemy, Hank Greenspun, who called McCarran a man of action and a fierce fighter.[25] Greenspun and McCarran actually were similar in their dedication to causes and willingness to engage in rancorous public debate.

Whatever his critics thought of McCarran's political views, the evidence all around Nevada that he had used his senatorial power for Nevada's economic benefit was indisputable. Therefore, a prime requirement for his successor would be to continue McCarran's economic blueprint. Chester Smith, who had driven the "boss" from his home in Reno to the Hawthorne rally more than 130 miles to the south, telephoned Bible within an hour of McCarran's collapse and asked if he wanted to run for McCarran's Senate seat. Bible agreed to run, but questioned whether his name would appear on the ballot in time for the general election in November.[26]

Meanwhile, Bob McDonald moved nearly as quickly as Smith in lining up support. That night McDonald and his brother Joe telephoned as many members of the Nevada Democratic Party central committee as they could reach.

Chester Smith and Senator Alan Bible at Secretary of Transportation office in 1973 in Washington, D.C. (Courtesy of Chester Smith)

Bible was the unanimous choice of the party, which soon formally ratified what had been informally agreed to within hours of McCarran's death.[27]

Bible's long apprenticeship to McCarran and his grass-roots political education in Nevada were finally rewarded in the early morning hours of September 29, 1954. He knew every prominent Democrat in the state, and even Democrats who belonged to the Pittman wing of the party liked him. Clearly the logical choice to succeed McCarran, despite his loss to Mechling in 1952, Bible had name recognition, an enormous circle of friends and supporters, and status as McCarran's unofficial yet de facto heir-apparent, not to mention his two terms as state attorney general and acknowledged expertise on local and regional water issues. The other leading Democrat was beyond consideration: as the party's nominee for governor in 1954, Vail Pittman was out of the running for McCarran's Senate seat.[28]

Still, some people, even within the McCarran machine, would have supported almost any candidate other than Bible. Biltz and Mueller preferred their friend, Reno lawyer William Cashill. McCarran's administrative assistant Eva Adams, who had assumed a leading role in McCarran's Senate office operation, had little regard for Bible. Her administrative skill, competence, and loyalty made her McCarran's key employee, but she considered Bible stuffy and methodical, with a tendency toward indecision—all valid criticisms.[29] In turn, Bible questioned her judgment due to her relationship with Biltz and Mueller. By the late 1940s Biltz had accumulated a fortune through speculation in real estate, particularly around Lake Tahoe, and had become a key political supporter and fund-raiser for McCarran. Mueller was arguably the most influential lobbyist in Nevada state government.

Furthermore, Bible worried about the impact of Biltz's money on McCarran's Senate decisions. Aware that Biltz had helped McCarran financially on more than one occasion, Bible knew firsthand of McCarran's fiscal disorganization: as early as 1934 many people had complained to him about McCarran's refusal to pay his debts, thinking that Bible would bring the matter to the attention of the "boss."[30] In exchange for gifts, money, and fund-raising, McCarran had used his influence in Washington to provide Biltz and Mueller with favors that benefited them financially.[31] Consequently, Bible could never be sure if Adams represented his interests or those of Biltz and Mueller. He had no desire to continue the tainted alliance. Biltz and Mueller knew Bible's feelings, and so did Adams.

Meanwhile, the Democrats moved swiftly to place Bible on the November ballot, and Republicans acted just as quickly to block him. On the day after McCarran's death Governor Charles Russell wrote to the attorney general, William T. Mathews, for an opinion on his power to appoint a replacement for McCarran and how long the appointee could serve. Two days later Mathews told Russell that his power to appoint a replacement was temporary, meaning that the appointee could not serve out the unexpired term. In this case, the term of Russell's appointee would expire after the validation of the November election results by the state Supreme Court—roughly two months away.[32] Notwithstanding the opinion, Republicans believed that the appointee should finish the term, which would keep a Republican in McCarran's Senate seat until the November 1956 elections. Even if defeated in the general election, they argued, the appointee would remain in the Senate until January 3, 1957.

On October 1, 1954, Governor Russell appointed Ernest Brown, a relatively unknown and uncontroversial Reno attorney, to fill the vacancy. The Democrats unanimously selected Bible as their choice to succeed McCarran, whereupon Republicans moved to keep Bible's name from appearing on the ballot. The Democrats brought suit to settle the matter. On October 8, 1954, the Nevada Supreme Court quickly disposed of the issue along the lines Mathews had cited in his opinion; Bible's name went on the statewide ballot in time for the November elections.[33]

The Bible-Brown senatorial contest was boring and brief. The two found little on which to disagree. The election proved to be a lopsided popularity contest, with Bible defeating his lesser-known opponent by 12,573 votes statewide. More importantly, this time Bible ran well in predominantly Democratic Clark and White Pine counties, rolling up impressive majorities: 15,650 to 8,088 in Clark, and 3,020 to 1,294 in White Pine. Even in strongly Republican Washoe County, Bible ran even with Brown.[34]

In 1954 Bible had a clear advantage over Brown. Relatively unknown statewide, Brown received little outside support from the Eisenhower administration. The deepening recession of 1953 and 1954 and the short time in which to campaign also hampered Brown. Although Republicans did win most state contests in Nevada, they fared poorly across the country, where Democrats took advantage of high unemployment and the recession to gain two Senate and seventeen House seats.[35]

Bible's performance represented an impressive turnabout from 1952. He proved that he could win a statewide election by carrying a large majority of Clark County voters. The results also increased his standing in the party because no other Democrat won a major office in Nevada in 1954: candidates for Congress, state controller, governor, and lieutenant governor all went down to defeat.[36] Indeed, Bible had replaced Vail Pittman as the state's leading and most popular Democrat. His prospects seemed bright, but Nevada politics would never be the same after McCarran's departure.

After growing in scope and power since 1932, the McCarran machine soon disintegrated. It had been held together less by ideology than by the force of McCarran's personality. He never seemed to forgive anyone or to mend political fences, causing lifelong feuds and quarrels that severely damaged the Nevada Democratic Party.[37] Though loyal to McCarran in life and death, Bible was his mentor's opposite in personality and temperament. Unlike McCarran, Bible stirred no deep-seated passions in people: a core of supporters worked for him out of dedication and commitment, not because of fear or the profit motive. The differences between McCarran and Bible in 1954 were as stark as those between Eisenhower and his vice-president, Richard Nixon. Eisenhower and Bible liked people, whereas McCarran and Nixon were both emotional haters.[38]

Bible had a more easygoing nature than McCarran. He stayed out of purely state matters unless asked to intervene. He had no desire to be governor as well as senator. Perhaps the greatest difference between the two was Bible's willingness to share credit for his achievements with the other members of the Nevada delegation, which he saw as a team working for the best interests of the state, not as junior partners to do his bidding.

Still, the continuity in the McCarran and Bible years was clear. While the two men exhibited vastly different personality traits, they agreed on fundamental issues. Sharing the premise that Nevada's interests superseded all others, Bible proved as tireless as McCarran in expanding the state's economic potential with federal dollars. Regional solidarity on matters of water and power commanded center stage. Like McCarran, Bible used his office to aid young Nevadans who attended college in the nation's capital, particularly his alma mater, Georgetown. But unlike McCarran, he placed no demands on their loyalty afterward, although he understandably expected to benefit from their support once they returned home.

Ironically, Bible was sworn into office on December 2, 1954, the same day the Senate voted to condemn Senator Joe McCarthy.[39] Within three months in 1954 the nation's two leading red-baiters fell from power, one through death and the other through dishonor. Although Bible shared many of the same concerns about the dangers of worldwide communism, he wisely kept his views to himself, avoiding the finger-pointing and character assassination of the McCarthy-McCarran approach.

Thus, 1954 was a turning point for Nevada's freshman senator and for America. After 1954 McCarthyism declined almost as rapidly as it had arisen as a force in American politics, signaling a new direction in the political life of the nation. As the post-Stalin era began amid expectations of new diplomatic initiatives, America started down the long, dark path toward involvement in Vietnam after the French defeat at Dienbienphu. Domestically, the AFL-CIO merged into a single unified labor force, ending decades of bitter dispute between skilled and unskilled labor. The Supreme Court ruled in *Brown* v. *Board of Education of Topeka, Kansas* that the separate but equal doctrine was inherently unequal and unconstitutional. Democrats regained control of the United States Senate, aiding Lyndon Johnson's rise to power. All of these events would affect Bible in some way, but none more so than the changing of the Senate guard.

The careers of Lyndon Johnson and Alan Bible would be intertwined through much of the two decades in which Bible served in the Senate. Bible had his own agenda, but he understood his limitations and those of Nevada. When Johnson quickly and clearly established himself as the Senate's leader, Bible became one of his staunchest supporters, first when he was majority leader for six years, then as vice-president (and thus the Senate's presiding officer) for three years, and finally as president for another six years. The relationship benefited Johnson, who rewarded Bible's loyalty. But even amid all of the controversy to come, Johnson's ascent would serve Nevada in general, and Bible in particular.

Chapter Four

Signs of Things to Come:

The Quest for Land, Water, and Metals,

1955–1956

On January 15, 1955, only a month after being sworn into office, Alan Bible appeared on the national CBS radio program *Capitol Cloakroom*. When questioned by newsman Bill Shadel about his main goals in Congress, Bible listed "development of the West's water, power, and natural resources, protection of its industries against foreign imports and the nation's internal security." Asked to elaborate on the justification for the tremendous cost of reclamation projects, Bible replied, "The country must not forget that these projects repay every dollar to the federal treasury. They build the country's economic wealth, increase our industrial level and bring into cultivation vast areas of land adding to our food output." He noted that water, mining, and power issues had been an important part of his political background.[1]

Thus, from the beginning, Bible showed little concern for anything beyond his region and state. But while his statement represents a clear and unequivocal expression of legislative ends, it also reflects his view of federalism. He believed that the federal government's job was to aid in economic development of western states by providing money for projects to attract industry and increase agricultural production. Bible also felt strongly that the federal government should not expand its control over any project simply because it was the source of money. He wanted federal money with no strings attached.

Furthermore, in his enthusiasm for diverting federal dollars to the West, Bible ignored the fact that the western states rarely repaid the entire cost of development, simply writing off huge sums of money for flood control or recreation development expenses. Moreover, the Bureau of Reclamation's figures on cost-to-benefit ratios of mammoth western water projects were deliberately misleading because they failed to include repayments for recreation, flood control, and wildlife maintenance. By excluding these costs, water users, in effect, received a subsidy from the federal government, which kept down the cost of water development.[2] Still, Bible's views on water reclamation reflected mainstream western thinking in the postwar period, particularly in states like Nevada, which benefited tremendously from the expanded federal presence in regional economic development.

But with the Eisenhower landslide in 1952 came a dramatic shift in philosophy regarding the government's role in developing western resources. The 1952 election culminated the conservative attacks on Roosevelt's New Deal and Truman's Fair Deal that had been gathering momentum since the end of World War II. While Eisenhower refrained from dismantling the structure of Roosevelt's welfare state, as many in his party would have liked, he committed himself to a balanced budget by reducing government expenditures and decentralizing authority based on states' rights.[3] No one reflected the Eisenhower ideal better than Douglas McKay, the administration's first secretary of the interior.

More than any other administration official, McKay became the target of those who opposed Eisenhower's domestic policies and longed for a return to the more liberal days of the New Deal. The one-time Chevrolet dealer and Oregon governor was an unpopular choice for interior secretary among development-minded western Democrats. McKay's troubles began even before his confirmation hearings. Senator Wayne Morse (D-Oregon) called McKay "very good for reactionary forces that are out to plunder the people, as the nominee was a well recognized stooge of the Tidelands thieves, the private utility gang and other selfish interests."[4] Rumors even circulated that McKay would trade favors with oil and power interests to pay Republican campaign debts. While his confirmation hearing did nothing to help McKay's image or alleviate fears that his friends would raid for profits, his news conference following the hearing harmed him even more. McKay appeared so confused and detached from the issues that columnist and historian Bernard DeVoto commented, with a flair for euphemism, "McKay does not know the lower outlet of his alimentary system from a hole in the ground."[5]

In truth, McKay simply followed the party line, first from the White House and then from Congress, because conservative Republicans enacted the 1952 party platform plank on resource management into law. Seeking a complete restructuring of federal land-use policy, they wanted to turn over federal lands in the West to state and private developers. Initially, Republicans and their Democratic allies managed to pass legislation that transferred offshore oil lands from federal to state control. But when it came to western grazing lands, the Eisenhower administration faced continual opposition to its efforts to pass legislation known collectively as the Barrett-D'Ewart bills, which would transfer millions of acres of federally owned land to states for development and livestock maintenance. Senator James Murray (D-Montana) summed up the case against the plan, the work of Senator Frank Barrett (R-Wyoming) and Representative Wesley D'Ewart of Montana, calling it "another monumental giveaway."[6]

From 1952 to 1954 the Barrett-D'Ewart plan lost ground both in the White House and in Congress. The charges of "giveaways" hurt Republican congressional candidates in 1954, particularly in western states, which contributed to the Democratic return to power. Bible provided a prime example of the motives and results of opposition. Although he supported Nevada's livestock industry, he did so with considerably less zeal than his predecessor, Pat McCarran, who had unmercifully attacked the Grazing Service just for doing its job. Like Barrett and D'Ewart, McCarran wanted the states to control western land—a position Bible consistently opposed.[7] Viewing the federal government as better suited to protect the public domain (and the people's interest in it) than the western states, which he knew all too well were concerned mainly with development and profits, Bible believed in the need for some limits on growth and development. By drawing the line at the wholesale dismantling of the public domain, Bible proved that he was no "Sagebrush Rebel," willing to sacrifice public lands on the altar of private financial expediency.[8]

In addition to battling Eisenhower's public lands policy, Bible challenged the administration on reclamation. Soon after the 1952 presidential election the president announced his no-new-starts policy, designed to slow the reclamation projects under construction and to eliminate those under consideration. The administration had similar ideas on electric power development, announcing that new power plants were unnecessary unless private interests proved unable to meet the needs of consumers.

The administration's purpose was clear, but western Democrats understood the connection between regional economic development and federally financed water and power projects. Nevada was incapable of producing great quantities of cheap electric power because it had so little water. Because Southern California consumers received most of the power from Hoover Dam, the rapidly expanding populations in other western states needed new dams along the Colorado River to meet their needs. Bible and others wanted another New Deal in the West in which the federal government would finance reclamation projects to provide the water and power for growth and development to continue.

Eisenhower, however, believed that the private sector should bear the burden of development. In such areas as the Snake River, where private power advocates had been battling with supporters of proposed new federal projects, the administration favored private enterprise.[9] Clearly, the administration wanted to avoid another Tennessee Valley Authority or Columbia Valley Authority along the lines planned by the Truman administration. Eisenhower considered the TVA a prime example of what he called "creeping socialism."[10] Meanwhile, Democrats like Bible opposed the president's assault on the citadel of public works.

Leading the charge against the president's policy were Senators Morse and Murray, along with future majority leader Mike Mansfield (D-Montana). These development-minded Democrats questioned not only the wisdom of the president's land and resource policy, but the larger issue: which branch of government had the authority and responsibility to make policy in these vital areas. From their perspective, the best judge of regional needs and priorities was Congress, not the president. Conversely, the president maintained that water and power issues were politically charged, which more often than not resulted in wasteful and costly legislation. Eisenhower concluded:

> Bigger and better reclamation projects had been authorized merely to meet political demands. In place of such opportunism, the partnership emphasis could be defended as a long-term plan, adequate enough to meet all the water and power of the nation, but fiscally sound and equitable in its arrangements. The participation of private and local organizations was not inconsistent with furthering the interests of the people.[11]

Meanwhile, echoing Senator Murray's earlier "giveaway" charge, congressional Democrats attacked the administration's land-use policy, now extended to western water and power projects. As with the land, the federal government was giving away water and power to private developers. Indeed, the whole issue of western development pitted the advocates of centralized government control against supporters of private enterprise who wanted to exploit natural resources for profit. Ironically, Bible supported centralized authority while claiming the mantle of states' rights—as he did throughout his Senate career, at least when it suited his purposes.

In the view of western Democrats, the 1954 election which brought Bible to the Senate had been a referendum on private versus public interest politics.[12] The "giveaway" charges had hurt the Eisenhower administration. Although Bible's triumph over Ernest Brown had little or nothing to do with public interest politics on regional issues, it had the effect of a victory, since Bible quickly aligned himself with Senate Democrats who opposed Eisenhower's policies. Bible endorsed the utilitarian concept of natural resource management along the lines of Progressives Gifford Pinchot and Theodore Roosevelt and, later, Franklin Roosevelt's New Deal. For Bible, the newly elected majority leader, Lyndon Johnson, represented a logical extension of the New Deal philosophy as it applied to western issues. In 1955 Johnson announced,

"I believed then, and I still believe in many of the causes Roosevelt backed. That includes development of water power and all other natural resources." Bible and Johnson soon became close political allies, their ties cemented by their common understanding of western issues and shared commitment to an expansive federal role in the development of western land, water, and power. Both men owed much of their political success to water development. In the words of Tommy "The Cork" Corcoran, a leader of FDR's brain trust, "LBJ's whole world was built on water." [13]

In 1955, when Johnson became Senate majority leader, the clash over water and power development shifted from the Pacific Northwest to the Colorado River Basin—the area of Bible's expertise. The issue that galvanized the debate was the Upper Colorado Storage Project, which pitted upper basin interests against lower basin users (see fig. 2). This battle had a tremendous impact on Bible's Senate career and his outlook on land-use policy. Indeed, the mid-1950s proved to be the springboard for heightened environmental concerns during the 1960s. The Upper Colorado Storage Project triggered considerable support for protecting the region's natural wonders.

The Upper Colorado Storage Act brought Bible into contact with one of the Senate's most powerful Democrats, Clinton P. Anderson of New Mexico. Bible and Anderson became political allies because they had similar concerns and opinions on most public policy questions affecting the West, believing that the federal government should spearhead western development, with the Bureau of Reclamation leading the way. They both saw the development of the Colorado River, which New Mexico and Nevada shared, as the key to the economic expansion of their states. Both supported an expanded and revitalized national park system. [14] Anderson was a Senate leader in these matters. As a newcomer—and as usual—Bible was prepared to follow.

Anderson shared Bible's determination to protect his state's claim to the Colorado's waters for agricultural, hydroelectric, and municipal uses. In 1947 the Bureau of Reclamation had unveiled its Central Arizona Project (CAP) with a price tag of $700 million. The following year Anderson entered the Senate, took a seat on the Interior and Insular Affairs Committee, and immediately became a key player in all matters concerning the river's development.

In the spring of 1949 the Senate Interior and Insular Affairs Committee held hearings for six weeks on the Central Arizona Project. Anderson wanted to pin down the exact source from which Arizona would draw water if the CAP were approved. He and others worried that if California extended its water rights through future use, Arizona would have no alternative but to get its water from the shares intended for the upper basin states. In a typical display of humor, Anderson summed up New Mexico's position, and

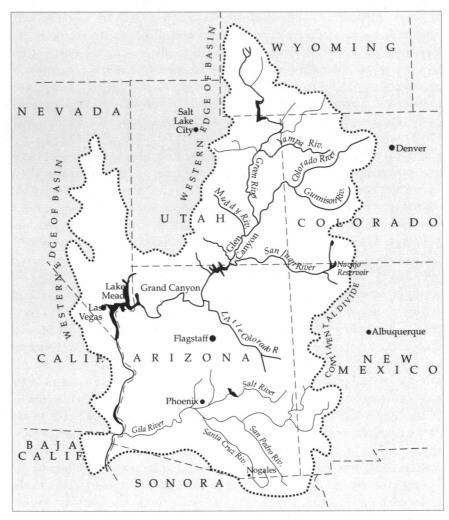

Fig. 2. The Colorado River Basin. (Courtesy of Nancy Peppin;
from A River Too Far, *Joseph Finkhouse and Mark Crawford, eds.)*

Nevada's, when he observed, "I am not particular as to which person picks
our pocket, but I just want to be sure you realize we understand we are
about to have it picked." [15] The more Colorado River water California used
and the longer it kept Arizona from using the water, the greater California's
claim would be; as the first in time to use it, the state was also the first in
right. In theory, California could lay claim to most of the 7.5 million acre-feet
a year set aside for the lower basin in the Colorado River Compact of 1922.

Anderson was determined that Arizona's water problems would have a limited impact on New Mexico's right to use 800,000 acre-feet a year from the Colorado. In 1950, only a year after Anderson and the full Interior and Insular Affairs Committee voted to approve the CAP, the Bureau of Reclamation released its proposal for developing the upper basin. The price tag was a staggering $1.5 billion, more than twice the cost of the CAP. The plan called for six high dams, storage facilities, power-generation plants, flood control, and irrigation and included seventeen lesser projects strung all along the upper Colorado River basin.[16] The Bureau of Reclamation proposed that New Mexico receive its share of water by way of a transmountain diversion from the San Juan River across the Continental Divide to Albuquerque. The entire project faced tremendous obstacles; two of the foremost problems, Indian water rights and objections from preservationists, had implications for Bible and Nevada.[17]

The conflicting demands of Indian and Anglo water users along the river could have destroyed the whole upper basin plan by smothering the project beneath an avalanche of litigation with unforeseeable results. The Navajo Reservation Indians of New Mexico insisted that reclamation plans include irrigation projects for their use along the San Juan. If approved, these might drastically reduce the amount of water available for use in Albuquerque. To Anderson's credit, he worked hard to resolve the dispute, which ultimately paved the way for enacting the entire project. When Bible encountered a similar problem along the Truckee River in northern Nevada, however, he proved unable to settle the quarrel between Anglo irrigation users and Paiute Reservation Indians, who demanded their water rights.

With the Indian demands met, Anderson moved quickly. Early in 1955 he became chairman of the Senate Interior and Insular Affairs Subcommittee on Irrigation and Reclamation. He wasted little time in introducing the Upper Colorado Storage Act, S. 500, which was identical in scope and content to his earlier proposals for river development. Bible reacted just as quickly on behalf of his southern Nevada constituents. On February 25, 1955, he announced that the Bureau of Reclamation had set aside $66,000 to study the feasibility of pumping water from Lake Mead to the Las Vegas Valley. This proved to be the beginning of what later became known as the Southern Nevada Water Project (SNWP), the key to continued growth and development in the state, particularly in the Las Vegas area.[18] Aware that he needed Anderson's help for the SNWP to become a reality, Bible began by supporting Anderson's drive to enact his upper basin plan. Bible saw that his colleague's proposal would do no harm to Nevada's water rights and had the potential to increase the state's ability to generate power.

Power, politics, and preservation soon found a common ground. On January 23, 1955, a month before the hearings on Anderson's bill, Bible received a letter from Horace M. Albright, representing the Council of Conservationists. A former director of the National Park Service and respected conservationist, Albright called for support of the Anderson plan, but only if the Senate deleted the Echo Park Dam from the bill. Furthermore, Albright insisted on two provisions: one to protect the Rainbow Bridge National Monument from water behind the Glen Canyon Dam, and a second to prohibit Congress from constructing any future dam within the boundaries of a national park or monument.[19] Bible agreed with Albright. So did Anderson, who removed the Echo Park Dam that would have destroyed the Dinosaur National Monument and inserted the two provisions that the Council of Conservationists had recommended.

This clash between the Bureau of Reclamation and preservationists introduced Bible to conflicting concepts of land use. The developers, who saw profits for everyone, and environmentalists, who were concerned with protecting the landscape for future generations, pushed Bible toward a middle position. The Upper Colorado Storage Act forced Bible and Anderson to strive for balance in resource management.

As the February hearings on Anderson's bill began, Bible worked to get as much as he could for Nevada without jeopardizing either the bill or Anderson's friendship. On March 8, 1955, Bible wrote to Governor Charles Russell to ask him if Nevada would support Anderson's plan if it guaranteed a share of the electrical power from the Glen Canyon and Bridge dams to the lower basin states.[20] Russell responded that he supported the Anderson plan because of the potential economic advantages for Nevada. Bible and Russell always considered additional power sources a high priority due to the state's inability to generate its own hydroelectric power. Indeed, power considerations had dominated the debate over the original 1922 Colorado River Compact and, later, during construction of Hoover Dam, from which Nevada received 17 percent of the power generated. But by 1955 Nevada's needs had grown substantially beyond the Hoover Dam allotment, requiring more power for the population and economic boom in the Las Vegas area.

Initially, Bible objected that Anderson's proposal banned the sale of power to lower basin states. When the full Senate Interior and Insular Affairs Committee considered the bill, Bible requested that the exclusive power use clause be omitted and the following language be inserted: "The Committee intends that full equality of treatment be accorded to both upper and lower power customers . . . and it is not intended that lower basin customers should be discriminated against in any respect."[21] Anderson accepted Bible's amendment, a small price to pay for the support of Bible and other lower basin senators whose votes Anderson needed to enact legislation that would be the cornerstone of upper basin development.

Lower basin states such as Nevada would benefit, too. Bible was elated that Nevada, through the state's Colorado River Commission, would get a share of the 800,000 kilowatt electric capacity generated from the Glen Canyon installation. On June 22, 1956, he said, "Nevada's industrial growth cannot be stopped and a vital element of this growth is electric power . . . Glen Canyon will help greatly and later Bridge Canyon. . . . Southern Nevada will get another boost in this cycle of programs which the entire state of Nevada is enjoying." [22] From Bible's perspective, Nevada's future prosperity was inextricably linked to federal water and power development in the far West.

Nor could Anderson's timing have been better calculated to win presidential support. On March 6, 1956, President Eisenhower announced his candidacy for a second term. Two weeks later House and Senate conferees struggled to resolve the differences between their respective versions of the Upper Colorado Storage Act. Candidate Eisenhower, careful not to alienate western voters, signed the legislation and heartily endorsed the concept underlying it. Thus, the Anderson bill swept away all remnants of his partnership ideal, except the rhetoric.

Still, the path to development was strewn with casualties. Anderson's Upper Colorado Storage Act further reduced the river to little more than a plumbing and hydraulic system serving the needs of a society dedicated to never-ending expansion (fig. 3). It was the beginning of what journalist and author Philip Fradkin has called *A River No More*.[23] In the mid-1950s the Colorado was the one essential resource for water and hydroelectric power in the semiarid Southwest. In Nevada, Colorado River water enabled the Las Vegas gaming industry to expand its hotel and casino operations, attracting those fleeing the urban jungle for a desert oasis. Las Vegas is an artificially created playground that would crumble under the unrelenting desert sun if not for the benefits flowing from the mechanized river. To many, the river's death seemed a small price to pay for profits and jobs, not to mention soaring land prices and home sales. While eliminating the Echo Park Dam saved the Dinosaur National Monument, the federal government turned the entire Colorado River over to developers.

In the process, the Upper Colorado Storage Act had brought together all the diverse groups seeking to influence land and water policies in the West. While preservationists lost the war over the river, they won the battle over the Dinosaur National Monument, which had a lasting impact on the public and politicians alike. Bible left the battlefield with a diversified perspective on western development that reflected a new regard for parks, recreation, wilderness, and preservation of scenic wonders.[24] For Bible, "ecopolitics" was a lesson in accommodation that tempered his zeal to exploit the region's

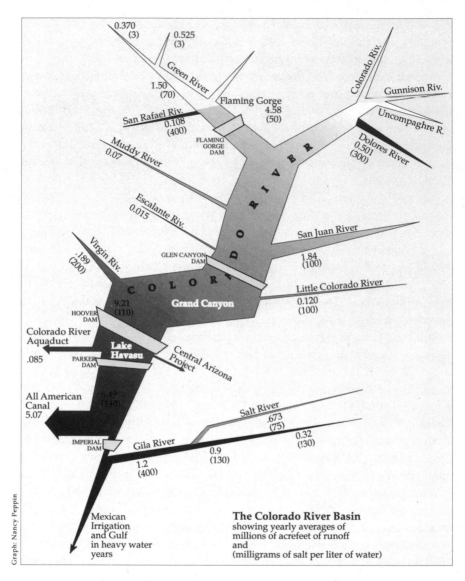

Fig. 3. *Impact of the Colorado River Storage Act on the river water. (Courtesy of Nancy Peppin; from* A River Too Far, *Joseph Finkhouse and Mark Crawford, eds.)*

natural resources purely for economic reasons. After 1956 he worked for a balance in western land use, just as Anderson had been compelled to do to pass his pathbreaking legislation.

Bible's diversified perspective proved necessary for his success; the fight to save the Dinosaur National Monument showed that preservationists had

to be taken seriously. They clearly had the political muscle and the ideological will to influence the course of legislation. Likewise, the wishes of
California's congressional delegation had to be considered in any water plan
that affected its interests. More than any other basin state, California was
the focus of suspicion because it had long been the most selfish water user
in the West.

Beginning in 1955, Bible was consumed with trying to authorize a complex
reclamation and flood control plan for northern Nevada, while adjusting
conflicts over water rights among the Paiute Indians and the Anglo farmers
who relied on reclamation. California even laid claim to some of the waters
of the Truckee, Carson, and Walker rivers in northern Nevada.

Lake Tahoe, high on the east side of the Sierra Nevadas, feeds the Truckee.
The water flows east through Nevada, terminating at Pyramid Lake. Historically, the Truckee has been a life line, providing water for domestic
and municipal use, but also serving as a dumping ground for California's
waste products, which contaminated the drinking water and killed the fish.[25]
But in 1902 the federal government passed the Newlands Reclamation Act,
which earmarked the Truckee and Carson River basins for irrigation projects.
Almost immediately, problems multiplied faster than crops. The United
States Reclamation Service (now the Bureau of Reclamation) greatly exag-
gerated the available water supply and fixed the cost of construction at an
unrealistically low level. It originally estimated that the Truckee could supply
enough water to reclaim 232,000 acres of arid land. But by 1964 only about
60,000 acres were actually receiving irrigated water.[26]

By 1918, disillusioned by government mismanagement, high-handed administration, and escalating costs, Nevada farmers moved to create a private
operating entity—the Truckee-Carson Irrigation District (TCID). In 1926
the government and the TCID agreed to transfer control of the Newlands
Project from the federal government to the private sector and provided for
the repayment of the original costs. The deal included the Lahontan Dam
and Reservoir on the Carson River, the Lake Tahoe Dam and Derby Diversion Dam on the Truckee River, the Truckee Canal, four pumping stations,
and almost 900 miles of canals, laterals, and drains.

From the taxpayer's standpoint, the Newlands Project was a bad investment. The Department of the Interior estimated that the Newlands Project
cost $7,947,000, and wrote off $4,438,000, reducing TCID's liability to
$3,509,000. From 1926 to 1964 the TCID paid about $3,204,000 and still
owed the government $305,000 in 1964,[27] leaving more than half of the origi-
nal cost of construction unpaid, with the balance not paid back for more
than thirty years. It was an expensive subsidy that irrigated about 60,000
acres of land used to grow alfalfa to feed cattle. Congressional critics cor-

rectly charged that eastern taxpayers were bearing the major burden of a reclamation project that benefited few outside the West.

The Newlands Project was only the beginning of what became a massive federal subsidy for western development interests. From its inception in 1902 construction costs greatly exceeded estimates, stretching Nevada farmers' meager resources to the breaking point to repay the government for projects described to them as affordable. Legal expenses incurred in expensive litigation over water rights added to the costs and contributed substantially to the farmers' overall liability. The Reclamation Service, overly optimistic in calculating how much water was available for reclamation, failed to consider such factors as soil composition in estimating land productivity. All of this deepened the Eisenhower administration's opposition to federally financed reclamation projects.

But Bible and others in northern Nevada continued to praise the success of western reclamation in general and the Newlands Project in particular. On June 14, 1955, Bible introduced S. 2218, a bill to authorize the conveyance of the Newlands Project, land, and works to the TCID, when it completed the repayment schedule in the 1926 contract. He declared, "The Newlands Project was a wonderful and successful experiment. It charted a great future for reclamation development in this country." Reclamation was to Bible what Social Security was to most of his colleagues: the most sacred of all government acts. Bible went even further in expressing his sentiments: "The Nevada farmers who assured this success paid in dollars and cents for the trial and error experience it gave the federal government in pioneering this field from which the entire nation has benefitted." [28] He correctly argued that Nevada farmers paid dearly for the government's experiment in reclamation, since the original predictions of low-cost water for irrigation were unrealistic. But to say that western reclamation projects substantially enriched the whole nation distorted reality.

Indeed, after the Newlands Project, the government kept pouring money into northern Nevada's water schemes. Beginning in 1937, the Bureau of Reclamation authorized the Truckee River Storage Project and the Boca Reservoir on the Little Truckee. The Boca Reservoir would hold up to 40,000 acre-feet of water, supplement the irrigation of 27,000 acres of Truckee Meadows farmland near Reno, and provide an alternate water source for municipal and industrial purposes in Reno. In 1948 the bureau created the Stillwater National Wildlife Refuge between the Newlands Project (TCID) and the Carson Sink. But this multipurpose waterfowl area depended upon water from the Newlands Project, putting more pressure on a system unable to meet the needs, let alone the demands, for more water.

This need for additional water sources was apparent to Nevadans as early as 1927, when developers sought to expand the potential water delivery from the Truckee and Carson rivers further upstream in California. But the real push came in 1952, when Senator George Malone persuaded the Senate Public Works Committee to hold hearings in Reno on flood control, water and power development, and the commercial possibilities of the Truckee and Carson. In May 1954 Senator McCarran introduced legislation to authorize construction of what became known as the Washoe Project—a multipurpose system to provide flood control, irrigation, and municipal water delivery to supplement the Newlands Project and service the needs of western Nevada's growing population. But the McCarran plan stalled when the Bureau of Reclamation failed to complete its studies in time for Congress to take action. With McCarran's death in September and the Democrats regaining control of Congress in 1955, the burden immediately fell on Bible to steer the Washoe Project through Congress.

Bible moved quickly. After meeting with Secretary of the Interior Douglas McKay about the project, he dashed off to Reno to chair more hearings, this time by the Senate Interior and Insular Affairs Committee. On January 18, 1955, just after the congressional Christmas recess and about a month after Bible took office, he and Malone introduced S. 497, which authorized the Washoe Reclamation Project for Nevada and California. On April 26, 1956, Bible's Washoe Project finally passed the Senate and later the House. Like Anderson's Upper Colorado Storage Act, its timing to gain White House approval was perfect. President Eisenhower, still reluctant to antagonize western voters, signed the Washoe measure on August 1, 1956.[29]

Bible was elated. The Washoe Plan promised to aid northern Nevada's growth and development, as the Upper Colorado Storage Act aided southern Nevada. Commenting on the bill, Bible said, "This is a great day for Nevada. This project will halt costly floods and bring economic growth to our state. This will reclaim new agricultural lands, provide sorely-needed electrical energy, and provide a new economic base on which new generations can build."[30]

For all of this, the Washoe Project's price tag was indeed low, at least compared with the Upper Colorado Storage Act. The original estimate was $43,700,000, later revised to $52,000,000, to build Prosser Dam and Reservoir, which would impound 30,000 acre-feet of water. It also included a 175,000 acre-foot storage facility to be built at Stampede Dam on the Little Truckee River in California and a 115,000 acre-foot reservoir at Watasheamu on the Carson River's east fork. In addition, the plans included two power plants, the Cal-Vada installation below Stampede Dam and the Watasheamu facility near the Carson Valley (fig. 4).[31]

As with the Newlands Project, Nevadans did not need to repay the full

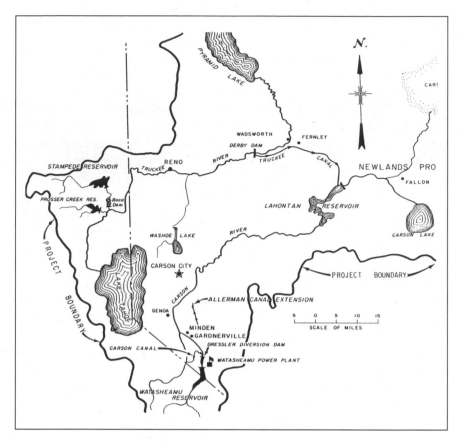

Fig. 4. Washoe Project, 1961. (Alan Bible Collection, Box 101)

cost of the Washoe Plan. The government immediately eliminated $8,000,000 in flood control costs. By deducting another $2,000,000 for fish and wild-life protection and $100,000 for recreation purposes, $41,900,000 remained to be repaid; about $35,000,000 would come from power revenues and the balance, nearly $7,000,000, from water users over a fifty-year period.[32]

While the Newlands Project, with its one-dimensional irrigation plan, was clearly wasteful and costly, the multipurpose Washoe Project could be justi-fied in the public interest. The Reno-Sparks area badly needed flood control measures. In extremely wet years, as recently as 1950 and 1955, the runoff from the melting snow pack in the Sierra Nevadas overflowed the Truckee River, resulting in extensive property damage. The Army Corps of Engineers planned to improve the Truckee River channel, but more permanent works were necessary to halt the periodic devastation.

The project served other useful purposes. The proposed dam construction would not only hold back potential floodwaters by regulating the Truckee's flow, but provide needed water for municipal and industrial use in dry years. Western Nevada sorely needed its hydroelectric power, because most of the available sources were stretched to their limits. Still, the Washoe Plan left several major problems unresolved, principally in the area of the conflicting water rights of California and Nevada, the federal government, the TCID, and the Paiutes of the Pyramid Lake Reservation. Any or all of them could destroy the whole project.

So, too, could the United States Supreme Court. In 1955 the court confused the issue of water rights in the West with its ruling in *Federal Power Commission* v. *Oregon et al.*, more commonly known as the Pelton Dam case. The State of Oregon opposed building the Pelton Dam along the Deschutes River and refused to issue construction permits or to allow the federal government to impound water behind the proposed site. In ruling against Oregon, the high court held that Congress had not given the states control over water flowing through the public domain and that the government did not need state permits for construction wholly on public land. The court's decision came as it was taking testimony, through a special master, in *Arizona* v. *California*, which also could drastically alter the structure of state water laws, causing economic upheaval in the process.[33]

The court's line of reasoning in the Pelton Dam case reached as far back as 1899 in *United States* v. *Rio Grande Dam and Irrigation Company*.[34] Speaking for the court, Justice David Brewer said, "In the absence of specific authority from Congress, a state cannot by its legislation destroy the right of the United States, as the owner of lands bordering on a stream, to the continual flow of its waters; so far at least as may be necessary for the beneficial uses of the government property."[35] Trying to resolve the issue of state versus national supremacy over water rights, western congressmen countered with section 8 of the Reclamation Act of 1902. In *Kansas* v. *Colorado* (1907), the Supreme Court seemed to indicate that state water laws were supreme. But by saying otherwise on the Pelton Dam, the justices threatened to wipe out the structure western states had relied on to control the flow of water within their borders.[36] This was an issue of great significance, since about 60 percent of the western water supply originated from sources located on federal lands.

While many western leaders were confused, federal water officials were elated. Supporters of the doctrine of federal reserve rights and the supremacy of federal water rights had long maintained that the federal government was the original owner of the public domain and all of the water attached to it. They argued that the government sold land to private persons and allowed the states and territories "to parcel out water to make the land productive." As with the land, title to water passed directly from the federal government to private hands, with states acting merely as administrative agents for the federal government. In short, western states never had owned the water on the public domain.[37]

From the standpoint of federal reclamation officials, the doctrine of federal reserve rights provided a comfortable framework for control of federal water projects, unencumbered by conflicting state water claims. The conflicts between California and Nevada over the Washoe Project provided a classic case. Lined up solidly against the project, the counties in northeastern California threatened the plans of Nevada and the Bureau of Reclamation.[38]

Still, western states were not about to surrender their perceived dominance in water matters without a fight. Western senators moved at once to repair the damage from the Pelton Dam case. On February 1, 1956, Senator Frank A. Barrett (R-Wyoming) led the charge with twenty of his Republican and Democratic colleagues, including Nevadans Malone and Bible, to regain through the legislative process what western states had lost in the courts. Barrett introduced S. 863, officially known as the Western Water Rights Settlement Act, "to govern the control, appropriation, use, and distribution of water." Point by point, the bill refuted the court's ruling in the Pelton Dam case and denunciation of the federal reserve rights doctrine. Beginning with section 2, the act clearly outlined Bible's view of federalism as it applied to water resource policy:

> Neither the proprietorship functions of the United States derived from the ownership of the public lands nor the exercise of its powers relating to interstate commerce and the general welfare should be permitted unduly to interfere with priority rights in the use of water or the orderly acquisition of such rights in the future. . . . It has not been and is not the intention of the Congress that federal agencies, in pursuing their programs for water resources development in these arid land and semi-arid areas, shall have any prerogative to preempt the field or cast clouds on the security of prior rights under state law acquired for beneficial purposes.[39]

Barrett, Bible, and their western colleagues badly wanted federal reclamation projects, but without the reserve rights that many federal water experts advocated. Likewise, section 6 of Barrett's proposal went to the heart of the matter, the issue of supremacy. The act specified:

> All unappropriated navigable and nonnavigable ground and surface waters are reserved for appropriation and use of the public pursuant to state law, and rights to the use of such waters for beneficial purposes shall be acquired under state laws relating to the appropriation, con-

trol, use, and distribution of such waters. Federal agencies . . . in the
use of water for any purpose in connection with federal programs . . .
shall acquire rights to the use thereof in conformity with state laws and
procedures.[40]

It was the clearest possible statement of Bible's view. For Bible, as for other
supporters of the Barrett plan, the federal government's role in the development of water resources was that of financier only.[41]

Section 9 took on the issue of federal supremacy that the Supreme Court
raised in the Pelton Dam case by making all federal withdrawals of water
from federal land "without prejudice to the beneficial use of water originat-
ing in or flowing across such lands, theretofore or thereafter initiated under
the laws of the states in which such lands are situated."[42] Thus, the federal
government could control no water in the West unless it conformed to state
law and received the state's permission to use such water. This was exactly
what Newlands intended to accomplish in section 8 of the 1902 Reclamation
Act, and the Barrett bill of 1956 just as clearly sought to restate and clarify
what western leaders believed to have been the law for more than fifty years.
The bill ignored the practical and difficult problems of conflicting claims and
rights between states like California and Nevada, however. Nor did it address how to settle disputes between states sharing the same water source
and reclamation projects.

The irony is evident. Unable to work out their water rights without resort-
ing to a costly litigation process, the western states were incensed that the
federal government had done what the states clearly failed to do themselves.
The government was unwilling to withdraw from the field of water rights.
In its comments on the Barrett bill, the Bureau of the Budget recommended
against enactment, pointing to the legal and constitutional problems the
Interior and Justice departments were studying.[43] Indeed, the unresolved
issues continued through almost every legislative session thereafter, with
unforeseen consequences for California and Nevada. Water rights remained
as uncertain as ever, with the federal government chipping away at the
supposed supremacy of state water laws.

Meanwhile, Nevada and California tried to solve their water problems and
assure the Washoe Project's continued success. On March 10, 1955, Senator
William Knowland (R-California) introduced S. 1391, co-sponsored by his
Republican colleague Thomas Kuchel and Nevadans Malone and Bible. The
measure gave congressional consent for California and Nevada to negotiate
a compact to distribute the waters of the Truckee, Carson, and Walker rivers,
Lake Tahoe, and their tributaries.[44] By July both houses had passed the bill,
which President Eisenhower signed on August 11.

Afterward Bible called the California-Nevada Compact bill a necessary outgrowth of the Washoe Project, which Congress had approved earlier. California and Nevada shared the water needed to fuel Nevada's $52 million project. Lake Tahoe, which empties into the Truckee River, lies partly in each state. After flowing through eastern California, the Truckee runs through Reno in western Nevada and is the area's primary source of water. From Reno, the river continues east and ultimately empties into Pyramid Lake. Between Reno and Pyramid Lake, nearly half of the water is diverted south to the Carson Sink, where it irrigates farmland under the TCID's control. Californians, in turn, made little use of the much smaller Carson and Walker rivers, but western Nevada farmers relied on them as a primary source for crop irrigation. Other water uses soon forced Bible to rethink his policies. By the mid-1950s the same forces fueling the environmental movement became involved in water issues in Nevada, and Bible would have to pay heed to them. The central question was whether water was more important for recreation—boating, camping, and outdoor activity—or for farms and industry. As Lake Tahoe grew into an important recreation area, its population, homes, and businesses placed greater demands on the water resources needed to stimulate further expansion. Clearly, growth and development were in the interest of both states, but their approach differed: Nevada wanted to enhance its agricultural and municipal use; California saw tourism in the Tahoe Basin as the best use for the limited water supply.[45] Unless negotiators of the California-Nevada Compact could resolve the water use issues, the entire Washoe Project was in jeopardy. California's powerful congressional delegation could easily cut off funding, as it had done earlier with the Central Arizona Project.

Similarly, the dispute over the Carson River involved Nevada and California—and the federal government. Beginning in 1902, the Newlands Project used Carson River water to irrigate crops in Fernley and Fallon. In 1925 the federal government filed suit in behalf of the Newlands Project to determine its right to Carson River water and the rights of California and Nevada. The federal court refused to enter a decree, prolonging the uncertainty for all of the water users who depended on the river. In the late 1940s the government renewed the controversy when it refused to build new reservoirs along the river until the issues raised in its 1925 suit had been settled. Moreover, farmers in California and Nevada who were not beneficiaries of reclamation water feared that the government would establish water rights by virtue of its contract obligations to the TCID, which could force those not using the project to supply additional water for district farmers downstream.[46]

The Walker River presented a different set of problems: fairness and equity. Nevadans dominated the water control board, created in a 1936 court decree, that decided water allocation, raising the suspicions of California's farmers. The issue reached a fever pitch in the 1940s when the Walker River Irrigation District's directors considered building more reservoirs without regard to the needs of California's users.[47]

While California and Nevada water users staked out their positions, the unknown factor was the Pyramid Lake Paiutes, whose needs Bible had to take into account. Since 1905 economic conditions had steadily worsened for the nearly 700 inhabitants of the 475,000-acre Pyramid Lake Reservation, due to the 32-mile diversion canal from the Truckee River to the Carson Sink. With the loss of one-half of the natural water flow into the lake, the spawning pools dried up and the fish population declined, jeopardizing the mainstay of the Paiute diet and economy. By the 1930s the problems had reached crisis proportions: the Cui-ui Sucker was nearly extinct, the famous Cutthroat Trout appeared destined for a similar fate,[48] and the Paiutes knew that state and federal governments and the farmers to the south were to blame.

Between 1850 and 1880 the federal government removed most of the far western Indian tribes to reservations consisting mainly of poor land that Anglo settlers considered useless. In the flood of treaties, executive orders, and congressional acts setting aside Indian land, the question of water was ignored. The focus of conquest shifted from Native Americans to the land, first with the miners, later with settlers, and afterward with land speculators, railroad builders, cattle grazers, and loggers—then water rights became critical. The doctrine of prior appropriation worked well for Anglo Americans bent on conquest and pursuit of profits. But for western Indians, like the Paiutes of Pyramid Lake, prior appropriation threatened their very existence.

The first case involving Indian water rights affecting the situation in Nevada concerned the Fort Belknap Reservation Indians who had established ranches and farms along the Milk River in Montana. Anglo farmers began to divert water from the Milk River for their own use. This reduced the amount available to the Belknap Indians—a situation similar to that of the Paiutes when the Carson Sink farmers diverted Truckee water from Pyramid Lake. After the drought of 1904 and 1905 the Belknap Indians asked the federal government for help. Thereafter, the Justice Department sought a federal court restraining order to prohibit non-Indians from diverting water that the Indians on the reservation needed to survive.

From 1905 to 1908 *Winters* v. *United States* traveled through the federal courts and ultimately to the Supreme Court. In a controversial landmark decision, the high court concluded that Indian water rights differed from riparian and appropriative claims because Indians had reserve rights to water whether or not they used it, for whatever beneficial purpose they desired.[49]

This established the doctrine of reserve rights, which expanded to include areas and situations beyond Indian reservation rights. Still, a perplexing question remained: who reserved the rights—Indians, the federal government, or both?[50]

When the Supreme Court failed to explain how the Indians had reserved their water rights, two theories developed. The first held that the Indians themselves reserved them, so it followed that their rights had existed since they first occupied North America, making their claim superior to all non-Indian landholders. The second argument rested on the assumption that the federal government had reserved water rights for the Indians, making their claims dependent on the time when a reservation was established. Consequently, Indian water rights differed from reservation to reservation and in some cases might be inferior to earlier claims established by non-Indians.[51] The implications were of enormous importance. The whole structure of economics in the West, including land values, settlement patterns, and future development, was at risk.[52]

While most westerners ignored the implications of *Winters*, Nevada and the federal government took advantage of the nonagricultural economy of the Paiutes. In 1944 the federal government settled all conflicting claims to the Truckee's waters. In *U.S. v. Orr Water Ditch Co., et al.*, the Bureau of Indian Affairs (BIA), which was part of the Department of the Interior, and the Bureau of Reclamation, which brought the suit, represented the Paiutes, an inherent conflict of interest that received little notice. Claiming only enough water to irrigate a few acres of reservation land, the BIA made no demand for enough water to maintain the lake at its 1859 level or at any height that would stabilize the reservation's only industry. As a result, the *Orr Water Ditch* decree gave the Paiutes very little Truckee River water.[53]

By 1956 the condition of western Indians had changed little since the Supreme Court's pronouncement in *Winters* and the *Orr Water Ditch* decree. Clearly, Native Americans living on reservations west of the ninety-eighth meridian were the poorest, sickest, and most disadvantaged of all Americans, and few tried to relieve their plight. The federal government, usually in concert with state and local economic interests, opposed Indian claims, as in the *Orr Water Ditch* case. Moreover, the Department of the Interior consistently supported the Bureau of Reclamation over the Bureau of Indian Affairs, since the western senators and congressmen with whom Interior officials had to work cared more about water projects than about Indian rights. Nevada, and its newest senator, differed little from their western counterparts.

Indeed, Bible is representative of a whole generation of western leaders who, in their drive to develop resources for the prosperity of Anglo Americans, ignored the plight of Native Americans. It was not that the welfare of Nevada's Indians meant nothing to Bible; but civil rights differed substantially from status quo economic rights. His boyhood experience exposed him only to the benefits of federal reclamation, not to the horrors of the economic dislocation at Pyramid Lake. Believing in the progressive management of natural resources for the benefit of the many, Bible naturally concluded that Truckee River water could be better used in the Carson Sink rather than at the Pyramid Lake Reservation.

More importantly, if Bible had supported Indian water rights in northern Nevada, he would have repudiated the cornerstone of western economic expansion, not to mention states' rights. Under the *Winters* doctrine, either Indian water rights were unlimited or the federal government reserved them for beneficial use. If they were unlimited, the whole body of western water law, which had developed over decades and supported the doctrine of prior appropriation, could be wiped out. If not, federal reserve rights meant federal control and domination, the direction in which the courts had moved since the Pelton Dam case. Bible and other western leaders responded quickly to any threat to states' rights, as their support for the Barrett bill indicates. Western political leaders resisted any perceived federal encroachment, especially in the vital area of water rights. Minority rights, or the status of a disadvantaged group, had little effect on their basic concern or argument.

Practical political concerns tempered Bible's private attitudes. Had he supported the *Winters* doctrine and opposed the Washoe Project because it failed to deliver more water to Pyramid Lake, he undoubtedly would have been committing political suicide. In the West water projects represented not only material development, but also political capital. In strictly political terms, the welfare of 700 Paiute Indians meant little when compared with that of the northern section of the state. Finally, Bible was a product of his times. In the mid-1950s the nation was just beginning to be sensitive to minority rights. From a later perspective, it is easy to be critical of Bible for allowing the injustice at Pyramid Lake to continue. It must also be remembered, however, that neither Congress nor the executive branch had acted to protect Indian water rights since the *Winters* decision was first handed down in 1908. While Bible may have been morally blind, he was far from alone.

If Bible was uncomfortable about his stand on the Washoe Project and the California-Nevada Compact, he never said so publicly. Nor did he express any second thoughts about the water troubles of Nevada's Paiute Indians. In fact, he took great pride in his support for the state's Indian population, pointing to his efforts to advance the quality of reservation life through better medical facilities, grants for economic diversification, and improved educational programs.[54]

While Bible enjoyed political success in legislating water and power projects during the Eisenhower years, he met stiff resistance when he defended the cause of mining in the West, particularly in Nevada. Mining had been the lifeblood of Nevada and its politicians for nearly a century. From the silver discoveries in the 1860s to the copper and tungsten boom in the 1950s, political officeholders and aspirants were inevitably tied to the only economic activity that promised prosperity. Nevada produced a continuous line of United States senators dedicated to aiding the mining industry with federal support and subsidies. Bible was an important part of that tradition. From 1954 through 1974 he constantly championed Nevada's mining interests.

The mining boom in Nevada in the 1950s went virtually unnoticed, although its profits rivaled those of the legendary Comstock Lode of the nineteenth century and the spectacular finds at Tonopah, Goldfield, and Ely early in the twentieth century. The 1950s boom differed from the earlier ones in several ways. First, it lacked the flamboyant personalities who dominated the Comstock era—by then, gambling had a monopoly on colorful, roguish figures. Also, unlike the earlier periods, gambling was becoming Nevada's mainstay, so the mid-twentieth-century boom was less crucial to the state's economy than the previous bonanzas. In addition, silver production was less important in the 1950s; uranium, mercury, manganese, copper, and tungsten led the way. Finally, by 1957 the boom was over—much more quickly than the others—and mining's fortunes in Nevada were again in decline.[55]

The Korean War had fueled Nevada's mining comeback, led by tungsten. Before the war depressed prices had stunted the development of Nevada's massive tungsten deposits. But with government subsidies, the industry again became profitable. When Bible entered the Senate in 1955, Nevada ranked second among the states in tungsten production; between 1953 and 1955 total production reached $77.4 million.[56] The market was only temporary, however. After the war the defense industry no longer required Nevada's tungsten to manufacture armor-piercing shells, and the ensuing decline in the state's mining economy was entirely predictable.

Bible consistently argued that the federal government should stockpile tungsten because defense priorities in the postwar era remained in a state of flux. Until the nation's strategic plans were certain, he reasoned, it should continue to store whatever metals it might need. Given his record of support for defense appropriations, Bible was no doubt sincere, but his line of argument could not have been better tailored to boost Nevada's mining interests. As in the case of atomic testing and special military bases, Nevada's pure self-interest was linked to national security. The senator estimated that 7,500 jobs were at risk in Nevada, a significant number, considering its small population.[57]

Early in his Senate years Bible combined a dual approach in his support for the nation's mining industry. First, and most importantly, he sought to guarantee a market for its products. Mineral and metal prices were set on the world market, which resulted in considerable fluctuation and instability. That left domestic producers hesitant about moving ahead with large investments in development, exploration, and production. Bible supported government purchases of strategic metals along the lines of the Pittman Silver Purchase Act of 1934. The second aspect of his mining policy established him as a leading opponent of foreign imports, which became the cornerstone of his views on foreign policy.

Bible quickly made his views known. Little more than three months after taking office he introduced S. 1583 to extend the Critical Materials Stockpiling Act of 1946 and the Domestic Minerals Program Act of 1953, to "encourage the discovery, development, and production of certain domestic minerals."[58] The bill excluded foreign imports in setting production limits covering chromite, mica, asbestos, beryl, tungsten, and manganese. If approved, Bible's plan would significantly boost Nevada's mining production: it was the largest producer of manganese and the second biggest supplier of tungsten in the United States. S. 1583 was a staggering subsidy for the domestic mining industry.

Throughout the spring and summer of 1955 Bible and other western senators presented a united front in behalf of western mining interests. The result was S. 922, introduced by Senator Barry Goldwater (R-Arizona) and co-sponsored by Malone and Bible. S. 922 was essentially the same as the earlier Bible proposal, but it would extend government purchases for twelve years instead of six.[59] On May 17, 1955, the full Interior and Insular Affairs Committee approved S. 922 and sent it to the Senate floor for debate. Two days later the Senate approved the measure, which the House soon passed (H.R. 6373). Apprising his constituents of the Senate's action, Bible insisted, "Domestic mining industry is just as important for peace as it is for war. Our dependence upon foreign sources must be abrogated in every possible way. Therefore, this domestic purchase program must be continued."[60]

But not everyone saw the issue as one of national defense. Speaking for the opposition, Senator John Williams (R-Delaware) called the measure a "price support for western mining." He pointed out that government stockpiles were already at record levels; over the next twelve years it would cost the taxpayers another $750 million to increase supplies of metals that the government would neither need nor use.[61] Echoing Williams, Arthur Flemming, director of the Office of Defense Mobilization, said, "There would be no justification in the name of national defense for either extending or enlarging these programs in the manner proposed."[62]

S. 922 was unquestionably pork-barrel legislation designed to aid the slumping mining industry. Clearly structured to protect the industry from foreign competition, it required the government to purchase metals at prices higher than world market levels. President Eisenhower recognized the bill's implications and let it die by pocket veto on August 17, 1955. He said, "Government assistance to the producers of several minerals will not be continued under the guise of defense needs when such needs do not exist."[63] But the 1955 Domestic Mineral Program bill laid the philosophical foundation for Bible's support for western mining. He wanted price supports in the form of subsidies and protectionist legislation to curb imports that competed with domestic producers. The 1955 measure merely began a twenty-year battle to save a declining industry. For Bible and at least some of his constituents, this became a central part of their lives.

Thus, Bible and his colleagues were back again in early 1956, knocking at the door of the federal vault on behalf of western miners. This time Bible and his cohorts decided to start with a modest proposal, S. 3379, introduced by Senator James Murray, "to provide for the maintenance of essential production of tungsten ores."[64] The Murray plan called for the purchase of a million short tons of tungsten ore a year for a three-year period, ending on June 30, 1959. But a week later Murray, Bible, and other supporters of western mining scrapped S. 3379 in favor of S. 3982, a replica of the failed Goldwater bill of 1955. Western senators hoped to cash in on election-year politics and pass a domestic minerals measure, just as they had done with regional reclamation projects.

To be sure, presidential politics played a key role in the overall strategy of the mostly Democratic mining senators. Believing that Eisenhower's domestic policy was unpopular with western voters, they hoped to capitalize on the plight of miners, just as they had used water and power issues in 1954 to help regain control of the Senate. Combining partisanship and pork, Bible kept the pressure on the administration. "Many of us would like to change the Eisenhower free-trade policy so our country's big metal demands could be met by our own metals, rather than the cheaply produced foreign products coming in today," he declared on April 6, 1956. "As a second choice, we wanted to see our mines kept operating by supplying defense stockpile metals" (see fig. 5).[65]

Bible's statement was a straightforward assessment of the problem of the western mining industry. It was indeed a battle between American mine workers and the cheap foreign labor importers relied on to undercut the price of domestic-based firms. The jobs of American workers were at stake, including those of Nevadans, and that concerned Bible more than larger concepts of free trade and foreign policy considerations.[66] He reasoned that

Fig. 5. "Let's Forget the Good Old American Competitive Spirit a Minute."
(Las Vegas Review-Journal, *August 23, 1959*)

if the government could not, or would not, reduce foreign imports, then it should subsidize the mining industry—particularly tungsten production.

In 1955 annual domestic production of tungsten reached about a million tons, nearly all bought by the government at $63 a ton, or $63,000,000. Conversely, domestic demands met by foreign imports cost $43 a ton, a $20,000,000 difference in the cost between domestic and imported tungsten. Taxpayers were subsidizing the domestic mining industry.[67]

The Eisenhower administration wanted to avoid the appearance of favoring foreign competitors over American workers, however. Coupled with election-year politics, this attitude forced the administration to compromise by offering some financial support, provided that the mining industry cut production as quickly as possible. On May 24, 1956, Secretary of the Interior Fred Seaton wrote to Murray, chairman of the Senate Interior and Insular Affairs Committee, to offer administration support for a two-year program with total mineral purchases not to exceed 1,000,000 tons at $52 per ton.[68] Shortly thereafter Murray introduced S. 3982, co-sponsored by Bible and others, calling for 1,250,000 tons to be bought over a two-year period at $55 a ton. But the Senate Appropriations Committee approved only $35,000,000 for metal purchases, which the Senate and House Conference on Appropriations promptly removed from the budget.

When the appropriations bill returned to the Senate for approval, the western bloc swung into action. Murray, Bible, Malone, and others worked furiously to persuade their colleagues to reject the Conference Committee's appropriations bill and refer it back to committee. These efforts probably would have failed without majority leader Lyndon Johnson's support. On July 27, 1956, the Senate rejected the conference committee's appropriations bill, which went back to the joint House-Senate committee. This time the committee agreed to spend $21,000,000 for mineral purchases. President Eisenhower signed S. 3982 just one month before the Democratic Convention in Chicago.[69]

On August 14, 1956, Bible went to the Democratic Convention seeking help for his beleaguered mining constituents. He pressed the cause of western miners to friendly members of the Platform Committee, like fellow Nevadan Grant Sawyer and Senator Joseph O'Mahoney of Wyoming. Just hours before the platform reached the full convention Bible, O'Mahoney, and Sawyer succeeded in gaining approval of a strong mining plank that charged the Eisenhower administration with ignoring the nation's mining industry and pledging the Democratic Party to support a long-range minerals policy.[70] Afterward Bible flew home to campaign for a full term in the Senate.

Bible's abbreviated first term in the Senate had been a successful one, continuing the policies of his predecessors and laying the groundwork for a solid tenure for himself and Nevada. He had demonstrated his clear interest in issues of land, water, and power—all crucial to the postwar West's development. Yet, strangely enough, it was almost over before it began. Bible faced a tough race for reelection, and it was of his own making. Senator Alan Bible nearly became citizen Alan Bible.

Chapter Five

Home Folks and Folkways:

The Senate of the 1950s

Alan Bible launched an uninterrupted twenty-year career in the United States Senate in 1954 when Nevada's Democrats chose him to succeed Pat McCarran. Bible believed in serving his constituents. But he also understood longtime Speaker of the House Sam Rayburn's dictum: "If you want to get along, go along."[1] Indeed, Bible's political life is a study of one man's rise to power in an institution that rewarded loyalty and seniority. Tailor-made for the Senate of the 1950s, Bible moved quickly in his first term to establish a base of power, which he expanded in later years despite the reforms of the 1960s.

Bible's decision to run for reelection in 1956 was the hardest of his career. From the beginning, his children disliked Washington, D.C., because they were forced to leave behind their friends and relatives in Nevada. Paul and Bill were more affected by the separation from friends than David, who was only seven at the time. They also missed the open spaces, along with the more relaxed lifestyle of the West. Similarly, Mrs. Bible found the adjustment difficult, particularly the formality expected of a senator's wife and the demanding schedule of meetings, tea parties, and charitable work. The continuous round of cocktail parties and social gatherings placed further demands on the Bibles' time and energy. For the most part, Senator and Mrs. Bible ignored the party circuit, spending their available free time at home with the children, who never stopped telling them how much they missed Nevada.[2]

Under pressure from his family Bible announced in late 1955 that he would not seek reelection in 1956. But in April 1956 he changed his mind and entered the race to retain his Senate seat. His sudden turnabout embarrassed him, and he always maintained that he was under tremendous pressure from powerful Senate Democrats, led by majority leader Lyndon Johnson, along with Robert Kerr of Oklahoma, Stuart Symington of Missouri, Carl Hayden of Arizona, and Richard Russell of Georgia. Bible candidly admitted, "I got my arm twisted by these various emissaries, particularly LBJ, and got back into the race."[3]

Johnson had a huge stake in the outcome of the Nevada Senate election, and the legendary "Johnson treatment" was hard to resist. He was primarily concerned with retaining his position as majority leader because the Democrats held a slim two-seat majority in the upper chamber in 1956, and President Eisenhower's candidacy probably would affect state races. With Bible out of the Nevada contest, Johnson feared that lesser-known Democrats like Harvey Dickerson, Mahlon Brown, and Jay Sourwine, all of whom announced their candidacy to succeed Bible, would be an easy mark for popular two-term Republican Congressman Cliff Young. And a Republican victory in Nevada spelled trouble for Johnson, especially in a presidential election year.

Moreover, if Bible retired from the Senate, Johnson would lose one of his most devoted followers. Their friendship had blossomed almost from the moment Bible took office. Three days after his swearing-in Bible asked Johnson to meet with the Western Conference of Senators to discuss issues of mutual concern. Johnson accepted the offer and remained a dedicated supporter of western economic development throughout his Senate years and beyond. When Johnson suffered a heart attack in 1955, Bible visited him almost daily in the hospital. When Johnson was recuperating at his ranch in Texas, Bible delivered a speech to the Reno Rotary Club in which he predicted that Johnson would one day be president if his health permitted.[4] Two weeks later Johnson thanked Bible for his kind words and encouraged him to "boost his own stock for next year's election."[5]

Soon after Bible's Reno speech he informed Johnson that he was considering not running in 1956. On September 30, 1955, Johnson wrote to Bible to encourage him not to retire from the Senate because the country, Nevada, and the Democratic Party needed him. In a return letter, Bible thanked Johnson, adding in a handwritten postscript, "First, last, and always I am on your team, whether here or in Washington. Lyndon, I only hope that team leads to the presidency." Johnson told him, "I just want you to know that anytime anywhere Alan Bible needs some help, he is going to find Lyndon Johnson backing him to the limit."[6] Although there may have been an element of blarney, both men kept their commitments. Bible sincerely wanted Johnson to become president and remained a Johnson man throughout his career. And Johnson gave Bible overwhelming support, beginning with the Tungsten Purchase Act and the battle over the 1956 appropriations bill.

Bible's announcement that he would run for reelection in 1956 was embarrassing, because his Democratic friends Brown, Dickerson, and Sourwine had entered the primary based on his word that he was out of the race. Each had spent time, money, and political capital to seek an office he had little hope of capturing if Bible was a candidate. It was particularly difficult for Sourwine, because he was a staff member for the Senate Judiciary Committee. Senator James Eastland (D-Mississippi), chairman of the committee, asked Bible if he wanted him to fire Sourwine. Bible told Eastland no, that it had all been his fault, not Sourwine's.[7]

Predictably, the primary was a rout. Bible outpolled his nearest opponent by 18,741 votes, 26,784 to Brown's 8,043. Dickerson and Sourwine received a little more than 2,000 votes each.[8] The general election would be a much more formidable task. Young had political experience, a proven record of accomplishment, and support from a popular president, the first Republican to win Nevada's electoral votes since Herbert Hoover in 1928.

Bible and the Democrats pulled out all the stops to win in Nevada. Powerful, nationally known Democrats like Johnson, Kerr, Symington, and John F. Kennedy came to the state and campaigned for their colleague. Even Estes Kefauver, the party's vice-presidential nominee, made an appearance in Las Vegas to assure voters that, while he personally disapproved of gambling, he nonetheless considered it a matter for the state to decide, not the federal government. In October Lyndon Johnson made a speech in the heavily Republican town of Ely in which he referred to Cliff Young as "a little phoney." At the end of the speech, he asked to borrow a cowboy hat from a spectator, then flung a twenty-dollar bill inside and told the crowd, "Now I want to see this hat full of campaign greenbacks by the time it gets back to me." John Kennedy spoke in Reno and Las Vegas, with considerably less flare than the majority leader.[9]

Bible also relied heavily on newspaper endorsements. The state's traditional Democratic organs, such as the *Las Vegas Review-Journal* and Reno's *Nevada State Journal*, backed him. He also picked up help from Jack McCloskey, owner and publisher of the influential *Mineral County Independent* and a Republican who had previously crossed party lines to support McCarran.[10] They constantly reminded voters of Bible's legislative accomplishments, while rarely, if ever, mentioning why he had changed his mind about seeking reelection. Meanwhile, Bible told voters that, if elected, he would remain in the Senate for as long as Nevadans approved of his record. He wasted little time in explaining his change of mind after publicly announcing his retirement, instead pointing to accomplishments such as the Washoe Project and the Minerals Purchase Act.

Bible campaigned furiously. He stressed that he would continue to deliver for Nevada's miners, as he had during the previous summer when it looked as if the industry would lose government support. His reelection campaign purchased full-page newspaper advertisements showing a photograph of Bible with a list of his legislative triumphs, with water and mining receiving top billing. He also won the endorsement of Nevada's mining association, which helped his campaign by printing editorials in its newsletter describing Bible's role in the fight over the appropriations bill.

Bible also cited his achievements beyond the fields of water, power, and mining: in behalf of airport expansion, airline service, defense spending, home rule for Boulder City, and increased allotments for cotton production in Nye County.[11] Suggesting that he would become a powerful figure in the Senate in the tradition of Key Pittman and Pat McCarran, Bible's campaign literature pointed out that his colleagues had named him acting majority leader in Lyndon Johnson's absence, assistant Democratic whip, and acting president pro tempore of the Senate. To be sure, these titles were largely ceremonial—and distributed among several senators—but to voters they conveyed an impression of power that could be transformed into benefits for them.

While Bible sought to impress voters with his list of bills, projects, and titles, Young assailed his indecisiveness and "old-boy" connections. Touring the state, he told Nevadans that, unlike Bible, he was a man of his word and a loyal Republican President Eisenhower could rely on. Young also tried to capitalize on the issue of machine politics, as Mechling had done four years before, by charging that Bible had the support of a bipartisan coalition of moneyed interests that would back anyone for favors, no doubt referring to the Biltz-Mueller contributions to McCarran's campaigns. But Young's charges failed to stick with the voters and never became an important issue during the campaign. In fact, the charge was untrue, because Biltz and Mueller did not support Bible.[12]

On November 6, 1956, President Eisenhower rolled over Adlai Stevenson in Nevada by 15,000 votes, while Bible won by a 5,000-vote margin. Democrat Walter Baring captured Young's former congressional seat by an even greater margin of nearly 8,000 votes. Clearly, the president's popularity in Nevada was great, but not transferable to other Republicans like Young.

An analysis of Bible's victory over Young shows that the honesty issue, raised when he changed his mind about seeking reelection, caused him no damage. He carried Clark County with 57.2 percent of the vote, compared with 65.9 percent in 1954. While this indicates a substantial drop in support, it must be remembered that Young was a far more formidable opponent than Ernest Brown, a little-known political novice in 1954. In addition, a popular Republican headed the ticket in 1956, unlike 1954, when Bible benefited from Republican weaknesses: the majority party or president's party traditionally suffered in midterm elections and the precipitous, nationally televised decline of Senator Joseph McCarthy also hurt the Republicans. Bible carried every county considered strongly Democratic or leaning in that direction. He also carried nominally Republican Lyon County with 53 percent of the vote—

in Yerington, *Mason Valley News* publishers Walter Cox and Jack Carpenter were supportive—and did well in most other Republican areas, where he garnered about 40 percent of the vote. Overall, he carried the state with 52.6 percent of the vote, a drop of 5.5 percent from his 1954 race.[13]

The 1956 election in Nevada was important for three reasons. First, it showed that Bible was popular with the voters and could defeat a well-known and respected Republican candidate. Second, his message that he could deliver federal dollars to help Nevada was effective. Time and again he reminded the voters that he had supported the Upper Colorado Storage Act, authorized the critical Washoe Project, and fought long and hard for the minerals purchase bill. The infusion of federal dollars to develop land, water, and power resources in Nevada was vitally important in the mid-1950s, and Nevadans responded to Bible's contention that he could deliver on his promise of continued economic expansion. Third, Eisenhower's ideal of a partnership between government and private industry to develop the West's resources was a dead issue. Young tried to insert the issue of private versus public power development (along with the evils of big government) into the campaign, but voters showed no interest in what had been the cornerstone of Eisenhower's domestic policy for economic development.[14] For Bible and like-minded western senators, the 1956 election signaled a return to the New Deal philosophy of federalism. Unlike the New Deal, with its emphasis on executive planning, this time the Senate would move forward and play the key role in formulating land, water, and power policies in the West. In the years to come Bible would play an important part in these developments.

Bible's rise to power in the Senate can be traced to four interrelated factors: his easygoing, friendly personality; his close association with Johnson, who dispensed favors and political capital; his acceptance of traditional Senate customs and methods of operation; and his mastery of subcommittee government, which allowed individual senators to have a large impact within a narrow range of expertise. In addition, Bible was extremely fortunate that his party controlled the Senate throughout his tenure, thereby enhancing his influence, which would have been much weaker as a member of the minority.

Mild-mannered and unassuming, Bible was unfailingly courteous to his friends, colleagues, and employees. A warm, instantly likeable man who made time for others and their problems, he rarely lost his temper and seldom uttered an unkind word in public. Unlike his predecessor McCarran, who ruled largely by fear and manipulation, Bible was happy to share credit with others in Nevada, the Senate, and his party. In the words of Grant Sawyer, a fellow McCarran protégé who served two terms as governor of

Nevada during his Democratic colleague's Senate tenure, "I never heard anyone say they didn't like Alan Bible." [15]

Bible certainly wanted to get along in Congress, and he made a concerted effort to accommodate others. [16] His reputation as a helpful colleague was well known even among members of the House. A letter from Representative Frank Chelf of Kentucky offers a revealing insight. On June 16, 1964, the Democrat wrote to plead for Bible's help in restoring a $25,000 appropriation item for flood relief in his district. Chelf explained that he faced a stiff challenge from his Republican opponent in the upcoming election and needed to show his constituents that he was an effective advocate in their behalf. He began by saying, "Help me, Alan," and concluded with the statement, "Please help me—I really need it: Thanks a million and God bless you." [17] This was typical of the way his colleagues saw Bible. As a fellow member in good standing in the congressional club, he understood and shared their views, their problems, and their solutions.

Bible's relations with other senators were even more important. His colleagues were fond of him, and the feeling was not only mutual, but crucial to his success. Like most successful politicians, he had the ability to get along with others. [18] He disliked controversy and acrimony. Clearly, his personality was a key to his career in the Senate. Far less intellectual or ideological than Richard Russell, Eugene Millikin, or J. William Fulbright, and certainly less of a string puller than Russell or Lyndon Johnson, Bible was a bread-and-butter politician who paid close attention to the needs of his colleagues, his constituents, and his state.

Bible's personality, temperament, and legislative priorities made him an ideal candidate for the Senate's "inner club"—the elite, informal power structure. He developed instant ties with such powerful colleagues as Johnson, Russell, John Stennis, Clinton Anderson, Robert Kerr, Carl Hayden, and Henry Jackson. From the beginning of his Senate career, Bible fell under Johnson's spell, and he remained a loyal Johnson man. The two had a great deal more in common than their differences in personality might indicate. As westerners, they shared many of the same ideas about economic development. Both were wise pupils who learned from their mentors, McCarran and Rayburn. They both knew how to get along with others—although their techniques differed—and Bible quickly became one of the majority leader's favorite followers.

Johnson had idolized Franklin D. Roosevelt, and Bible was similarly devoted to Johnson. Bible's position on issues often became known only after Johnson had stated his views, just as Johnson had waited for signals from the White House during the Roosevelt years. Roosevelt had first interested Johnson in water and power projects to provide jobs, loans, and expanded

The Bibles and the Johnsons at a reception in 1959. (Bible family collection)

business opportunities for his constituents. Although Bible brought a well-developed position on federal reclamation to the Senate, he soon fell under Johnson's influence in judging public works projects on the criterion that FDR had employed: "Was it good for the folks?"[19] Indeed, the FDR-Johnson formula was well suited to Bible's dedication to helping people and building political support through economic development. Bible returned in support and loyalty to his mentor what his constituents received in government projects, loans, and jobs. Just as Johnson was a devoted New Dealer in the 1930s, Bible committed himself to Johnson's Great Society in the 1960s.[20]

When the Democrats regained control of the Senate and chose Johnson as majority leader in 1955, his mandate was to heal the divisions that had existed within the party since the adoption of Roosevelt's liberal New Deal agenda. An eminently practical politician, Johnson enjoyed close ties to southern senators without sharing their deep prejudices.[21] He sought to bring together the various warring factions through accommodation and balance. As a preeminent Senate type, Johnson taught Bible the institutional folkways he had learned during his first term in the upper house. In return, Bible gave Johnson his loyalty, assisting Johnson's quest for consensus rule and personal power. Bible's reward came in 1957 with his appointment to the Democratic Party Steering Committee, assuring Johnson of another vote in the selection of committee chairman.[22]

Upon arriving in the Senate, Bible requested assignment to the committees on which McCarran had served—Judiciary and Appropriations. Bible's lack of seniority meant that he had to settle for his second choices, the Interior and Insular Affairs and the Interstate and Foreign Commerce committees. Johnson also asked Bible to sit on the Committee on the District of Columbia, a thankless task, given its heavy workload, low prestige, and lack of constituent appeal.[23] He became its chairman in February 1958, which brought him into close contact with other committee chairmen, easing his entry into the Senate's "inner club."

Bible's committee assignments proved extraordinarily advantageous for him and for Nevada. The Interior Committee truly reflected his interests in water, power, mining, and public land policy. Bible won appointment to the Subcommittee on Mining and became the chairman of its Subcommittee on Public Lands in 1961. In 1965 he exchanged the public lands post for the chairmanship of the newly created Subcommittee on Parks and Recreation, which he kept until he retired in 1974. Consequently, Bible was at the center of the debate over legislation for wilderness, parks, and recreation from the beginnings of the environmental movement in the 1950s. In 1969 Bible consolidated his power over environmental issues by switching chairmanships from the Appropriations Subcommittee on Military Construction to Interior-related agencies which ruled on budget requests for the National Park Service, Bureau of Land Management, U.S. Geological Survey, Bureau of Mines, Bureau of Sport Fisheries, Office of Water Resources Research, Bureau of Outdoor Recreation, Bureau of Indian Affairs, Office of Saline Water, and Environmental Protection Agency. He was a member of the Appropriations Subcommittee on Public Works and Lands, which approved the budget requests for the Bureau of Reclamation and the Army Corps of Engineers.[24] Little wonder that Bible was instrumental in the formulation of land and water policy in the West for nearly two decades.

The key to power in the Senate of the 1950s—indeed, the nerve center of the Senate establishment—was the Appropriations Committee. It controlled the flow of money for projects in a member's home state. The inevitable result was horse-trading and evolving friendships for the senator who played by the rules of the game, as Bible did. Government agencies requesting increased budgets for their programs constantly courted members of the Appropriations Committee. Senators on the committee were at the apex of power and uniquely positioned to influence the course of events through favors and distribution of money.[25]

Naturally, Bible coveted a seat on Appropriations. He soon formulated a plan to force Johnson to choose between preserving Senate harmony and elevating Bible to the "money" committee ahead of others such as Stuart Symington, a Missouri Democrat with greater seniority. Bible would use his chairmanship of the Committee on the District of Columbia as a bargaining chip. He planned to tell Johnson that he wanted to be removed from the Committee, which would elevate Senator Wayne Morse (D-Oregon), the next in line to be chairman. An unpredictable liberal, Morse had the potential to disrupt Johnson's coalition and legislative plans through a variety of tactical and procedural means.

Bible's chance came in November 1958, when Johnson visited Las Vegas for a vacation after the fall elections and to get to know Howard Cannon, the newest Democratic senator from Nevada. After a brief initial meeting, which also included Cannon and former Bible aide Chester Smith, Johnson, Bible, and Smith adjourned to the majority leader's room at the Sands Hotel. Bible told Johnson that he wanted off the Committee on the District of Columbia. Johnson quickly proposed that if Bible would remain as its chairman and Smith would return to Washington to run the committee, he would let him have the vacant seat on Appropriations. Symington would be unhappy because he was senior to Bible, but Johnson thought he could handle him.[26] Johnson kept his promise and appointed Bible to the Appropriations Committee in January 1959.

With the assignment to Appropriations, the last piece of Bible's power base was in place. Bible accumulated power and emerged as a Senate insider. In 1967 columnist Clayton Fritchey of *Harper's Magazine* went in search of the Senate's legendary "inner club" and was immediately told to go to the Appropriations Committee. Fritchey identified twenty-seven full-fledged Senate insiders, including Alan Bible and thirteen of his fellow members of Appropriations.[27]

Complementing Bible's personality and his ties to Lyndon Johnson was his readiness to embrace the Senate's customs. Bible furnishes a case-study in institutional behavior and the exercise of power within an established framework. In the Senate of the 1950s the southerners held the strings of power and set the rules for admission into the inner club.[28] In 1955 southerners chaired seven of the nine powerful standing committees, although they made up only about one-third of the Senate membership.[29] Southerners such as Richard Russell evaluated others for admission into the club based on their concept of the ideal Senate man. From the very beginning, Bible qualified.

The southern bloc of senators attracted Bible because of their compatibility with his legislative goals and moderate stand on public policy issues. Practical and easygoing, he always tried to understand their positions—even on civil rights—for while he diverged from their racism, he understood and shared their qualms about federal interference in local affairs, given his desire to protect gaming and his view of the federal role in western development. Sensitive to the political problems and needs of his colleagues, he was at the same time loyal and generous. He fit the ideal Senate type by practicing accommodation and balance in his approach to issues and by speaking softly and infrequently. On September 13, 1956, Johnson wrote to Bible and in essence outlined the qualifications for admission to the inner club: "I learned a long time ago that a man who combines hard work, ability, and loyalty to his friends is a man destined for success. I never met anyone who fits that description any better than Alan Bible."[30] To be sure, this flattery was part of the famous "Johnson treatment," but his statement nonetheless contains the essential truth about Bible's qualities and qualifications.

Bible shared a common characteristic with some of the most effective senators of his time: they were little known outside of the Senate and their home state. Eugene Millikin (D-Colorado) was a man of extraordinary intellect whom his colleagues deeply respected. Another Colorado Democrat well-established in the Senate's inner circle, Edwin C. Johnson, was largely invisible to the public, but his colleagues held him in high regard. Virtually unnoticed beyond the Senate, Frank Carlson (R-Kansas) won respect and admiration within the institution. These men shared inner circle status with Carl Hayden, Richard Russell, John Stennis, and other conservative Democrats who wielded formidable power and exercised painstaking care in deciding with whom they were willing to share it.[31]

While personality and temperament were crucial to being a Senate insider in the 1950s, acceptance of its folkways counted even more. Donald R. Matthews, the preeminent scholar of the Senate for that period, has likened the institution to living in a small town.[32] The pressure to conform to the Senate's ways of operating was enormous. But for Bible, adjustment to these norms proved remarkably easy. He had always been a team player and a follower, and he preferred the small-town life the Senate resembled.

Initially, senior senators expected freshmen to serve a period of apprenticeship in which they were seldom seen and rarely heard. Their senior colleagues asked them to demonstrate respect while performing without complaint the same thankless senatorial tasks that their predecessors had completed. For Bible, this meant service on the Committee on the District of Columbia. Senior senators also placed a high value on the work ethic and attention to legislative detail. Early in Bible's career, Carl Hayden told him that he could be either a "work horse" who paid attention to his legislative business or a "show horse" who continually made speeches in and out of the Senate.[33] Bible chose to be a work horse. It was natural for him and earned him the gratitude of his peers. The transaction of Senate business depended on the willingness of all members to pull their weight, which meant that a senator who was faithful to committee assignments had little spare time for outside activities or public recognition. Some of the most respected and effective senators were little known beyond their state and the committee rooms.

Specialization complemented committee work in the operation of the Senate. Expected to concentrate on a few matters connected with their committees and their constituents, senators became experts in those fields, helping their colleagues reach decisions on issues beyond their individual expertise.[34] "Table hopping" from one committee to another was frowned upon. For most of Bible's career he kept his original committee and subcommittee assignments except for the Commerce Committee, which he traded for Appropriations in 1959, and the Committee on the District of Columbia, from which he resigned in 1968, having earned the seniority to give up his least important and most thankless committee.[35]

Paralleling dedication to committee business were the personal requirements of courtesy and reciprocity. Here Bible excelled. From the beginning in 1955, the conservative politics and gentlemanly manners of the southern Democrats appealed to him. Democratic senators like Russell of Georgia, Stennis of Mississippi, and Earle C. Clements of Kentucky were ideal role models. Bible kept political disagreements from influencing his personal feelings. A good example of this was his relationship with Republican Thomas Kuchel of California. The two men often sparred on the numerous and complex water issues affecting the Colorado River in the 1960s, yet remained close friends throughout their careers. Bible saw Kuchel's water politics simply as a matter of defending his state's interests—an action he expected, understood, and admired.[36]

Bible was a "pork-barrel" politician and the practice was crucial to his success. He followed the Senate tradition of reciprocity and adhered to the belief that all politics is local. Logrolling was a way of life in the Senate, and Bible never hesitated to join in slicing the pork or assuring his colleagues of their fair share. He rarely stood in the way of another colleague's pet projects, unless they affected Nevada interests.[37] Constituent need was the glue that held the inner club together.[38]

By contrast, reformers such as Senators Joseph S. Clark (D-Pennsylvania), Paul Douglas (D-Illinois), and, indeed, most northern liberals had a hard time getting along in the Senate of the 1950s. Because they failed to conform to the institution's mores and traditions, rebellious members received less desirable committee assignments and few favors for their state, reducing their influence, prestige, and effectiveness.[39] Back home, a senator on the outs often had little to show for six years in office. Campaign funds from the Democratic Party could dry up, and powerful and popular colleagues might prove unwilling to campaign in the maverick's home state.

Because of the Senate folkways, particularly the concept of reciprocity, legislative policy tended to gravitate toward the middle, where negotiations produced a working consensus acceptable to the inner group. Smaller states, southern Democrats, and northern Republicans worked to produce a conservative legislative record, thwarting northern liberals who sought civil rights, public housing, and better education.[40] Bible fit into this tradition—as did his mentor and predecessor—in more ways than one. In *Pat McCarran: Political Boss of Nevada*, Jerome Edwards called the senator's office operations the "linchpin of power": "The chief reason McCarran was reelected three times was that he succeeded in convincing the voters of Nevada of his deep commitment to them and the state. National issues had little to do with it." According to the *Nevada State Journal*, edited by McCarran's close friend and ally Joe McDonald, Sr., "There has never been a senator in the history of the state who paid as close attention to the needs of the state." McCarran used his influence and his "boys" in Nevada to keep track of what Nevadans wanted and needed and, so far as possible, keep them happy and satisfied. He accumulated power through seniority and his assignments on the Judiciary and Appropriations committees.[41]

McCarran's conception of a senator's role influenced Bible. While his personality kept him from emulating all of McCarran's political style, he followed closely in the realm of office operations and shared his mentor's views of a senator's part in the federal government.

Bible's office was typical of the Senate as a whole. He employed about twelve people, ranging from an administrative assistant to a part-time clerk-typist. Like McCarran, Bible delegated to his administrative assistant a great deal of power in office affairs, from answering constituent mail to formulating press releases. Also, he turned over office functions such as public relations and legislative affairs to professional newspapermen and lawyers trained and interested in these areas.[42]

Back home, Bible maintained two urban offices, one in Reno and one in Las Vegas. Both were one-person operations with limited authority to solve constituent problems. For the most part, these local offices simply relayed requests to Washington, where the main staff handled them. However, the Reno and Las Vegas offices were a center of activity when Bible was in Nevada, which averaged about sixty days a year.[43] During these visits Bible kept his staff busy holding open-house sessions and inviting constituents to his office to hear their complaints, problems, and suggestions.

Besides maintaining the flow of press releases and serving constituent needs, Bible kept in touch with Nevadans by way of a newsletter, *Washington Round-up*, mailed out four times a year. It typically contained news about his stands on current issues, legislation important to Nevada, and a generous dose of information about the senator's hard work on behalf of the state's economic interests. Bible considered these quarterly issues of the *Round-up* important because of the feedback he received from Nevadans, many of whom told him that the newsletter was about the only mail they ever received.[44] Bible also insisted on meeting personally with all Nevadans who dropped by his Washington, D.C., office. Whenever possible, he sought to communicate directly with his constituents.

This was in keeping with the McCarran tradition. Initially, Bible kept the staff he inherited from McCarran, including administrative assistant Eva Adams. Bible and Adams had known each other since their college days at the University of Nevada. Bible respected her skill and intelligence, but their relationship lacked the necessary element of trust. Her association with Biltz and Mueller left her loyalty to Bible in doubt. Adams, in turn, doubted that Bible could measure up to her former boss, Pat McCarran.

When time and a close working relationship failed to heal the breach, Bible faced a problem: a smart and talented administrative assistant whose loyalty is questionable is a dangerous employee.[45] Still, Bible declined to replace her because he preferred not to fire anyone. More importantly, he felt that she could and did help him learn the workings of the Senate and avoid problems with the powerful Nevadans with whom she had a close relationship.

But from 1954 until 1960 he was unable to shake the feeling that Adams had some hidden agenda. According to Bible, President Kennedy asked him if he could help with any problem in 1961. Seizing the moment, Bible told the president that appointing Adams to the vacant position of director of the Mint would be a boon to him. Bible's recollection of the event is probably inaccurate, because he met in January with Robert Hardy, Sr., president of

Alan Bible and Eva Adams in 1962, celebrating the Senate's confirmation of her as director of the U.S. Mint. (Eva Adams Collection)

the Sunshine Mining Company, Kellogg, Idaho. Hardy proposed to Bible that Adams be considered for director of the Mint. Afterward, Bible talked with Chester Smith about the appointment, but said not one word about what impact Adams's appointment would have on Nevada or silver mining in the West. Bible then telephoned the White House and spoke directly to President Kennedy, saying that he had an important matter to discuss with him. Bible and Chester Smith went to the White House the following day to see about Adams's appointment. Two days later Smith drove Adams to the White House to be interviewed by staff assistants for the post. On the way Adams expressed misgivings about leaving the Senate for the Mint. Smith told her that she had no future with Bible—an accurate assessment of their relationship—and Adams overcame her hesitancy. Kennedy nominated her on September 23, 1961, and she was confirmed by the Senate. Johnson later reappointed her to another five-year term. Bible was not sorry to see her go.[46]

The appointment proved controversial. On September 26, 1961, columnist Drew Pearson reported that Adams, dubbed the "Silver Mama," was a tool of silver producers, specifically J. B. Lynch, who had extensive holdings in Canada. According to Pearson, Lynch and others had engineered Adams's appointment to get the government to stop selling "free silver" on the open market, which, the producers claimed, would boost silver prices above 90 cents an ounce. While Adams, and Bible, sympathized with the plight of mine owners and may have had every intention of supporting their cause, Adams's appointment had nothing to do with their desires. Pearson reported only half the story. He would have been much closer to the truth, and more in keeping with his frequent reporting of backroom political dealings, if he had said that Bible wanted to get rid of her and the timing was perfect.[47]

Additional changes solidified Bible's office operations. After the 1956 election Chester Smith resigned as Bible's executive secretary and returned to Las Vegas to practice law. Bible then hired Jack Carpenter, a Yerington newspaperman, to assume the duties of public relations and press expert in the Washington office. After Adams left in 1961, Carpenter became administrative assistant for the rest of the senator's career.

Bible and Carpenter immediately hit it off and established a relationship of trust and affection that lasted until Bible died in 1988. Easygoing and friendly, with a marvelous sense of humor, Carpenter was an ideal match for Bible's personality and temperament and well suited to set the relaxed tone and atmosphere that Bible liked in general, and in his Washington office in particular. When Carpenter agreed to join Bible in Washington, he told the senator that he wanted to stay only a couple of years. He sold his half-interest in the newspaper to Cox and set out on a career that spanned twenty years in the Senate and House, and afterward many years with the American Mining Congress.[48]

Initially, Carpenter impressed Bible because of his work in the 1956 campaign. He and his wife gathered signatures and lined up voters at barbecues, teas, and other public gatherings. At a grass-roots level, Carpenter wrote supportive editorials in his newspaper, the *Mason Valley News*, and tried to influence delegates to the state Democratic Convention to support Bible's Senate candidacy. In addition, Carpenter's appointment to the Economic Development Commission for Lyon County and his election as president of the Nevada State Press Association in 1956 made him a well-known figure among leading Nevada Democrats. Carpenter also strengthened Bible's ties to rural newspaper editors and political powers such as Jack McCloskey of the *Mineral County Independent* in Hawthorne, and Walter Cox, Carpenter's longtime partner in Yerington. Close friends of Carpenter and of each other, McCloskey and Cox were conservative Republicans who had supported McCarran through much of his Senate career and were willing to offer similar aid to Bible.

Carpenter fit well into Bible's concept of how his office should function and how it should differ from McCarran's model of tyrannical efficiency. For his part, Carpenter always got along with Adams, although he knew that her relationship with Bible was strained. Nonetheless, the differences between Carpenter and Adams were striking. Carpenter never tried to establish or accumulate power in Washington as a means of dominating Nevada's political life, as McCarran and Adams had done. Carpenter's approach was low-key and easygoing, unlike Adams, who was personable, but far more demanding and precise. In short, Carpenter was very much like Bible. The senator never could have felt as comfortable around Adams as he did with Carpenter.

While Carpenter ran the office from 1961 to 1974, he was not involved in several aspects of its operation, particularly the details of pending legislation, unless it directly concerned Nevada projects and politics. Because of the functional division of work, the legislative assistant met regularly and privately with Bible to discuss the senator's position on pending bills.[49] However, Carpenter maintained a record of all financial assistance given to Nevada, by county, which the senator had a hand in obtaining to remind the voters during election years that Bible had delivered on their behalf.

Bible treated his staff with friendly consideration. He generally paid them as much as Senate rules allowed and rarely withheld raises. Still, little things, such as being late for work or regularly leaving early for personal reasons, sometimes irritated Bible. Only once in eighteen years could Carpenter recall an occasion when Bible became angry at him—for his answer to a letter, which incorrectly stated the senator's position. But he did not embarrass Carpenter by changing it and quickly forgot the matter.[50]

In many ways, Bible and his staff reflected the Senate in the 1950s—congenial and accommodating. The institution was restrained in its legislative outlook and rewarded senators like Bible who were loyal to Senate traditions. Thus, Bible began his first full term poised to take advantage of the rules of the Senate game to advance the economic interests of Nevada and the West.

Chapter Six

Rolling Out the Pork Barrel, 1957–1962

The quest for economic prosperity has reinforced western regionalism since the New Deal, giving a sense of direction to its senators like Alan Bible. Indeed, this has been a vital force in the development of western culture. Because the West must compete with other sections of the country and against other interests to advance and keep pace economically, western regionalism has often united otherwise partisan politicians.[1] Since World War II the key factor has been the decreasing importance of mineral extraction and the expanding need for water development.[2]

Senate work horses like Bible dominated the key committees with power over the course of western economic development. The Interior and Appropriations committees, both vital to the West, included four joint members to guarantee that key pieces of legislation faced a minimum of opposition and that money would be available. Senators Gordon Allott (R-Colorado), Henry C. Dworshak (R-Idaho), Thomas Kuchel (R-California), and Bible kept a watchful eye on appropriations to assure that western states received their fair share of the federal pie.[3] Although northern and eastern liberals have received far more attention in their quest for welfare and poverty programs, western senators were among the leaders in supporting an enlarged federal role across a wide range of public policy issues. A sample of fourteen roll call votes on whether to expand the presence of the federal government shows that Bible voted in favor of more activist government 86 percent of the time. The same was true of Democrats James Murray of Montana and Clinton Anderson of New Mexico. Others were even more supportive: Henry "Scoop" Jackson and Warren Magnuson of Washington voted 100 percent of the time to support a greater role for the federal government in the lives of the American people, while Mike Mansfield of Montana, Gale McGee of Wyoming, and Ernest Gruening of Alaska went along 93 percent of the time.[4] These men are not generally remembered as liberals, especially when compared with senators like Hubert Humphrey or Paul Douglas. Nor did they play a particularly active role in designing and passing social welfare legislation in the Kennedy and Johnson administrations. Rather, their work in behalf of economic growth and prosperity, which was more regionally focused, resulted in their commitment to an activist government. Their brand of liberalism was rooted in economic betterment, not in ideas of social equality.

Bible's motivation for supporting a larger role for the federal government was abundantly clear. Between 1903 and 1938 Nevada received only about $15 million in federal funds.[5] While that figure increased substantially in later years, Bible nonetheless felt that Nevada had been slighted compared with other western states. He was not alone. When McCarran organized the Western Conference of Senators in January 1947, he did so partially with Nevada in mind. Although the organization was largely inactive after McCarran died, its ideas continued with the reorganized Conference of Western Democratic Senators, formed in January 1959 to support public works projects in the West. Its purpose was also partisan: criticizing the Eisenhower administration's "partnership" approach to western development.[6]

The Conference of Western Democratic Senators did wield significant power on regional issues. In 1959 Eisenhower nominated Admiral Lewis L. Strauss to be secretary of commerce. Strauss not only shared the president's "partnership" approach, but was openly hostile toward public power projects. Following Clinton Anderson's lead, the conference leaders, including chairman James Murray and vice-chairman Alan Bible, vigorously opposed the nomination and carried majority leader Lyndon Johnson with them. Strauss was not confirmed, due largely to western senators who resented his views.[7] Getting water and power projects for the West remained the primary concern of conference senators, and they spearheaded the formation of the Senate Select Committee on Water Resources, chaired by the ardently pro-development Robert Kerr of Oklahoma. The Kerr Report (discussed below) was probably the conference's most important contribution in the 1960s.

The conference's public policy agenda was clear. Neal A. Maxwell, who has written extensively and thoroughly on the effects of western regionalism in the Senate, has concluded that the development of western resources was the dominant shared interest of fully one-half of western senators. Bible was no exception. About 25 percent of his Senate speeches and comments concerned mining and mineral issues, the same percentage as for New Mexico Democrats Dennis Chavez and Clinton Anderson.[8]

Bible's position on western mining reflected his constituent base in Nevada and was, in fact, atypical of western senators. By 1960 the West had become a diverse economic region united by water and power concerns, not mining. While core interests have bound together the western states, other issues and interests have divided them. California, Oregon, and Washington have been concerned with Pacific Rim trade and cheap imports, while the mountain states have been more involved with local mining and livestock

TABLE 4
United States Industrial Mix, 1967–1978

Industry	Percent Employed			
	1967	1970	1974	1978
Total Wage and Salary Employment	100.00	100.00	100.00	100.00
Agriculture	2.24	2.02	1.96	1.90
Mining	0.81	0.74	0.75	0.84
Construction	4.55	4.57	4.71	4.65
Manufacturing	26.32	24.74	23.33	22.25
Transportation	3.51	3.39	3.20	3.00
Communications	1.31	1.44	1.41	1.35
Public Utilities	0.88	0.88	0.88	0.84
Trade	18.85	19.62	20.25	21.32
Finance, Insurance, and Real Estate	4.46	4.77	5.09	5.19
Services	16.58	17.12	17.95	19.02
Government	20.48	20.69	20.46	19.63

Source: Gregory Jackson, *Regional Diversity: Growth in the United States, 1960–1990,* 100.

issues that often conflict with the positions of senators from the West Coast. Both industry and branch businesses were also taking root in the mountain states. With 30 percent of the work force tied to government contracts, mining and other extractive industries remained vital sections of the privately based economy with potential for future development.[9]

The regional differences in mining's economic importance are apparent. Mining ranked last in wage income for the United States in 1967 and tied for last in 1978 (see table 4). By contrast, in the mountain states mining ranked ahead of communications and public utilities in economic importance (see table 5). By 1978 mining was more important to the regional economy than agriculture and transportation. This economic reality inspired Bible to move to the forefront as the spokesman for mining interests in the Senate.

Bible's advocacy of mining had both ideological and political overtones. In the 1956 campaign he emphasized his previous support for mining, stressing that he could obtain aid for Nevada's miners as he had in the summer, when it had looked like the industry would lose government support. Newspaper

TABLE 5

Mountain States: Industrial Mix for Selected Years

	Percent Employed			
Industry	1967	1970	1974	1978
Total Wage and Salary Employment	100.00	100.00	100.00	100.00
Agriculture, Forestry, Fisheries	4.43	3.63	2.90	2.72
Mining	2.89	2.48	2.66	2.74
Construction	5.04	5.35	6.38	6.78
Manufacturing	11.87	12.01	12.05	11.78
Transportation	3.19	2.98	2.77	2.25
Communications	1.57	1.57	1.60	1.50
Public Utilities	1.26	1.17	1.16	1.15
Wholesale and Retail Trade	20.98	20.99	21.76	22.82
Finance, Insurance, and Real Estate	4.18	4.32	4.87	4.97
Services	14.62	17.26	17.47	19.01
Government	29.95	28.22	26.39	24.29

Source: Gregory Jackson, *Regional Diversity: Growth in the United States, 1960–1990,* 186.

advertisements lauded Bible for working tirelessly for the tungsten interests, and the Nevada Mining Association helped his campaign by printing editorials in its newsletter that described the budget fights over tungsten, with Bible playing a prominent role.[10] On election day Bible enjoyed a comfortable margin of 5,000 votes, but he had little time to rejoice because he faced a renewed fight in Congress over metals.[11]

The new year had barely begun when Bible and other senators from tungsten-producing states testified before the Interior Committee on the need to keep stockpiling vital metals. They requested a supplemental appropriation of $30 million, which the Interior Committee approved on February 19 and rushed to the Senate floor for action. The measure passed easily, 64 to 17. In a statement released that day Bible emphasized that this was only the first step in a long-range program. Criticizing the Eisenhower administration, which Nevadans had overwhelmingly supported in the 1952 and 1956 elections, he said, "We were promised a long-range minerals program by the administration over two years ago. The action taken today is a stop-gap measure to keep western mines and mills open until a better program is devised." [12]

Nevada's junior senator continued to press Congress in behalf of tungsten. In March he forwarded a joint resolution from the Nevada legislature to the Committee on Interior and Insular Affairs. Nevada lawmakers offered essentially the same arguments that Bible had made in February—tungsten mining was essential not only to Nevada's economy, but also for the nation's defense needs. Exactly one month later the irrepressible Bible appeared before the Senate Appropriations Committee with a five-page statement outlining his cause, the patriotism of Nevada miners, and a general history of tungsten mining in the United States. [13]

Shortly thereafter Bible collared majority leader Lyndon Johnson on the Senate floor. After hearing Bible's case, Johnson asked for a letter setting forth his ideas. Bible returned to his office and dictated a two-page letter that detailed his concerns. First, he accused Congress of breaking faith with western miners by failing to appropriate the necessary funds to carry out P.L. 733, which authorized the stockpiling of strategic minerals such as tungsten. Second, he emphasized that he had recently campaigned in Nevada on the Tungsten Purchase Act, giving his word that Congress would fulfill the intent of P.L. 733; miners had relied on his promises, and he must come to their aid. Third, he argued that the United States had spent twice as much to buy foreign minerals as it would expend under P.L. 733. In conclusion, Bible warned that the Democratic Party might face political disaster in the western states in 1958 unless Congress reversed its position on western mining. Thus, he appealed to Johnson's sense of party loyalty (the same tactic Johnson had employed on Bible two years earlier to induce him to seek reelection) and to his concern about retaining a Democratic majority in the Senate. [14]

As Nevada miners continued to lose their jobs, Bible bristled over the spending to aid mining industries in foreign countries. In the second week of April 1957 the Riley Mine in Nevada closed, bringing to 900 the number of people who had lost their jobs since that 1956 election in which Bible had promised to protect the tungsten industry. [15] He felt helpless to aid those who had relied on him and voted for him in 1956.

Although Bible had struggled for two years to reverse Eisenhower's policy of reducing the stockpile of strategic metals, the outcome was never really in doubt. While western senators were sympathetic, House members were not, since few of their constituents relied on a mining-based economy; they continually slashed appropriations earmarked for the western mining industry. The administration's fiscal outlook and the end of the Korean War worked against Bible's efforts. Postwar cutbacks were inevitable as the country looked toward a balanced budget and continued prosperity. Still, the Nevada senator, reared in a mining tradition, would be heard from later.

In response, Bible opposed foreign aid programs throughout his twenty years in the Senate, in part because he felt that American economic interests would suffer. Regional and state interests—particularly mining—shaped his foreign policy views. Like so many other western senators, including Kerr of Oklahoma, Bible felt that money should be spent on western projects rather than in foreign countries. Moreover, the plight of western miners in the late 1950s and 1960s convinced him that to support foreign aid ran counter to the interest of his mining constituents. He fought hard to impose quotas on imported metals and to increase the government's commitment to buying surplus metals and encouraging exploration. But with 350,000 American jobs directly tied to the nation's foreign aid policy, and only 41,622 of those in the West, mostly in California and Washington, he stood little chance of persuading others to join his cause.[16]

More importantly, Bible was battling long-established ideals in American diplomacy. Since the early nineteenth century, when President Thomas Jefferson sent Meriwether Lewis and William Clark westward, American policymakers had seen the region as a road to the Asian market. After World War II the West extended its highway deep into the Pacific Basin, with California leading the way in corporate expansion and trade. The two interrelated goals were to expand American exports and to secure a world safe for the advance of a global capitalist economic system.[17] Both the Truman and Eisenhower administrations saw Japan as the key to American security and economic expansion. American policymakers moved swiftly to create a new Japan. As the industrial center, Japan would become the primary trading partner with the smaller nations of Southeast Asia, which would supply raw materials in exchange for finished products, creating an interlocking capitalist system in which the United States would be the primary economic and political player.[18]

Bible had little use for such lofty ideals. His goals were simple and parochial: he was interested in what was best for his constituents. Nevada voters overwhelmingly opposed foreign loans to support industrial growth that ultimately competed with their own extractive and land-based businesses. Not even his own party's presidential leadership could change his mind. He opposed not only Kennedy, but later Johnson, on policies that allowed a flood of foreign imports to compete with livestock and mining interests. Bible joined his southern cohorts in the Senate, who shared his fear of competition with their own textile industries and sought protection, particularly higher tariffs and lower import quotas.[19] It was unusual for him to break with his party's leaders in so forceful a manner, but his actions were due to his commitment to his constituents.

Bible saw the trend toward the globalization of American business, with increased investment in Asia, Latin America, and Third World countries. Between 1940 and 1967 American investment overseas skyrocketed; by 1970 more than one-third of American investment in petroleum and mining went overseas. In fact, direct overseas investment grew faster in the postwar period than did the gross national product. Reduced investment at home meant reduced employment, Bible's primary concern because of the loss of jobs in the region's mines, while extractive industries were clamoring for capital to finance expanded exploration.[20]

By the 1950s the American West had become a full-fledged industrial economy, exporting manufactured goods and importing cheap raw materials. Casting off the financial hold of northeastern banking, the West established its own capitalist class in aerospace, real estate, and computers. For a time high-tech industry and mechanized agriculture, with their supporting industries, created a boom through increased trade, particularly to Asia. But by 1967 the boom was over and the American economy showed sign of decline.[21]

Bible's analysis of America's economic problems later proved partially correct. While the Pacific states, particularly California, created a dominant new center to match the Northeast, Nevada and the mountain states were unable to share in the boom. Nevada remained on the periphery, as before. A key reason was the nation's foreign economic policy, with increased reliance on foreign sources of raw materials, which opened the American economy to foreign competition. By 1970 foreign imports accounted for 25 percent of the growth in consumer goods, while 75 percent of all goods produced in the United States faced foreign competition. American companies preferred to import raw materials because their unit costs were lower. In fact, 80 percent of eight basic raw materials were imported by the end of the 1960s, and imports from Chile had devastated the West's copper industry.[22]

The decline of mining resulted from the western economy's integration into the world economy.[23] As American business leaders traveled abroad, they increasingly saw America as a lucrative market, just like any other. Many of these American multinational corporations, more interested in profits than patriotism, flooded the United States with cheap finished products and low-cost raw materials. The United States was the largest market for cheap foreign imports from overseas-based American mining companies doing business throughout the world. To the amazement of Bible and his supporters, America's mineral policy had abandoned all reliance on domestic production.[24]

Bible and others believed that the United States relied too heavily upon imported metals. This left the nation vulnerable to blackmail by Third World countries and its security in the hands of foreigners—or so they argued. The Joint Chiefs of Staff supported Bible's contention, but it was extremely unlikely that all of the producing countries would unite in refusing to export critical metals to America.[25] Yet Bible argued that a policy of expanded domestic metals production, coupled with government subsidies and reduced imports, would alleviate the possibility of a massive cutoff that could harm American industry and security.

Bible's assault on American policy began early in his career. On March 31, 1958, he chided the Tariff Commission for importing New Zealand beef to the West Coast. In a rare display of anger, Bible told the commission, "Nevada's mining industry has already been laid prostrate by indiscriminate importation of foreign metals. It is not unreasonable to ask: is another of Nevada's few productive industries to be subjected to the same cavalier treatment?"[26] Almost two years later he again assailed the commission for failing to protect domestic sheep producers from the reduced tariff rates on live lambs. But Bible soon learned that appealing to the Tariff Commission in behalf of mining and livestock interests was usually fruitless. Thereafter, he concentrated his efforts on increasing the flow of federal money to Nevada to aid the state's miners and ranchers.[27]

Bible and other western senators acted to protect their constituents. On January 4, 1961, Senator Kerr introduced S. 115, co-sponsored by Bible and Cannon, to stabilize the lead and zinc industries and their mining byproduct, silver. Nevada was typical of what was happening to the industry as a whole. While the value of lead and zinc mining in Nevada stood at $8,400,000 in 1951, production had plummeted to about $320,000 annually by 1960. On June 23, 1961, Bible wrote to President Kennedy to outline his explanation for the industry's decline: with foreign imports depressing the domestic market price, western miners could no longer operate at a profit and were rapidly going out of business. The president, in an almost routine way, told Bible that he was sympathetic and would consider the matter.[28]

The western senators made it clear that they wanted action, not consideration. Introduced by Anderson and again supported by Bible, S. 1747 modified the Kerr bill to increase the duties on lead and zinc and subsidize domestic producers at 13½ to 14½ cents per pound. But the State Department, calculating American foreign policy interests in Canada, Mexico, Australia, and Peru, opposed S. 1747, prompting Bible to comment that "charity begins at home." Apparently having no desire to incur the wrath of western senators, particularly Kerr and Anderson, Kennedy signed the lead and zinc stabilization bill on October 3, 1961. Bible kept a watchful eye on the act, pressuring the Bureau of the Budget for the $4.5 million to fund it, and the money was approved on April 17, 1962.[29]

Dissatisfied with the lead and zinc bill's limited success, Bible continued throughout 1962 and 1963 to press the Kennedy administration and the Tariff Commission to help western miners. Writing to Kennedy on January 25, 1962, he complained about the president's plan to barter surplus agricultural products for beryl ore. Bible pointed out that stepped-up exploration and development, especially in Nevada, could meet all future domestic needs. A month later he appeared before the Tariff Commission to plead for higher tariffs on quicksilver to stave off the industry's domestic collapse. Only one month before Kennedy's assassination Bible wrote to the White House to express his dismay that the nation's poultry industry was receiving presidential attention while the mining industry went virtually unnoticed.[30]

To be sure, Bible overdramatized the condition of the mining industry. Cheap foreign imports did depress domestic prices, causing the loss of jobs. Yet domestic production of all metals continued to rise, although exports failed to keep pace with the rate of imports. What worried Bible was the strategic metals sector of the industry, which suffered from government cutbacks and layoffs. Nevada was rich in metals like tungsten that could be mined if not for the greed of American investment overseas and a foreign policy that encouraged it, to the detriment of American workers. While Bible spoke for the industry as a whole, his primary concern was the jobs tied to the artificial market in defense-related metals.

While Bible met limited success in his drive to improve the lot of western miners, he was more fortunate in the area of water resource development, which received a substantial boost. After early initiatives like the Upper Colorado Storage Act, the Washoe Project, and the report of the Select Committee on Water Development, Bible expanded his efforts between 1957 and 1962. In the process, he did much to lay the groundwork for future important projects, and thus for much of southern Nevada's rapid growth in the 1970s and 1980s.

Bible began his second term by once again introducing legislation that would transfer the Newlands Project in Nevada to the Truckee-Carson Irrigation District (TCID), a private corporation of Fallon reclamation farmers. From his youth to his Senate career, Bible had heard complaints from farmers about government inefficiency, and he believed that the local farmers could better manage their own affairs than government officials sent from Washington. This transfer of operating authority was consistent with Bible's concept of home rule, which he espoused throughout his career, whether as chairman of the Committee on the District of Columbia or back home in Nevada, where he sponsored the Boulder City emancipation bill to convert the town from a federal reservation to an independent city.[31]

While fighting for home rule, Bible continued to push for more federal water development projects in northern Nevada. On January 3, 1957, he obtained a $25,000 appropriation for a plan to study flood control along the Walker River. The following year the Walker River Irrigation District received a $563,000 loan from the federal government to be repaid over forty years and $130,000 in nonreimbursable flood control benefits. Authorized by the Small Reclamation Act of 1956, the improvement loan for the Walker River added 6,000 acre-feet of water to existing supplies.[32]

More importantly, Bible moved ahead on the Washoe Project, which his influence on the Appropriations Committee clearly helped bring to the state. Early in 1959 the House had cut $1 million earmarked for construction of the Prosser Dam and Reservoir near Reno. Bible successfully lobbied his committee colleagues, who restored the budget request, making possible the construction of a power transmission line from Burns, Oregon, to northeastern Nevada. The plan called for additional power capacity to serve isolated ranchers in Nevada, and the Harney Electric Cooperative, which was laying the lines, needed the money. Without it, the Rural Electrification Administration would turn down the cooperative's request for the $5 million loan needed to complete the project.[33]

A year later Bible was again immersed in the affairs of water and power affairs in the Southwest. On April 5, 1960, he moved to reduce power costs to users receiving service from the Davis Dam. Bible had opposed the 1944 treaty that guaranteed Mexico delivery of 1.5 million acre-feet of water a year from the Colorado River. Now he sought to shift a percentage of the cost of building the dam from Southwest Power customers to the general public to meet the Mexican demand. The bill, S. 3331, was identical to S. 33, which Bible had introduced in 1957. Although Congress failed to pass the measure, it reflected the thinking of a large group of western senators working to finance western reclamation across as broad a tax base as possible, rather than making it a regional obligation.[34]

Even more critical than the Mexican treaty—or the "Mexican burden," as informed water experts called it—was the problem of saline, which was extraordinarily high in the Colorado system and affected the quality of water ultimately delivered to consumers. But for Bible and others, this paled in comparison with the long-range implications for converting seawater for domestic and industrial use. Indeed, by converting the seawater, the water problems that had plagued upper and lower basin states for decades could be solved almost overnight. Southern California could be transformed from a water-deficient area into a section with little concern for its annual allotment of 4,400,000 acre-feet from the Colorado.

Bible was more interested in southern California's conversion of seawater than in the quality of the Colorado, and he was not alone. On May 16, 1960, majority leader Lyndon Johnson introduced S. 3557 to expand the Saline Water Conversion Program first authorized on July 3, 1952. The bill authorized a maximum of $20 million for research and expanded plant construction to reduce the salt content in rivers and seawater, recognizing the necessity to convert brackish water to domestic use because too little fresh water was available to serve all the needs of a rapidly expanding population. Although S. 3557 died in Congress, it set the stage for later successes.[35]

Long dedicated to reclamation, Johnson was one of the early and most influential leaders in the area of saline water research. After he received the Democratic nomination for vice-president in 1960, Johnson and presidential nominee John F. Kennedy established a National Resources Advisory Committee to make recommendations for national resource development policy in the Kennedy administration. Along with Bible, Kennedy appointed Representative Wayne Aspinall (D-Colorado), and Senators Kerr, Murray, and Magnuson. The appointment of these development-minded westerners was the harbinger of the direction the new administration would take in the West, and its course rapidly became clear.[36]

Almost at the moment Kennedy took office, the Kerr Select Committee on National Water Resources issued its report. To no one's surprise, the study emphasized water resource development for economic growth and totally ignored the environmental consequences of reclamation that had inspired the controversy over the Echo Park Dam a few years earlier. The report's foreword set the tone: "If the economy of the United States is to continue to grow and prosper, there must be adequate supplies of water available." The report stated, "It is becoming more apparent each year that lack of water may deter growth unless early action is taken to assure a continued supply." Finally, "The committee also stresses the importance of research and development in order to promote more efficient use of available water."[37] The Kerr committee had outlined the blueprint for the western empire in the postwar era.

The Kerr report stressed that economic growth would be unlimited if the complex technical, legal, financial, and political problems could be solved— and "the national interest demands their solution." Again, environmental issues or problems connected with the mass plumbing system required for the redistribution of the West's natural water routes went unmentioned. In accordance with the tenor of the study, Kerr recommended the development of comprehensive plans, "keeping in mind the ultimate need for . . . development of all water resources," including dams, reservoirs, desalinization plants, cloud seeding (weather modification), and flood control.[38]

Bible enthusiastically embraced Kerr's recommendations, which would mean more "pork" and water for the "Iron Triangle" of western development: banks, real estate developers, and merchants seeking growth and development in pursuit of profit. At the most basic level, local economic interests found congressmen and senators their most responsive supporters. Kerr and Bible certainly needed little prompting to swing into action. Likewise, the Bureau of Reclamation, always searching for an expanded bureaucratic role, found merit in almost any plan for building dams in the West. Better yet, as far as the bureau was concerned, everyone profited from the enterprise. After all, it reasoned, growth was good for the country.[39]

Bible enjoyed considerable support from Kerr because they agreed that western water development was the key to economic growth. Kerr's primary concern was his state's economy. Indeed, Kerr and Bible shared a great many views. While Kerr became identified as a spokesman for the oil and gas interests in Oklahoma, Bible played a similar role for mining and water interests in his state. Both avoided ideological causes such as civil rights and stuck to the bread-and-butter issues of western politics, which usually meant devising new ways to funnel more federal money into western states. Kerr and Bible believed that the federal government's proper role was to fund and expand the economy; what was good for Oklahoma and Nevada was good for the country.[40]

Even before the Kerr committee had published its findings, Clinton Anderson, a member of the study group and another ideological soulmate whose leadership Bible often followed, pushed ahead on one of the report's recommendations—expanded commitment to desalinization. On June 27, 1961, Anderson introduced S. 2156, co-sponsored by Bible and others, to expand and extend the Saline Water Conversion Program of the Interior Department. The next day, Representative Aspinall introduced H.R. 7916, which was identical to the Anderson bill. The plan called for a ten-year commitment to fund research and build "demonstration plants" capable of conducting experiments in saline water conversion. In addition, it would provide loans and grants to states willing to undertake research in the field.[41]

Bible shepherded the bill through the Senate. On August 31, 1961, as acting majority leader in the absence of Senator Mike Mansfield, Bible served as the floor manager for the Anderson bill, which passed unanimously. Later that day Bible said, "In my opinion the water saline program is of vital importance to the West and the entire world." Although he clearly overstated the case, he expressed the exuberance and zeal of the Kerr committee and

Senators Alan Bible and Clinton Anderson and Secretary of the Interior
Stewart Udall at a Senate committee hearing ca. 1961, Washington, D.C.
(Courtesy of Chester Smith)

like-minded western senators. On September 22, 1961, President Kennedy
signed the saline water plan, launching the West into yet another rush for
federal dollars to obtain more water to fuel never-ending development.[42]

Bible and his fellow Nevadans were ready to join the scramble. On October 10, 1960, Bible, Cannon, and Congressman Walter Baring attended a
meeting with state and local leaders in Las Vegas to consider a project to
bring water from Lake Mead to the Las Vegas Valley. Bible agreed to press
the Senate for money to fund a Bureau of Reclamation study. In February
1961 he pledged his support, and indeed his political future, to deliver the
Southern Nevada Water Project—which became the most important political
success of his career and had far-reaching implications for Las Vegas.[43]

Bible enjoyed success in related areas. On September 20, 1961, the Senate
Appropriations Committee approved $968,000 to finish the Prosser Dam,
the cornerstone of the Washoe Project. Bible not only had written the measure as a freshman senator in 1955, but had, in part, based his reelection
campaign on it in 1956. On October 30, 1962, the dam was completed and
dedicated just in time for the full political effect to be felt in northern Nevada
before the November election.[44] A clear message had been driven home:
Bible had delivered for Nevada's water development enthusiasts throughout
his eight-year Senate career and could be expected to do so in the future.

While mining and water issues seemed to dominate Bible's political life, he still devoted considerable time and attention to land and power problems. Bible and fellow Nevadan Howard Cannon became pioneers in the development of solar energy. On July 1, 1959, Bible introduced S. 2318 to provide for research into practical means for its use. Although his bill died in Congress, it provided a forum for hearings on the issue and elicited the opinions of the Interior Department and the Bureau of the Budget. Interior officials supported the plan despite its $10 million price tag, due largely to growing energy shortages throughout the country. The department was anxious to undertake long-range studies on energy alternatives, and the Bible bill presented an excellent opportunity to get into the infant but growing energy field.[45]

Meanwhile, Bible moved forward on land matters of another kind—parks and recreation development in Nevada and the nation. Unlike his thinking on water issues, which remained largely unchanged throughout his career, the creation of parks and recreation areas expanded his view of land issues to include environmental problems and the dangers facing many of America's last unspoiled scenic areas. Bible's perspective and ethic regarding land use changed over the years, beginning in 1957.

Chapter Seven

Dollars for the Environment, 1957–1962

In 1956, as a member of the Interior and Insular Affairs Subcommittee on Public Lands, Bible began his drive to expand and improve the National Park System. Initially, he saw national parks as a way to supplement local economies because they attracted visitors who would spend money in service-oriented businesses. With time, he developed a different perspective on parks and the environment, particularly the preservation of recreation and wilderness areas. Like most environmentally conscious people in the 1960s, he sought a balanced approach that emphasized both use and protection of scenic and wildlife areas. Not an environmental purist, Bible was a legislator who worked well in juggling competing interests—a statesman who wanted to represent all land users, whether homeowners, developers, miners, loggers, livestock owners, or environmentally concerned citizens. This view put him in the mainstream of environmental politics.

With the postwar period came a new interest in the idea of environmental balance. In 1948 Aldo Leopold, the father of wildlife management in America, published an influential essay, "Land Ethic," arguing that lands must be protected or they would become unusable. Leopold noted that with economic privileges came interlocking obligations. Utilitarian and ecological views of the environment allowed no either/or proposition. A balance was necessary for the survival of humans and nature.[1] This idea of balance was reflected in the 1956 battle over the Echo Park Dam versus the Dinosaur National Monument, which pitted esthetics-minded conservationists against western water developers. The result was a dramatic change both in the direction of the environmental movement in America and in Bible's outlook.

This environmental concern arose as millions of Americans were taking to the highways in search of places to spend their money and leisure time. Urban and suburban recreation enthusiasts joined with environmentalists of all varieties in a drive to force concessions from developers and traditional land users like ranchers and miners. The battle over recreation and wilderness represented as much a conflict of urban against rural as exploiter against preservationist.[2]

Bible was a major force in the evolution of politics and policies that accom-

99

panied these changing public attitudes. During most of the 1950s his desire to aid Nevada economically through water development left him firmly entrenched in the Gifford Pinchot school of conservation. Efficiency and equity were his concerns, not esthetics. He was fully aware of the growing influence of environmentalists and their ideas, especially after their victory over the proposed Echo Park Dam. More importantly, Bible knew that national parks were a good investment in local and state economic development. This desire to cash in on national parks motivated him in 1956 to embrace Mission 66—a ten-year, billion-dollar plan to publicize and commercialize the national parks.

The moving force behind Mission 66 was Conrad L. Wirth, director of the National Park Service from 1951 to 1964. Since the New Deal the size, scope, and responsibilities of the park service had doubled, but appropriations failed to keep pace with the expanded workload. With the increasing defense needs of the war years, money for park upkeep and improvements became scarce, and the facilities declined. By 1955 the national parks, once America's "crown jewels," were rapidly becoming a disgrace. Wirth's proposed Mission 66 to upgrade and modernize the park system received overwhelming congressional support and approval from President Eisenhower. Mission 66 blended nicely with the emerging recreation and wilderness movements just beginning to take hold in America.[3]

A year after the plan was announced Bible was claiming Nevada's share of Mission 66 money. Wirth had requested $10 million to develop Lake Mead's facilities over a ten-year period, starting with about $900,000 in 1958. In February 1957 Bible met with Wirth, who agreed to build two new roads not included in the original plan, with additional trails, campsites, picnic areas, a visitor center, lunching facilities, and expanded beaches. Based on Mission 66 expenditures, Bible correctly predicted, "We can expect the Lake Mead area to double its potential as a recreation area, insofar as tourist traffic is concerned."[4]

Thus, Bible contributed significantly to southern Nevada's recreation development. During the 1930s Nevada's congressional delegation of Senators Key Pittman and Pat McCarran and Representative James Scrugham had sought to advance Lake Mead's development as a recreational facility. In the process, Pittman and McCarran in particular had often fought over patronage, as they did on so many other matters, hindering their efforts more than they helped. Billing their town as "the Gateway to Boulder Dam," Las Vegas city leaders tied their budding tourism industry to the dam and the lake that resulted from its construction. Relying on his knowledge of park issues and willing to share credit, Bible was able to achieve a great deal more than had his predecessors.

Yet events proved that some things about Nevada politics remained the same when Bible followed up on his Lake Mead expansion program with a plan to create the Great Basin National Park in eastern Nevada. The move to establish the park began in 1957, when the Great Basin Range National Park Association was formed to preserve the natural wonders of Wheeler Peak, Lehman Caves, and the Bristlecone Pine. In 1958 Bible asked the Interior Department to investigate the possibility of a park along the Snake Range in eastern Nevada. Alarmed, the state's mining and grazing interests marshaled their forces to oppose the park plan, which they perceived as a threat to their traditional domination of land use in White Pine County. Making money was the mining industry's only concern. It gave little, if any, thought to the environment or other economic uses, like tourism.[5]

Mining production in eastern White Pine County, near the proposed park, was insignificant. Yet the industry took the firm position that any change in land-use policy would inhibit future production. Still, mining opposition paled in comparison with that of ranchers, who followed the time-honored Nevada pattern of opposing any regulation of the public domain that might conflict with their industry's welfare. Their power had traditionally been exercised in a negative manner—they acted to stop legislation they opposed rather than influencing the passage of laws they favored. The battle over eastern Nevada was no exception.

The livestock industry, the most destructive force on the public lands, has benefited from a welfare system rivaled in the West only by subsidized water for agribusiness. Some critics have called the system "cowboy welfare" and its recipients "welfare parasites."[6] Stock raisers argued that their "vested rights," extending back into the nineteenth century, entitled them to priority use of the range. In the 1950s stock producers still saw themselves as the victims of unfair regulation and braced for the assault on the public domain by recreation enthusiasts seeking additional national parks.

While the mining and livestock industries could depend on traditional political and economic interests to support the status quo, they lacked the momentum and force of the new ideas found in the arguments of recreationists. More importantly, the new constituencies, developing parallel with suburban growth, were influencing the views of politicians and agency employees. The actions of Alan Bible and Howard Cannon provide classic examples of balancing Nevada's traditional economic interests with the desire of urbanites for expanded recreational activity.

In addition to advocating continued support for mining and defense, Bible and Cannon supported the livestock industry with equal vigor. They denounced the importation of sheep and beef from New Zealand and implored the tariff commission to aid Nevada ranchers.[7] But their support for the state's customary economic base did not preclude economic expansion and diversification through the infusion of federal dollars into Nevada's depressed areas. By the mid-1950s, with the mineral industry slumping, White Pine County badly needed to expand its economic base.

To bolster the area's sagging economy and protect its natural wonders, Bible introduced S. 2664 to establish a 147,000-acre national park on the Snake Range. Walter Baring, the state's Democratic congressman, followed suit in the House with H.R. 9156, which was identical in wording and intent to Bible's bill.[8] On the surface, the Nevada delegation appeared united, and the state seemed well on its way to its first national park.

But the hearings on Bible's bill cracked the delegation's unanimity. On December 5, 1959, the Senate Subcommittee on Public Lands began a three-day forum to solicit opinions on the Great Basin National Park. Predictably, the American Mining Congress opposed it, citing evidence that the Snake Range was rich in mining potential. The industry's key witness was Bible's longtime friend W. Howard Gray, who made clear that the mining industry opposed not only this park, but all parks, because the park service forbade mining exploration.[9] Representatives of Kennecott Copper Corporation echoed Gray's sentiments.

Livestock raisers joined the chorus, claiming that the park threatened their present use of the range. Their chief objection was that Forest Service grazing permits would lack full force if the National Park Service administered the land. Local rancher George N. Swallow testified, "We also feel that a national park in this area will adversely affect our stock watering and agricultural use of water. We will be prohibited from cutting timber for use in our operation."[10] Besides the issue of economic hardship, Swallow stressed the dislocation of "innocent victims" of government regulation. The hearings hit a high note for the bizarre when Swallow invoked the plight of hunters and trappers in the Wheeler Peak region who would be unable to earn a living. Under questioning by Senator Cannon, Swallow admitted that he "probably" knew two people in the area whose living depended on trapping.[11] Still, his testimony appealed to the established principle that national parks should be carved only from areas considered economically worthless.[12]

The testimony in Ely revealed the land-use philosophy of the parks' opponents. They consistently argued that every acre of the public domain should be open to multiple-uses—specifically, mining, grazing, and timber harvesting. Single-use concepts such as national parks "locked up" the land by excluding agricultural and industrial activity. When Congress passed legislation in June 1960 to include outdoor recreation within the definition of multiple-use, park opponents ignored this change in land-use theory and practice; they continued to define multiple-use in commercial terms, while denying the claims of recreation advocates. They neither accepted nor under-stood the full meaning of the 1960 multiple-use and sustained yield act: a victory for recreationists, it still gave ranchers and miners economic access to the land.[13]

Throughout 1960 Bible worked to draft new legislation so that the park would accommodate as many of White Pine County's economic interests as possible. S. 1760, co-sponsored by Cannon, contained an important provi-sion in section 7 allowing grazing on park lands for twenty-five years. True to his instincts to aid western mining, Bible revised the park boundaries to exclude 24,000 acres in the northeast to allow beryllium exploration and, in section 6, protected existing mining operations within the national park.[14] Bible's proposal included the principal bristlecone pine groves, the Lehman Caves, the glacier at Wheeler Peak, and the surrounding scenic attractions. In addition, the National Park Service would spend $4 million in improvements over a five-year period and $2 million in operating costs.[15]

The Bible plan provided strong support for Nevada's mining and livestock industry while injecting large sums of federal money into eastern Nevada's economy. But in late 1961 regional forester Floyd Iverson told Bible that ranchers had overused the Humboldt National Forest along the Snake Range and grazing there would have to be curtailed for many years to restore the ground cover.[16] The implications were serious, and the forest service's timing could not have been better calculated to revive the fear and suspicion of the livestock producers. From their perspective, reduced grazing in the national forest, the hated park plan, and foreign competition all conspired to inflict economic hardship on eastern Nevada's ranchers. In early 1962 the Interior Department touched off another controversy by recommending a new in-crease in grazing fees. Although Bible and Cannon moved swiftly to repair the damage by securing a postponement, the cumulative effect solidified the resolve of park opponents and was probably the key to Baring's sudden change of position on the park plan.

At the height of the grazing-fee controversy, S. 1760 passed and went to the House, where Bible expected quick action because Baring was one of the Democratic majority on the House Subcommittee on Public Lands. But in June Baring met with members of the Ely Livestock and Mining Industry and agreed to introduce legislation to protect their interests. Upon returning to Washington, he received the draft bill by special delivery from Ely and introduced it at the committee hearing on S. 1760.

The draft bill completely surprised Bible and Secretary of the Interior Stewart Udall. Equally shocking, Baring never read the legislation before presenting it to the committee.[17] The new bill, H.R. 7283, proposed to re-duce the size of the park from 123,000 acres to 53,000, with mining and

TABLE 6

Areas Administered by the National Park Service, January 1, 1960

Types of Areas	Number	Federal Land (acres)
National Parks	29	13,205,071.01
National Historical Parks	7	31,841.66
National Monuments	83	8,984,449.45
National Military Parks	12	26,324.71
National Memorial Park	1	68,708.36
National Battlefield Parks	3	5,318.07
National Battlefield Sites	5	188.63
National Historical Sites	12	1,491.40
National Memorials	13	4,447.96
National Cemeteries	10	215.10
National Seashore Recreational Area	1	24,705.23
National Parkways	3	91,429.72
National Capital Parks	1	39,503.53
Total, National Park System	180	22,483,694.83
Other Areas		
National Recreation Areas	3	2,013,768.00
Total	183	24,497,462.83

Source: John Ise, *Our National Park Policy: A Critical History*, 2.

grazing allowed indefinitely. Hunting and fishing would be permitted under the Nevada Fish and Game Commission's supervision. Baring had informed neither Bible nor Cannon of his switch, and both senators were angry. In the face of these new developments, Wayne Aspinall, chairman of the House Subcommittee on Public Lands, refused to act on Bible's bill—besides the confusion, Baring himself was from the affected state—leaving the whole matter of the Great Basin National Park unresolved.

Meanwhile, Bible moved beyond the limits of his local constituency to embrace larger national goals. By 1960 Congress had established only one national seashore recreation area—Cape Hatteras, North Carolina (see table 6 for a list of all parks established by 1960). Congress responded to pressure from recreation users to expand shoreline areas for public use by including them in the national park system. On July 29, 1959, Bible and seventeen other senators co-sponsored S. 2460, to preserve and develop shoreline resources. With a price tag of $50 million, the measure fell short of congressional approval. But S. 543, which was almost identical in scope and purpose, passed Congress on August 28, 1961, paving the way for creation of the Cape Cod National Seashore and consideration of the Indiana Dunes National Lakeshore, Padre Island National Seashore, and Point Reyes National Seashore.[18]

Bible soon had another chance to expand his environmental horizons. The battle to protect the Indiana Dunes from destruction by developers was well underway when Bible assumed the chairmanship of the Subcommittee on Public Lands. Senator Paul Douglas, a liberal Democratic reformer from Illinois, was waging an often lonely, almost impossible battle in the Senate to pass legislation to protect the Dunes. He received help in 1958 when Congress created the Outdoor Recreation Resources Review Commission to make recommendations on the general state of recreation. While the commission's report was still pending, Udall and Bible gave Douglas a boost. On July 23, 1961, wanting a firsthand view of the area that had caused such an uproar, they accompanied Douglas on a well-publicized trip to the Dunes, which convinced them that the area needed protection.[19] In the process, Bible established an important precedent: not only did he visit all areas considered for inclusion in the national park system, but he also refused to allow witnesses to testify unless they, too, had seen the area for themselves. He learned from experience that this practice often converted critics to supporters.

With protection of the Dunes still years away, Bible's Subcommittee on Public Lands moved ahead with hearings on S. 857, sponsored by Senator Leverett Saltonstall (R-Massachusetts), to establish the Cape Cod National Seashore. President Kennedy, who had backed previous park proposals while in the Senate, threw the full weight of his young administration behind this measure. Although Congress had considered the plan since 1956 and held three hearings, it had taken no action—testimony to the problems and obstacles encountered in creating new national parks.[20]

The initial stumbling blocks were the proposed park's size and boundaries. Opponents, primarily real estate developers, bankers, and residents, sought reductions in its size to allow for as much economic development as possible to increase land values and thus profits from future resales. But in 1961 the realization that the nation's shoreline was rapidly disappearing to residential and industrial uses shocked Congress and Bible into action. Bible endorsed the National Park Service study's conclusion:

There is no longer any comparable area in the New England region that exhibits all the outstanding values desirable and suitable for extensive seashore recreation. For those reasons alone, the great beach area of Cape Cod merits preservation as a major public seashore of the North Atlantic Coast.[21]

Unlike previous attempts to save what remained of New England's coastline, opponents were unable to stop Congress, supported by environmentally conscious citizens and groups like the Sierra Club. The Cape Cod Seashore National Park bill sailed through Congress, and Kennedy signed it on August 7, 1961. It was a milestone that had awakened Bible's sense of commitment to preserve recreational areas.

At least as important as the 44,000 acres and nearly 40 miles of shoreline saved from destruction were two precedents set by Congress and Bible's Public Lands Subcommittee (and later the Parks and Recreation Subcommittee). First, Bible made clear to his Senate colleagues that Congress would have to spend about $16 million to acquire land for the park, unlike the Cape Hatteras Seashore Park, which had been a donation. It took almost 100 years from the creation of the Yellowstone National Park in 1872 for Congress to recognize that protecting and preserving America's vanishing beauty required large sums of money. Bible believed the country simply could not afford to rely on the generosity of concerned groups and citizens, like the Rockefeller and Mellon foundations. Second, Bible used Cape Cod to pave the way for other national parks carved mainly from highly urbanized areas (see table 7).[22]

Bible and his Senate colleagues also moved in 1961 to include rivers and seashore areas in the National Park Service's protective orbit. The Ozark Rivers National Monument Bill pitted future water development plans against the protection of several miles of the free-flowing streams of the Current and Eleven Point rivers in Missouri. At stake was the Water Valley Reservoir Project, planned on the Eleven Point River near Pocahontas, Arkansas. Pointing out that Arkansas needed the economic benefits the project promised to his constituents, both agriculturally and recreationally, Democrat J. William Fulbright made it clear that he opposed any bill that threatened the project. Timber and grazing interests in Arkansas also opposed the bill, because it would deny them the same free access to park land that they enjoyed in the national forest reserves—which Fulbright failed to mention.[23]

The key to legislative success was compromise. Park proposals not only created conflicts over land use, but revealed differences in economic interests. Senator Stuart Symington (D-Missouri), the bill's sponsor, emphasized the recreational advantages of protecting the river, which in turn would at-

TABLE 7

National Seashore Parks Established by Subcommittee on Parks and Recreation
(Senator Alan Bible, Chairman)

Area	Date Authorized or Established
Cape Cod National Seashore, Massachusetts (40 miles of Atlantic Ocean seashore and 44,600 acres)	Aug. 7, 1961
Point Reyes National Seashore, California (45 miles of Pacific Ocean seashore and 64,500 acres)	Sept. 13, 1962
Padre Island National Seashore, Texas (80 miles of Gulf of Mexico seashore and 133,900 acres)	Sept. 28, 1962
Assateague Island National Seashore, Maryland and Virginia (35 miles of Atlantic Ocean seashore and 39,630 acres)	Sept. 11, 1964
Fire Island National Seashore, New York (32 miles of Atlantic Ocean seashore and 19,300 acres)	Oct. 9, 1965
Cape Lookout National Seashore, North Carolina (58 miles of Atlantic Ocean Seashore and 24,500 acres)	Mar. 10, 1966
Pictured Rocks National Lakeshore, Michigan (35 miles of Lake Superior shoreline and 67,000 acres)	Oct. 15, 1966
Indiana Dunes National Lakeshore, Indiana (13 miles of Lake Michigan shoreline and 8,720 acres)	Nov. 5, 1966
Apostle Islands National Lakeshore, Wisconsin (140 miles of Lake Superior shoreline and 42,825 acres)	Sept. 26, 1970
Sleeping Bear Dunes National Lakeshore, Michigan (64 miles of Lake Michigan shoreline and 71,000 acres)	Oct. 21, 1970
Gulf Islands National Seashore, Florida and Mississippi (87 miles of Gulf of Mexico seashore and 125,000 acres)	Jan. 8, 1970
Cumberland Island National Seashore, Georgia (19 miles of Atlantic Ocean seashore and 41,600 acres)	Oct. 23, 1972

Totals: 648 miles; 682,575 acres

Source: Conrad L. Wirth, *Parks, Politics, and the People,* 199.

Senator Bible standing behind President Kennedy during Oval Office signing of the Point Reyes National Seashore bill on September 13, 1962. (Bible family collection)

tract tourists to his state to spend time and money. Clinton Anderson agreed, pointing out that the value of water is greatest when used for recreation rather than for agriculture or industry. The senators and their supporters considered recreation a good business investment, particularly when the federal government picked up the tab by creating a park or monument.[24] Consequently, after a prolonged battle, proponents of river recreation prevailed, and the Ozark Rivers National Monument became law in 1969.

While the Ozark Rivers bill demonstrated the almost endless struggle between park advocates and water developers in different states, the Sleeping Bear Dunes proposal in Michigan split the state's congressional delegation in one of the most heated environmental controversies in the 1960s. As with the Cape Cod act and the Ozark Rivers bill, the issue was again economics, but park proponents eventually prevailed.[25]

In the meantime, Congress enacted laws to create the Padre Island National Seashore in Texas and the Point Reyes National Seashore in California.[26] In a short period of two years seashore areas had received protection from Congress. As chairman of the Public Lands Subcommittee, Bible endorsed, supported, and often shaped the efforts of his fellow senators to protect and develop recreational areas for public use. Developers and land speculators found him less than receptive to their ideas of liquidation.

Thus, as 1962 drew to a close, Bible had come to believe in the creation of national parks for economic and esthetic reasons. Still, economic concerns were uppermost in his mind, especially the advantages of recreation development in Nevada and elsewhere. While water and mining issues continued to dominate his legislative agenda, the steady and unrelenting pressure of environmental groups clearly had an impact on Bible, who began his Senate career without regard for wilderness or recreation protection. He had revealed a capacity for growth—and greater accomplishments were still ahead.

Chapter Eight

Winners and Losers, 1963–1968

The Senate in 1963 was a far different institution than the one Bible joined in 1954. Previously dominated by conservative southern Democrats and their northern Republican allies, it had been an inward-looking group that rewarded its friends with plum committee assignments and projects to satisfy the folks back home. From 1955 until 1960, under Lyndon Johnson's leadership, the Senate became a symbol of consensus government. Johnson consciously tried to avoid ideological confrontations across a wide range of issues, from civil rights to education. The agenda of liberal northern Democrats, while not ignored, was dramatically slowed when compared with their later achievements in the 1960s.

The Senate and Bible had begun to change, and the consensus so carefully crafted by Johnson and his cohorts began to break down after the 1958 elections. This proved to be a bellwether; the election of fifteen liberal Democrats swelled their Senate ranks from a meager sixteen to thirty-one seats.[1] Unlike their colleagues, the members of this 1958 freshman class chose not to look exclusively to the Senate establishment for rewards and support. Instead, they looked outward, away from the business-as-usual Senate ways, to a broader constituency to define their legislative agenda. This resulted in a far more progressive approach to social issues. This liberal faction wanted to reform the Senate to make it more responsive to constituents on public policy matters.[2] Between 1958 and 1975 the Senate also became more democratic and more liberal as southern Democratic dominance waned. Equally important, standing committees and subcommittees proliferated, allowing freshman senators immediate influence and power undreamed of in the early 1950s. The enhanced role of junior senators meant the abandonment of the Senate norm of apprenticeship. New members took the floor to speak out on the issues of the day—a decided contrast to earlier times when freshmen were seen but not heard.[3]

Additionally, senators from the more populous northern states, traditionally underrepresented in comparison with the less populated states, were poised to attack the centerpiece of conservative domination. Northern liberals were united against conservatives on rule 22, which required a two-thirds vote to kill a filibuster. Under this relentless attack against rule 22 at the beginning of each legislative session Johnson's coalition, and his influence as majority leader, began to crumble. To compound Johnson's unhappiness, at the 1960 Democratic Convention disgruntled senators won approval of a party plank calling for majority rule in the Senate (a simple majority vote to shut off debate). While these events did not propel Johnson's drive to seek the presidency in 1960, they may help explain his surprising decision to accept the second spot on the ticket. If Johnson had chosen to stay in the Senate, he surely would have lost considerable influence and power as the target of northern liberals unwilling to accept consensus rule or politics as usual, both hallmarks of the Johnson style.[4]

These twists and turns mattered less to Bible than loyalty. He supported Johnson over Kennedy at the 1960 Democratic Convention and delivered the Nevada delegation for the majority leader, 6½ votes to 5½ for Kennedy.[5] Bible and others in Nevada remembered that Johnson had always been supportive of their state's economic interests (see fig. 6). Bible was as surprised as others, including many of his fellow senators, when Johnson accepted Kennedy's offer to run on the ticket as vice-president. But Kennedy proved no more threatening to the Senate's ruling elite than Johnson. He was unwilling or unable to challenge their hold on the process of that political body.

Kennedy's razor-thin victory over Richard Nixon was due in no small part to support from southern states, while in the Far West he carried only New Mexico and Nevada. Kennedy felt obligated to his southern friends and afterward paid careful attention to their needs. He moved cautiously on civil rights and other issues important to the party's southern wing.[6] But the flow of events soon pushed Kennedy and the Senate beyond the status quo. The civil rights movement was an irresistible force whose time had come. In response, the Senate changed during the 1960s, albeit more slowly.

As in the 1950s, power in the Senate of the 1960s grew out of a combination of factors: institutional acceptance, personal skill, and legislative expertise. Throughout most of the 1950s power had been lodged in legislative committees and regional blocs rather than in the hands of a few party leaders. As a result, subcommittee chairmen gradually became the key figures during the Johnson era—the full Senate usually deferred to their expertise. Johnson allowed Democratic senators to expand their political base and influence by giving each of them a choice committee assignment over a more senior member who already sat on at least one important committee.[7]

Bible was one of the beneficiaries, building an impressive legislative record from 1957 to 1962. He made sure that Nevada voters were well aware of his accomplishments and political connections as his quest for another term approached. He kicked off his drive for reelection with a testimonial dinner

Fig. 6. "This looks like your work!" (Las Vegas Review-Journal,
November 13, 1960)

in Las Vegas on February 16, 1962, with Senate majority leader Mike Mansfield as the principal speaker. The program also displayed a photograph of
Lyndon Johnson, who sent words of tribute to the Silver State's senior senator. The dinner set the tone for Bible's reelection campaign with a slogan that
emphasized his Senate achievements: "The man who gets things done for
Nevada."[8]

Bible's campaign literature dealt exclusively with his record as a lawmaker
and the benefits Nevadans received from his efforts. Advertisements listed
forty-one items, from water development to land transfers, from recreation
funds to military expenditures, from road improvements to new federal

Candidate John F. Kennedy (left), Governor Grant Sawyer (center), and Senator Alan Bible (right) on campaign trip to Las Vegas in 1960. (Bible family collection)

buildings. Above all, he emphasized his support for mining and opposition to foreign aid. In fact, like his mentor McCarran, Bible kept his office staff busy with a steady stream of news releases from Washington to Nevada extolling his hard work on behalf of the state. Jack Carpenter used his far-flung newspaper contacts to sell Bible as the can-do senator, publicizing Bible's record all over the state (see fig. 7). On September 4, 1962, Bible sailed to victory in the Democratic Party primary, trouncing Jack Streeter by 27,853 votes.[9]

The general election was a lackluster affair that might have been forgotten entirely, had the secretary of state not kept records. Bible's opponent, William B. Wright, was a political novice. A month after beating Streeter Bible trounced Wright by an even wider margin of 29,694 votes, nearly two-to-one. Democrats captured all of the major races except lieutenant governor, where Paul Laxalt beat former U.S. senator Berkeley Bunker.[10]

Bible's second full term, 1963 to 1968, proved to be the most eventful of his political career. While his personal political fortunes began and ended

*Fig. 7. "Carry Me back to Old Nevadee." (*Las Vegas Review-Journal, *August 19, 1962)*

on a high note, the nation experienced progress and despair, jubilation and tragedy. The nation changed dramatically during the heady years of the Great Society, and so did Bible. While he remained as dedicated as ever to Nevada's economic development, he moved cautiously closer to the ideas of environmental groups who wanted to protect America's remaining unspoiled lands.

Bible had cause for pride in his achievements and optimism about his

Senator Alan Bible (far left) during meeting of Democratic committee chairmen.
(Bible family collection)

political future. Following in McCarran's footsteps, he had "delivered the goods" for his state, particularly legislation for water development projects. He had made impressive strides as a senator, gaining power within the institution and winning some support in the White House, thanks to the presence of a Democratic administration more attuned to the needs of western senators and a vice-president he had served with and idolized. He had easily defeated his opponents in the primary and general elections.

Additionally, Bible began to benefit from the drift in power from subcommittees to individual senators. The movement was underway in the late 1950s, but the liberal onslaught in 1958 virtually guaranteed each senator ample opportunity to extend his power and influence. The ideal leader for the new Senate, Mike Mansfield, provided a stark contrast to Johnson's sometimes overbearing leadership; the equalitarian Mansfield rarely intervened, generally leaving his colleagues free to make their own decisions without interference from the party leadership.[11] Liberals, so long a second-class group in the Senate, applauded Mansfield's style, while many old-line inner club members could only bemoan their waning influence. But not Bible. He liked Mansfield and his style, which allowed him to benefit from the Senate's traditional ways and to expand his personal influence.

While subcommittee government had many advantages for both freshmen and more senior senators like Bible, the system was far from perfect. It reduced accountability for policy decisions, since each senator could find refuge deep in the subcommittee system. By creating closer ties among subcommittee senators, interest groups, and bureaucratic agencies, these links fueled the "Iron Triangle" and contributed to the escalating cost of government programs between 1956 and 1976. By the end of Bible's second term in

Bible (right) shaking hands with majority leader Mike Mansfield as Lyndon Johnson looks on. (Bible family collection)

1968 the Senate was drifting toward impotence caused by a lack of coordination, control, and, more importantly, leadership, which was extremely difficult for Mansfield—or anyone else, for that matter—to exercise in a 100-member institution run by 16 standing committees and 100 subcommittees.[12]

Mansfield's greatest attribute as majority leader was also his greatest fault. While his easygoing leadership style blended nicely with Bible's personality and legislative ambitions for Nevada, Mansfield lacked Johnson's drive and passion for legislative results, which at times proved frustrating.[13] Consequently, interest groups and coalitions, in and out of Congress, could work out their own compromises without interference or direction from the Senate leadership.

But all this changed after the tragedy in Dallas and Johnson's defeat of Goldwater in 1964. Johnson stepped into the vacuum and resumed the role of congressional leader in an effort to restore bipartisan agreement across a wide range of policy issues. He sought balance, compromise, and consensus—something for everyone—which produced an incredible legislative record until 1966, when his spell over Congress began to slip amid doubts about Vietnam, white backlash over civil rights demonstrations, urban unrest, and general social instability.[14] Despite the mounting criticism of the president as he moved further to the left at home and deeper into the quagmire abroad, Bible remained steadfastly behind Johnson, as he always had. Although the reasons for Bible's loyalty to Johnson were complex, it was also good politics for Nevada in terms of corralling federal dollars.

Still, keeping federal dollars flowing to Nevada could be a challenge. For most of Bible's career, the Nevada delegation consisted of fellow Democrats Howard Cannon in the Senate and Walter Baring in the House. While Bible and Cannon nearly always followed Johnson, Baring was another matter entirely. According to Bible, whose genial nature made him slow to criticize others, Baring rarely, if ever, accomplished anything requiring hard work. In Bible's view, he was unreliable and untrustworthy in an institution that valued a colleague's word of honor.[15] Worse yet, particularly for Bible and Cannon, Baring went out of his way to criticize and embarrass Johnson by voting against Great Society programs, including Medicare, food stamps, and civil rights—anything that required federal spending to help the poor or disadvantaged. Baring's politics angered and frustrated Democratic leaders in and out of Congress, and Bible put as much distance as possible between himself and the congressman (see fig. 8). Time and again, Bible and Cannon were called upon to repair the political damage inflicted by what they considered Baring's indiscretions. Indeed, they carried the Baring burden into their relationship with Johnson; according to Mike Manatos, White House liaison to the Senate, Johnson certainly would have vetoed legislation important to Nevada, if not for the support Bible and Cannon gave to the president and his programs.[16]

Still, Baring was extremely popular with Nevadans, who saw him much as they saw themselves—conservative and independent—not as lazy and difficult. The result was a series of tenuous relationships. Aware of Baring's popularity, Bible and Cannon concealed their feelings about the state's lone congressman to avoid a full-scale political break in the delegation, but Johnson let Nevada Democrats know exactly how he felt about Baring. On May 7, 1964, he wrote to Charles Springer, chairman of the Nevada State Democratic Convention, saying in part: "I need your help now in supporting Democratic programs for the good of all Americans and I continue to thank you for the support of your two great senators, Alan Bible and Howard Cannon, whose friendship and counsel are now more valuable today than ever before" (see fig. 9).[17] Johnson intentionally snubbed Baring; as the years passed, their relationship further deteriorated, which nearly scuttled projects vital to southern Nevada's economy (see chapter 10).

Fig. 8. *"We'll Be Campaigning Together, Pal."* (Las Vegas Review-Journal, March 18, 1962)

While Baring was a political problem for Bible, the most pressing economic concern remained mining—particularly silver. Friendly with Kennedy's administration, and later Johnson's, Bible disagreed with each when it came to western mining because he was a leading Senate spokesman for mining interests. While western mining, or more accurately the industry's plight, had formed the basis for Bible's foreign policy concerns in his first term, he altered his course somewhat in the second term. His defense of mining followed more traditional lines of domestic support for gold and silver producers. Bible became the leading post–World War II silver senator in Nevada. This was good politics because he never forgot his roots; like Tip O'Neill,

Fig. 9. *"One Sour Note."* (Las Vegas Review-Journal, *May 6, 1962*)

the future Speaker of the House, he believed that a politician was elected, and reelected, based on what he did for his constituents.[18]

The issue on which Bible worked particularly hard for his constituents, silver coinage, had been raised early in the Kennedy administration and continued well into Johnson's Great Society. When Drew Pearson charged that a Canadian silver producer engineered Eva Adams's appointment as director of the Mint, the Kennedy administration paused long enough to look into the allegations before allowing her to be sworn into office. Afterward Treasury Secretary Douglas Dillon removed all of Adams's authority over silver policy and placed it under the control of Undersecretary Robert V. Roosa. At the same time Dillon named Leland Hoard, former assistant director of the Mint, to head the new Office of Domestic Gold and Silver Production. Thus, Adams had no influence over the decision-making process on silver policy—a bad sign for the state's silver miners and the silver senator.[19]

These changes in the Treasury Department staff occurred just when silver stockpiles were being depleted in massive quantities. Although the exact amounts vary according to the sources used, it appears that between January and November 1961 treasury stocks fell from 123 million ounces to 47 million. The reason was clear: the Treasury Department had begun selling "free silver" (silver unnecessary to back the currency) to users and fabricators at 91.5 cents an ounce. Silver producers deplored these actions and urged an end to the sale of free silver or, as an alternative, that the price be raised above the Treasury Department's price of 91.5 cents an ounce, which was 2 cents below the world price.[20]

The federal response met neither the hopes nor the expectations of silver producers. On November 28, 1961, the Kennedy administration stopped selling free silver for commercial use. But the two-year period in which the Treasury sold free silver to commercial users had depleted its stocks by 55 million ounces. Worse yet, the Treasury Department's policy of selling at 91.5 cents an ounce kept the price artificially low, compared with world market prices. American silver users received a windfall, and the loss in Treasury stocks could only come from foreign imports—which, in Bible's view, would only depress the domestic market even further.[21]

But there was more. The Kennedy administration then sought to repeal the 1934 Pittman Silver Purchase Act and related laws, drawing Bible and Senator Frank Church (D-Idaho) to the White House to plead their case. Both westerners opposed the repeal because silver prices were uncertain, and a new policy direction could make them worse.[22]

Bible considered Dillon and his Treasury Department not only incompetent, but guilty of mismanaging the whole silver question and precipitating the crisis. He was not alone. *Barron's*, a respected national business and financial weekly, charged that both Dillon and Federal Reserve chairman William Martin were guilty of "mismanaged money." Dillon and Martin responded to the silver crisis by issuing federal reserve notes instead of silver certificates for one and two dollar bills. This prohibited redemption of silver certificates for bullion at the Treasury. Dillon explained that it became profitable to redeem certificates for silver as silver sales approached 1.29 cents an ounce. Unless Congress acted quickly, the result could be a shortage of dollar bills in circulation, constricting the money supply and further draining silver stockpiles.[23]

The silver mess and two years of foot-dragging by Treasury officials prompted further criticism. "Mismanaged silver, to be sure, is an ancient and honorable U.S. tradition, which, some would argue, dates back to William Jennings Bryan," *Barron's* declared. "On this score, however, Messrs. Dillon and Co. probably have set some kind of low."[24] Between the Treasury Department's policy of selling free silver and its failure to stop the silver drain, prices rose to 1.28 cents an ounce in March 1963, driving Dillon and Martin to Congress for help before silver users started to demand silver bullion for certificates. Dillon and Martin even expressed concern that, if silver hit $1.38 an ounce, Americans would melt down their coins for the silver content and hoard the bullion.

To be sure, the issue of silver stocks and money management was complicated and controversial. Still, the administration's answer to the escalating silver crisis sailed through Congress with amazing speed. The solution was H.R. 5398, which contained four features. First, it stopped the Treasury Department from selling silver for less than its monetary value. Second, federal reserve notes would replace $1, $2, $5, and $10 silver certificates, all retired from circulation. Third, it repealed the government's mandatory silver purchases (subsidy) at 90½ cents an ounce. Finally, it eliminated the silver transfer tax to permit a free silver market unencumbered by mandatory government purchases and taxes. The House Banking and Currency Committee held four days of hearings, allotting only two hours to opposition witnesses and two hours for floor debate. On April 10, 1963, H.R. 5398, known as the repeal of the Silver Purchase Act, passed the House. The Senate promptly took it up on April 29.[25]

Bible led the western senators lined up to assault the bill. Wasting little time coming to the point of producer versus consumer, he said, "Much testimony has been taken as to the hardship brought upon the silver users . . . in my opinion stopping sales of Treasury silver was action long overdue." Pausing only long enough to gather steam, Bible continued:

> Silver users state that this has caused untold hardships upon their industry and forced silverware, jewelry, and other articles of artistic character to be faced with a very large increase in production costs to the detriment of the industry. Well, I, for one, cannot weep, especially when I can drive through my state and other silver producing states of the west and see silver mine after silver mine shut down . . .[26]

But the administration clearly had the votes on the Senate Banking and Currency Committee to assure that it would follow the House's lead and report favorably on the bill. As a result, the Senate passed it on May 23, 1963.

On June 4, 1963, President Kennedy signed the repeal of the 1934 Silver Purchase Act.[27]

During the Senate debate, the bill's backers never told Bible and his supporters that silver might be reduced or eliminated in subsidiary coins like dimes, nickels, and quarters. Secretary Dillon gave every indication that after the silver act's repeal his department would have no trouble maintaining adequate silver supplies. In an exchange with Senator Wallace F. Bennett of Utah, Dillon testified that he had 1,600,000 ounces of silver on hand, enough to last fifteen to twenty years.[28] Once again Dillon and his experts were wrong, and within two years they were back to ask Congress to stop the drain of silver by removing it from the nation's coins.

Meanwhile, western senators were working to assure an increase in silver coins. Mansfield, Cannon, and Bible, to name only a few, stepped up their campaign to persuade Congress and the president to mint silver dollars known as cartwheels. The issue prompted political debate and speculation in Nevada and in Washington, D.C., in a most surprising way. In March 1964 Representative Baring told his House colleagues that Nevada's gaming industry needed cartwheels, which evoked little enthusiasm among other House members, who considered it a bail-out for Nevada's notorious criminal element. This prompted the *Las Vegas Review-Journal* to comment, "Walter Baring has proved himself totally ineffective."[29] Cartwheels were important to Nevada, not because casinos needed them, as many believed, but because they were a source of cheap publicity recognized around the world— important symbols in western states conscious of their frontier heritage.[30]

The Johnson administration proved sympathetic. In 1964 it requested $635,000 for silver dollar coinage. But when the House Appropriations Committee quickly rejected the plan, Bible and Cannon promptly launched a campaign to restore the cut. Later Mike Manatos, White House liaison to the Senate, attended a dinner commemorating Nevada's centennial and talked with Bible and Cannon about the silver dollar issue. Manatos found both senators deeply concerned and desirous of continuing the tradition of cartwheels in the West.

Having long enjoyed an unusual ability to manipulate Congress, Johnson and his aides saw the strings they could pull with Nevada's senators. "I believe we have the answer to cloture votes by Bible and Cannon in the palm of our hands" (vote to close debate in Senate filibuster against civil rights legislation), Manatos informed Lawrence O'Brien, special assistant to the president, on May 25, 1964. "I venture to say that if the president were to see Bible and Cannon and assure them he would see to it that new silver dollars were to continue to be minted if they cast a cloture vote, the pressures on them from Nevada would be so great they would be forced to cast their votes for cloture." Apparently, Manatos's plan to link the politics of silver with that of the civil rights filibuster never materialized. If it did, it failed to move Bible. He remained steadfast with the southern bloc of senators who opposed cloture. Manatos persisted in his attempt to change Bible's mind up to July 30, 1968—to no avail.[31]

With the repeal of the Silver Purchase Act and transactions tax in June 1963 came further changes. The New York Commodity Exchange permitted trading in silver futures for the first time since 1934, and silver prices rose about 38 cents an ounce over a three-year period. Responding to the worldwide shortage of silver and seeking to locate new deposits, the government offered financial aid to domestic producers, up to 75 percent of the cost of exploration. This incentive failed to stimulate exploration on the scale needed to keep pace with consumption, however.[32] Thus, an increase in foreign imports made up the difference.

In Bible's view, the government assistance program was too little, too late. In early 1965 the Bureau of Mines estimated that silver prices two to three times the level of $1.29 would be needed to stimulate new domestic production; but at the current rate of coinage demand, the Treasury stockpile of 1.25 billion ounces would be exhausted by 1968. Thus, the rate of consumption had to be reduced or the country would simply run out of silver. But if silver prices went as high as the bureau posited, the intrinsic value of all U.S. subsidiary coins would be greater than their face value. Consumers would hoard or melt down the coins, disrupting the retail business and industrial production of goods requiring silver.[33]

Bible disputed the remedy, not the facts. Since 1954 he had clamored in vain for a domestic minerals and metal policy. He clashed with the Eisenhower administration over tungsten and later copper, lead, and zinc, all hurt by foreign imports. Meanwhile, he continued to fume about a foreign policy that showed more concern for American business profits from foreign mining than for the needs of domestic miners. On August 13, 1963, he told the minerals subcommittee, "It is difficult for me to understand national policies while we will not permit at least an even break for our domestic mining industry."[34]

In the same statement, Bible touched on the key to western mining problems—U.S. investment overseas. In 1961 fifteen cents of every dollar of all corporate profits came from overseas operations. This affected the U.S. balance of payments and curtailed investment at home. Without trade restrictions such as quotas and tariffs, the domestic mining industry would be unable to compete with foreign sources that were better equipped and financed, principally from the outflow of American dollars. Finally, Bible cited Nevada's lead and zinc industry as a prime example of how a misguided foreign policy caused the collapse of western mining.

Bible considered the silver crisis and the overall plight of western mining inseparable. He reasoned that since silver is largely a by-product of copper, lead, zinc, and gold mining, silver production was an outgrowth of the demand for these metals. Thus, any reduction in the output from these sources would naturally reduce silver production, since roughly two-thirds of all silver mined in the United States comes from base metal ores. With base metal mining dipping to all-time lows, the government created a boom in silver imports to keep pace with the demand. Bible bristled at the staggering imports—15 million ounces from Mexico and 36 million from Peru.[35] Coupled with America's drop of 5.7 percent in the free market production of silver in fourteen years, this left Nevada's senator worried and perplexed about the future of western mining.

Throughout 1964 the silver coin crisis escalated. On May 31, 1963, the Treasury Department held $69,688,192 in silver dollars; in February 1964 it reached $25,300,700, a fall of $44,387,492. By March 25, 1964, Treasury vaults contained only $3,000,000. Nickels, dimes, quarters, and half dollars were also in short supply, limiting trade exchanges of all kinds, particularly vending machine operations.[36] Little had changed by the beginning of 1965. The 3,000,000 in silver dollars held by the Treasury had reached a value of $93 million to coin dealers and private collectors.[37]

With the coin shortage showing no signs of abating, the Bureau of Mines flatly stated that eliminating silver from subsidiary coins would free substantial amounts of silver stock for industrial use by 1967. In addition, silver prices would stabilize with corresponding production levels. Thus, the solution to the silver shortage was not to increase domestic production, but to remove silver altogether from the coinage system.[38] Naturally, silver users were elated.

The political forces for change in the nation's subsidiary coinage system included business leaders, banks, the national Chamber of Commerce, vending machine firms, and silver users. Vending machine makers were ready to alter the magnetic grabs from 90 percent silver and 10 percent copper to whatever formula the Treasury Department chose for the new coins. This alternative was preferable to the continued shortage, but western senators were unwilling to give up the fight completely. The 90-10 formula of silver and copper in coins meant that each silver dollar contained .77 ounces of silver. Therefore, when silver reached $1.29 an ounce on the open market, a cartwheel contained exactly a dollar's worth of silver. This ceiling was effective, but it forced silver users to pay more for their raw materials.

As an alternative, Senator Lee Metcalf (D-Montana) proposed to cut the silver content rather than eliminate it altogether.[39] Agreeing with most western senators on the need to reduce the silver content for subsidiary coins, Metcalf proposed a change in the ratio from 90 percent to 80 percent, which would make more silver available for coinage. Silver users countered that the Metcalf plan would only drive the world market price higher because cartwheels with an 80 percent silver content would contain .69 ounce of silver instead of .77, driving the price from $1.29 to $1.45 an ounce.[40] Meanwhile, on May 14, 1965, President Johnson ordered the Mint to produce 45 million silver dollars, no doubt in response to desperate pleas from his friends in the Senate, especially Mansfield. But the immediate response was mostly negative, because the new dollars were sure to be hoarded. The new dollars would end up in the hands of speculators.[41]

Only ten days after Johnson ordered the Mint to produce silver dollars the Treasury decided not to proceed. The next day Bible introduced S. 2036, co-sponsored by Cannon, Mansfield, Metcalf, and Frank Moss, to prohibit exportation, hoarding, and the use of silver coins as collateral for bank loans. Mansfield and Bible took to the Senate floor to present the case for silver miners.[42] Mansfield conceded that the Mint should not proceed with silver dollar production and that the silver content of subsidiary coins should be reduced. Although he agreed, Bible was far less conciliatory toward the Treasury Department for its lack of leadership during the silver shortage, which left Congress to deal with the problem. Clearly, Bible's bill was no solution: its provisions against hoarding and speculation were largely unenforceable and might just exacerbate the problems.[43] But it was a beginning that attempted to clean up some of the mess the Treasury Department had left behind.

Finally, the Treasury Department submitted its plan to deal with the silver crisis to Johnson, who wasted little time in prompting congressional action. On June 3, 1965, he sent the House and Senate his message and corresponding legislation. The president noted that the more than 10,000 tons of silver used yearly in coin production far exceeded free-world production. The deficit had to come from Treasury stocks, which had shrunk considerably since 1963, when the Silver Purchase Act was repealed and silver prices rose. While the penny and nickel would be unaffected, the dime and quarter would be a composite coin of copper and nickel alloy. Also, the silver portion of the half dollar would fall from 90 percent to 40 percent while the cartwheel's silver content would remain the same. Johnson speculated that with these changes a 90 percent savings in silver would be realized.[44]

Representative Wright Patman (D-Texas) introduced the House version, H.R. 8746, and A. Willis Robertson (D-Virginia) and Wallace F. Bennett

(D-Utah) did the same for the Senate bill, S. 2080. The House began hearings the next day in the Banking and Currency Committee, where Chairman Patman set the tone by emphasizing that H.R. 8746 had something for everyone, including incentives for silver producers. But industry users clearly would be the big winners, not western mining interests. Henry H. Fowler, who had replaced Douglas Dillon as treasury secretary, restated the president's message, which was based on a two-year Treasury Department study of worldwide trends in silver production and use.[45]

Patman led Fowler through a series of friendly questions. The treasury secretary concluded that whether a nation's coinage was made from gold, silver, paper, or any other substance was immaterial. What was critical was its acceptance as legal tender, with full faith and credit in commercial transactions. Fowler expressed the belief that current domestic production and employment levels would not suffer. While he probably was right, the point was that high costs, in comparison with foreign competitors, would keep silver production static.[46]

On June 9, 1965, the Senate Banking and Currency Committee took up the coinage act. While generally supportive, Mansfield and Metcalf wanted to amend S. 2080 to include portions of Bible's earlier bill, which prohibited the hoarding of silver coins used for collateral for bank loans. By contrast, Bible took dead aim at the bill and the Treasury Department's study with the most comprehensive testimony against the administration's proposal.

Beginning with a review of the Silver Purchase Act's repeal in 1963, Bible lashed out at the Treasury's rosy predictions of the past two years: "The Treasury Department said supplies of silver would last 10–12 years, which would maintain our coinage system. . . . They are wrong again. . . . They have now come up with another magic formula." Bible maintained that the silver shortage was the artificial result of the Treasury Department's mismanagement and the hoarding of silver dollars by speculators.[47] He proposed that the remedy was to force silver coins back into circulation, not to debase currency practices in use since 1800. Moreover, new coins with less silver content would only compound the problem by encouraging the hoarding of coins still in circulation. Circulating the two coins beside each other was impossible, and the result could only be more hoarding by speculators and a worried public.[48] Bible said that what had curtailed mining and exploration in the past was an unrealistically low silver price, due partly to a Treasury policy that proved to be a windfall for silver users while ignoring silver producers in the West.

But the predictions of a silver state senator who was also the spokesman for western mining interests went unnoticed. So did the pleas of Senator Milward Simpson of Wyoming, who charged the Treasury with providing a cheap source of industrial silver for manufacturers. Simpson and Bible were right: the senators who lined up to support the administration were also the spokesmen for silver users. Senator Edward Kennedy (D-Massachusetts) said, "Industrial users of silver in my state have indicated to me that every effort should be made to free silver from coinage so that there can be a greater supply of this metal available for domestic production." John O. Pastore (D–Rhode Island) echoed this theme: "My primary purpose . . . is the retention of American jobs. Silver is essential to industry not only in my state, where we have a large silverware industry and electronics industry, but in many parts of the country where silver is an essential manufacturing component."[49]

The most blatant expression of constituent interest in the silver fight came not from Bible, but from Pastore's colleague, Claiborne Pell. Citing the census of manufacturers, Pell maintained that in Rhode Island 289 firms employing 8,234, or 7 percent of the work force, depended on the manufacture of jewelry and silverware: "Silver means jobs, bread and butter . . . silver is an obsolete base for our currency. . . . A saving of some 90 percent of the silver now used for coinage comes as good news to Rhode Island."[50]

Bible had no illusions about the Coinage Act of 1965, which sailed through the House and quickly won Senate approval. The removal of silver from subsidiary coins had distinct advantages. First, the Treasury would save $300 million a year by buying cheaper copper and nickel instead of silver, making more silver available for use in missile parts, electronics, photographic plates, jewelry, silverware, and a host of other consumer items. More importantly, the coin shortage created by hoarding would be eliminated.[51]

Ironically, in the wake of his battle, the White House sent Bible a freshly minted quarter made of copper and nickel as a gift from President Johnson. In a letter bearing the president's stamp, rather than his customary signature on letters to Bible, Johnson said, "I want you to have this shiny quarter as a memento. Perhaps it may become a treasured keepsake in your family."[52] Perhaps it did not, because Bible continued to press the cause of western mining, including the dwindling supply of gold reserves.

Bible was concerned that America's foreign aid program and business investments overseas had endangered the nation's gold reserves. Statistically, he was correct. The gold stock was about $25 billion in 1950, but it had fallen to about $16 billion in 1962, due largely to foreign short-term claims against American gold that had risen from a low of 7 billion in 1950 to 20 billion in 1962. Finally, if all foreign claims against American gold were called in, the Treasury would find itself not only out of gold, but $16 billion in debt.[53]

It was even more distressing to Bible that some foreign countries exchanged their American dollars for gold, which they put back into their monetary systems to strengthen their own currency. The balance-of-trade deficit only exacerbated the problem by creating further pressure on American reserves. Unable to influence foreign policy, change foreign aid (which he had always opposed), or curtail American investments overseas, Bible reasoned that a partial short-term solution was to increase American gold reserves.

Exactly how additional gold reserves would strengthen America's economic position was unclear, but it gave Bible ammunition to aid yet another sector of the western mining industry. On September 9, 1963, he and Senator Ernest Gruening (D-Alaska) co-sponsored S. 2125 to revitalize the American gold mining industry. The bill would have subsidized gold producers to stimulate exploration and development of additional supplies. The rationale was that an executive order had fixed gold prices at $35 an ounce since 1934, while production and labor costs had soared, making gold mining unprofitable and a victim of federal discrimination. If production costs were subsidized, then gold mining could return to profitable levels, providing jobs in the West while strengthening America's economy. More importantly, gold need not rise above $35 an ounce to accomplish the desired results.[54]

On December 13, 1963, the Interior and Insular Affairs Committee unanimously approved the bill, but the Senate took no action due to the impending Christmas recess. The Treasury Department used the break to kill all hope of congressional approval by opposing the measure as a threat to financial stability. The Treasury's vagueness about the bill's potential for harm matched Bible's equally vague notions about its benefits. Western senators like Gruening and Bible, who saw President Johnson as sensitive to their problems, presented their case to him on August 19, 1965. As in the silver crisis, they blamed the Treasury Department for failing even to consider the plight of gold producers or to provide an alternative to legislation pending before the Senate.[55]

For nearly two years Johnson and the Treasury Department offered no constructive alternative to subsidizing gold producers, opting instead for the status quo. On September 24, 1965, Senator George McGovern (D–South Dakota) presented S. 2562, the Gold Miners Assistance Act of 1965, seeking an additional 5 percent depletion allowance to all gold miners based on yearly gross receipts. A month later Bible offered S. 2596 to increase the depletion allowance for gold and silver mine operators from 15 to 23 percent. The full Senate failed to act on either bill, and the continuing frustration of mining boosters carried into 1966. On May 4, 1966, Bible again pleaded with the president for help, but to no avail.[56]

Meanwhile, the House proceeded along the same lines as the Senate with H.R. 10924, 10925, 11081, 11667, 799, 5272, 6505, and 10681, all meant to accomplish purposes similar to the McGovern and Bible bills. On August 31, 1966, the Treasury and Interior departments issued their reports on the House and Senate plans. The Interior Department simply deferred to the Treasury's expertise, which Bible found questionable, given his battle with that department a year earlier over silver. However, the Bureau of the Budget agreed with the Interior Department's general impression that supporting the gold mining industry could cause instability in the $35 fixed price of gold.[57]

Clearly, the Treasury Department killed the support plan. The department's general counsel, Fred B. Smith, offered no specifics, only general feelings about the effect of the bills: "This would lead to uncertainty and speculation with regard to future gold prices. This could undermine confidence in international transactions tending to shake confidence in the dollar. . . . The monetary system of the free world is hinged at $35." That was enough, especially when the Bureau of the Budget concurred, implying that President Johnson had the same view on the issue.[58]

The Treasury Department's position was no surprise to Bible, but he was disappointed because massive gold deposits discovered near Carlin, Nevada, promised to pump as much as $120 million into the state's economy. He had hoped that S. 2596 would guarantee the profitability of the Carlin and other mines. Meanwhile, as with silver, the United States required large gold imports to keep pace with domestic needs. In 1966 alone demand outstripped supply by $140 million, while platinum added another $66 million and mercury still another $33 million. All heavy metal imports contributed to the growing imbalance in trade payments.[59]

At the end of the 1960s it was clear to many, including Bible, that the instability of western mining was due in part to a foreign trade policy that permitted cheap imports to compete with domestic metals. This led to declines in copper, lead, and zinc production, which contributed to the worldwide silver shortage, the 1934 Silver Purchase Act repeal, and the Coinage Act of 1965. Moreover, fears about worldwide monetary instability kept gold prices lower than production costs, inhibiting expansion and exploration of western gold reserves. Finally, the mining industry failed to consider the growing environmental movement, which contributed to the industry's declining economic and political influence and to Bible's most important legislative achievements, nationally and for Nevada.

Chapter Nine

The Triumph of Recreation, 1963–1968

While Bible and the mining industry savored few victories, water development advocates were the big winners in the years between 1963 and 1968—and so, therefore, was Bible. In April 1961 Senator Clinton Anderson unveiled his Water Resources Planning Act to help states prepare large-scale water development plans. The bill called for an annual appropriation of $5 million so that each state could hire water experts to evaluate needs and potential project sites. Even before Anderson could hold hearings on his bill, President Kennedy presented yet another plan to establish a federal Water Resources Council and a commission for each of the nation's major rivers. Unlike the Anderson proposal, the president called for more federal control than western senators would have preferred.[1]

In deference to the president, Anderson set aside his plan, but he was still suspicious of the administration. It appeared to him, and to others, that a council made up of the secretaries of agriculture, defense, and health, education and welfare would allow the Bureau of the Budget a greater role in deciding western water projects. Bible shared Anderson's distaste for the cost-conscious budget watchers when it came to water and mining legislation. He feared a repetition of his failed attempt to save silver and gold mining, which the Bureau of the Budget had refused to consider. Nonetheless, Anderson and Secretary of the Interior Stewart Udall supported the president until mail opposing federal control of river basin planning inundated western congressmen. Public opposition effectively killed not only Anderson's proposal, but also the president's.[2]

But Anderson persisted in his drive to coordinate research and planning for water development at the national, regional, and basin levels. The result was S. 21, the Water Resources Planning Act of 1965 (WRPA), which President Johnson signed on July 22, 1965. Bible co-sponsored the bill, which provided for expert evaluations of potential sites to gain congressional approval for costly water projects outside the western bloc. But in the West, where water and power projects were a religion, development interests never hesitated to appeal to their congressional delegations to influence decisions. Thus, the WRPA simply became irrelevant.[3]

In August 1963 Udall presented his ambitious plan to develop the Colorado River Basin. The Pacific Southwest water plan went to all seven basin states for review, since local interests had a vital stake in the outcome. From the beginning, Bible publicly supported Udall's idea, but privately he had reservations about the proposal for two hydroelectric dams within the Grand Canyon. The power-producing dams were to provide the money needed to underwrite the billion-dollar project. Recalling the battle over the Echo Park Dam in 1956, Bible sensed that trouble lay ahead in persuading environmentally conscious groups to go along with damming the Grand Canyon, and he was right. Udall's scheme also troubled Bible because it included southern Nevada's plan to bring water from Lake Mead to the Las Vegas Valley. He feared that the whole proposal might be rejected once the Grand Canyon became an issue, ending his plans and Nevada's hopes for expanding the Las Vegas area.

Meanwhile, the Supreme Court announced its long-awaited ruling in *Arizona* v. *California* (1963). It was a shocking announcement for states with vested interests in Colorado River Basin water development, especially California. Arizona was the big winner. The court decided that Congress had actually apportioned the waters guaranteed to the lower basin states in the 1922 Colorado River Compact by virtue of section 4(a) of the 1928 Boulder Canyon Act, which authorized 4,400,000 acre-feet to California, 2,800,000 acre-feet to Arizona, and 300,000 acre-feet to Nevada. Arizona also won its claim to exclude the Gila River's waters from its Colorado River allotment.[4]

While the court's ruling on allocation satisfied Bible, other aspects of the case troubled him, particularly the issues of federal authority and Indian water rights. The court gave the secretary of the interior the authority to divide future water surpluses and shortages within and among Colorado River Basin states. This meant that the secretary could ignore state water laws where water was secured by federal reclamation projects.[5] For Bible, this expansion of federal power in western water matters, coming on the heels of the Pelton Dam case, might limit Nevada's influence in basin water issues.

Equally troubling was the issue of Indian water rights, which affected the Washoe Project and California-Nevada Compact negotiations. The court sustained the reserve rights doctrine, first articulated in *Winters* v. *United States* (1908), by agreeing that Indian water rights dated from the reservation's establishment and that Indian claims were superior to those of non-Indians. While the court ignored water rights in tributaries, it ordered Indian water rights charged against the mainstream water allocated to each state.[6]

Clearly, the federal government reigned supreme in western water law, due to *Arizona* v. *California*. The court established federal reserve rights and the government's right to withdraw public lands for federal purposes. Also, the secretary of the interior won expanded powers to decide intrastate and interstate water issues involving federal reclamation projects. This spelled trouble for Bible, who had long supported the supremacy of state water laws while ignoring Indian water claims in northern Nevada. But the most perplexing problem for Bible was California's powerful congressional delegation, which sought to modify the court's decision in *Arizona* v. *California* through the political process. The plan was to hold the Central Arizona Project hostage, preventing Nevada from receiving its share of Colorado River water for the Las Vegas Valley.

While the federal government was wresting control of state water rights in the West, Bible backed a plan for Colorado River Basin states to transfer millions of acre-feet from watersheds in the Pacific Northwest. On April 20, 1964, he endorsed Idaho senator Len B. Jordan's idea of diverting Columbia River water to the arid Southwest. This was a blunt admission that the Colorado River was overappropriated and incapable of supplying the water needed for Udall's Pacific Southwest water plan or meeting the future needs of basin states. Additional sources had to be found to fuel the West's growing economic power; for Bible, "Progress is America's real destiny."[7] Indeed, he came out noisily for the Sierra-Cascade Project, also known as the Western Water Project. Overstating the case, he called it "a bold leap forward in America's history of progress which will begin a new era in western development." The very idea of 130 million acre-feet of Columbia River water flowing freely into the Pacific each year was simply a "tragic waste."[8]

Nor was Bible alone in his enthusiasm to prevent water waste in the Pacific Northwest. On September 2, 1965, he co-sponsored Senate Concurrent Resolution 55, recommending a joint United States–Canadian study group to investigate the feasibility of bringing arctic waters to the Southwest. Even bolder than the Columbia River idea, the proposal sought to divert surplus waters from Alaska, the Yukon, and British Columbia, across the Canadian plains to the Great Lakes and down to the Southwest and Mexico. The concept, dubbed the North American Water and Power Alliance (NAWAPA), never received serious consideration, due largely to the staggering costs involved and the impossible task of persuading others to part with their resources to benefit the Southwest.[9]

Still, the Sierra-Cascade Project and the NAWAPA demonstrate the incredible drive of western water development supporters to secure water rights, no matter what the environmental and financial costs. Both plans also reveal the fear generated by the Colorado River's inability to meet the future water needs of the Southwest, particularly with southern California's seemingly unlimited growth and Arizona poised to cash in on its guaranteed share of water from the 1963 Supreme Court ruling.

But Bible and his cohorts faced an obstacle: Senator Henry "Scoop" Jackson (D-Washington), who had succeeded the ailing Clinton Anderson as chairman of the Interior and Insular Affairs Committee. Jackson violently opposed the effort to free Columbia River water for use in the Southwest. He moved to enact a comprehensive review of water resources by introducing S. 3107 on March 21, 1966, to establish a national water commission with wide-ranging authority to investigate and recommend future use, development, and planning of all water resources. Aware of the time-honored congressional tradition of establishing commissions to avoid sticky decisions, Jackson sought to deflect the pressure that he was receiving from other western members of the Interior Committee. Nonetheless, he reintroduced the bill in the 90th Congress as S. 20, which the president signed on August 26, 1968, creating the commission.[10]

If Jackson was determined, so was Bible. In a prepared statement before the Interior and Insular Affairs Committee on May 17, 1966, Bible again stressed that high priority should be given to tapping water sources in the Northwest. He co-sponsored S. 1429, introduced by Senator Frank Moss, calling for a separate study and plan to meet the Southwest's water needs. But the Senate decided it had enough commissions on the water situation and took no action on the bill.[11]

Although the National Water Commission did not complete its study until 1973, it served Jackson's short- and long-term purposes. For the moment, it blunted discussion of interbasin transfers because the matter was under study. When the report came out, it alarmed Southwest water development extremists like Bible. The commission recommended that direct beneficiaries pay the full cost of interbasin transfers, including compensation to the area of origin. This meant that the cost of water development should be regional—a significant departure from nationally financed reclamation projects and a harbinger of future shifts in cost benefits from the federal government to local users.[12] Clearly, time was running out for Lower Colorado River Basin users. They had to reduce allocations or exploit additional sources to maintain current lifestyles. But coming to grips with the reality of living in an arid environment was never part of the heritage of southwestern congressional leaders, including Bible.[13]

While Bible remained on the front lines in the fight for additional water development projects and mining exploitation, his perspective on parks and recreation underwent a transformation. His legislative record as chairman of the Parks and Recreation Subcommittee was unparalleled in scope and in the number of new parks and monuments added to the system. For a decade he demonstrated leadership, patience, and a thorough understanding of the importance of preserving part of America's heritage. The result was a legacy of legislative accomplishment that extended far beyond his native state.

Bible's championship of national parks and recreation areas demonstrates the problem with labeling politicians conservative, liberal, or middle of the road. For most of his career colleagues and friends considered Bible a moderate to conservative politician who tended to move in circles dominated by southern Democrats, who were generally well to the right. To a limited degree, this remained correct. But at other times he supported the legislative agenda of the more liberal elements of the Great Society.

The key was that Bible wanted to improve the quality of people's lives. He supported a whole range of social programs, including traditional New Deal and Fair Deal approaches to Social Security and Medicare. He endorsed aid to education, civil rights, expanded minimum wage programs, food stamps, and Head Start, just to name a few. He saw national parks much as Johnson and others saw Great Society measures: as an investment in improving the way people lived.

Indeed, national park legislation ranks among the major achievements of the Great Society (see table 8). But until 1964 Bible willingly stood in the shadow of his friend Clinton Anderson, the acknowledged leader and expert on wilderness issues in the Senate. Afterward Bible's quiet manner and low-key temperament kept him largely anonymous, while Stewart and Morris Udall, Gaylord Nelson (D-Wisconsin), John Saylor (R-Pennsylvania), and Henry Jackson became more closely identified with parks, recreation, and wilderness legislation. But as every senator knew, recognition and identification paid few dividends in the legislative arena. It required hard work in the committee and hearing rooms, along with influence on the Appropriations Committee. Here Bible excelled, making his largest contribution to protecting the American landscape.[14]

Initially, Bible saw national parks in largely utilitarian terms: it was good business to have one around—in Nevada, for example—to bolster a sagging economy by attracting tourist dollars. He also felt that parks should be open for multiple-use programs and permit some grazing and mining as long as they did not threaten the park's most attractive features. Predictably, he strongly supported the efforts of Conrad Wirth, director of the National Park Service, to develop parks that would attract visitors who would use them. Mission 66 did that by commercializing the national parks while largely ignoring preservation. From Bible's perspective, the Mission 66 philosophy was the correct approach to park service management.

But as Mission 66 began, Senator Hubert Humphrey (D-Minnesota) un-

TABLE 8

Major Legislation, Subcommittee on Parks and Recreation, during the Johnson Administration, 1964–1968 (Senator Alan Bible, Chairman)

1964

Campobello International Park
Medicine Bow National Park
Ozark Scenic Riverway
Fort Bowie Historic Site
Fire Island National Seashore
Canyonlands National Park

1965

Assateague National Seashore
Whiskeytown National Recreation Area
Delaware Water Gap Recreation Area

1966

Cape Lookout National Seashore
Guadalupe Mountains National Park
Fort Union Trading Post National Historic Site
Chamizal National Memorial
San Juan Island National Historical Park
Bighorn Canyon National Recreation Area
Pictured Rocks National Lakeshore
Wolf Trap Farm Park
Indiana Dunes National Lakeshore

1967

John Fitzgerald Kennedy National Historic Site
National Park Foundation

1968

San Rafael Wilderness
San Gabriel Wilderness
Redwood National Park
Flaming Gorge Recreation Area

TABLE 8
Continued

1968 (continued)

Biscayne Park
Scenic Rivers Act
Scenic Trails Act
North Cascades Park
Colorado River Reclamation Act
Saugus Iron Works National Historic Site
Carl Sandburg National Historic Site

Source: Wirth, *Parks, Politics, and the People,* 326.

veiled a different plan to preserve the wilderness. He would remove large tracts of land from the Forest Service's jurisdiction, which would have prohibited mining and grazing—both traditionally allowed on Forest Service land, but not inside a national park or wilderness area. Bible moved in lockstep with Anderson in opposing Humphrey's "wilderness" plan, which posed a direct threat to a limited number of his Nevada constituents.[15]

While Anderson was concerned with his mining and grazing constituents, Bible feared that wilderness preservation would "lock up" valuable mineral resources needed for national defense—an argument the mining industry later used repeatedly. The mining and livestock interests formed a powerful alliance that senators from the mountain West could ill afford to ignore. Consequently, in 1963, Bible teamed with Colorado Republican Gordon Allott to amend Anderson's wilderness bill to allow mining in wilderness areas for fifteen years. While the Senate rejected the mining amendments, Bible and his supporters eventually reached a compromise with Representative Wayne Aspinall (D-Colorado), the House Interior and Insular Affairs Committee's powerful chairman, to allow mineral leases for nineteen years while creating the Public Land Law Review Commission to make future recommendations.[16]

By supporting the 1964 Wilderness Act with modifications, Bible signaled his approach to land-use policy in the 1960s. He accepted multiple-use because it accommodated all interest groups in the West; some areas were special and should not be open to multiple-use, while others with no particular economic value should be protected for their scenic value alone. Like Anderson, Jackson, and Aspinall, Bible sought balance while avoiding the

*Alan Bible (right) and Clinton Anderson (center) look on as Wayne Aspinall (left)
accepts pen from President Lyndon Johnson at the September 3, 1964, Rose Garden
signing of the Wilderness and the Land and Water Conservation Fund Acts.
(White House photo)*

extreme positions taken by some preservationists. The problem was how to determine a proper balance, given the circumstances of a particular case.

Bible also supported Anderson's Outdoor Recreation Resources Review Commission. Chaired by Laurence S. Rockefeller, the ORRRC issued a report that recommended establishing more parks and recreation areas closer to urban centers, allowing those unable to travel great distances to appreciate the beauty of parks and enjoy the benefits of recreation facilities. More importantly, the commission recommended increased federal funding to buy the land needed to carry out its first recommendation. This led directly to another Anderson proposal, the Land and Water Conservation Fund, which would purchase park land with National Park Service entrance and user fees.[17]

Both the Wilderness Act and the Land and Conservation Fund were major departures from earlier federal land-use policies. These changes reflected the rise of the postwar postindustrial society. Americans were becoming increasingly aware that wilderness areas were valuable not for commercial use, but for the sake of a human experience that could enrich lives and move the spirit. America could afford to protect 2 percent of its land mass, or roughly 48 million acres, purely for cultural and esthetic reasons.[18]

For the nation, Bible, and the environmental movement, the year 1964 was a watershed whose significance has been largely forgotten in the wake of the turbulent years that followed. Elected in a landslide over Republican Barry Goldwater, Lyndon Johnson used his huge Democratic majority in Congress to press ahead with a vast legislative program reminiscent of the New Deal, the Great Society, including parks, recreation, and wilderness areas on a grand scale. At that time, ill health forced Clinton Anderson to accept a secondary role in environmental matters and to relinquish his chairmanship of the Interior and Insular Affairs Committee to "Scoop" Jackson. As Jackson took over the full committee, Bible assumed leadership of the newly created Parks and Recreation Subcommittee in 1965. For nearly a decade Jackson and Bible worked closely together to pass parks and recreation legislation. They moved beyond the narrow confines of conservation ideals to embrace the much broader perspective of preservation.

Bible and Jackson were close friends who shared similar views and experiences. Influenced by the New Deal, both supported public power in the West and opposed Eisenhower's concept of partnership in developing water and power resources. Both worked hard in behalf of their constituents and readily engaged in the time-honored congressional practice of logrolling, believing that all politics is local. They were Senate insiders and work horses who deeply believed in the institution's established practices.[19]

In 1964 Johnson named George Hartzog, Jr., director of the National Park Service, succeeding Conrad Wirth, whose emphasis on commercialism and opposition to the Outdoor Recreation Resources Review Commission disturbed Udall. The secretary believed that Hartzog would be more attuned to the direction in which the administration was headed, and he was right. Hartzog and Bible became close personal friends who worked well together. Their goal was always the same—to do what was politically possible to protect America's vanishing scenic wonders while erecting new parks and recreation facilities.

Thus, what emerged in late 1964 was a national team assembled to capitalize on, and contribute to, a balance in the environmental movement. The president himself led the way. Lady Bird Johnson provided encouragement and publicity through her beautification program. Secretary Udall was a tireless worker who was always helpful to congressional committees. Senator Jackson supported Bible's committee decisions and rarely interfered in its business, while Hartzog wanted an expanded park service to fulfill his agency's mission, which sometimes conflicted with the goals of purely environmental organizations. But Bible was the key man in the Senate not only because of his power as subcommittee chairman, but also through his membership on the important Appropriations subcommittee.

Just as Bible assumed leadership of the Parks and Recreation Subcommittee, public opinion was moving inexorably in the administration's direction. Rachel Carson's *Silent Spring* and its indictment of pesticide use aroused the public's indignation. In 1963 Stewart Udall's *The Quiet Crisis* alerted Americans to the dangers facing the environment. Udall argued that some rivers like the Ozark should be kept wild and clean, "a part of a rich outdoor heritage." As Edward Abbey suggested in *Desert Solitaire*, "Wilderness is not a luxury but a necessity of the human spirit." For many, a river was a way of thinking about the world. Bible certainly had two sets of ideas, one utilitarian and the other esthetic, and both related to politics. When it came to the Colorado, complete exploitation was acceptable, especially when his constituents benefited. But for the Ozark River, Bible had other priorities.[20]

The Ozark National Scenic Rivers Bill was another landmark measure that did for the nation's rivers what the Wilderness Act did for land preservation. The first bill designed to protect scenic riverways—in this case, portions of Missouri's Current River and Jacks Fork River—the park proposal covered about 94,000 acres.[21] But it never would have become a reality without the congressional delegation's full cooperation, which Bible had found over the years to be a prerequisite to establishing any national park.

Senators Stuart Symington and Edward V. Long of Missouri introduced the Ozark National Scenic Rivers Bill, S. 16. Representative Richard H. Ichord, who spoke for the district in which the park was to be located, brought a companion bill, H.R. 1803, before the House. Before the hearings on April 8 and 9 and May 22, 1963 the Interior Department and the Bureau of the Budget reported favorably on the proposal. While the parade of witnesses was largely friendly, Bible questioned Udall closely about the Park Service's plans for the area. Udall replied that the Scenic Rivers Act would provide a foothold for the park. Bible was concerned that the government's intention to acquire nearby easements at some future time would, in effect, enlarge the park area without additional congressional authorization. While Udall was vague on the issue, he did say there were no immediate plans to enlarge the proposed site.[22]

More important to Bible was Ichord's assessment of the degree of local support. The representative told Bible that his poll showed a 2-to-1 margin for the bill, thanks to changes that accommodated some local residents worried about losing their homes. Other residents, including Francis L. Ederer, were more concerned with government and taxes. Ederer told Bible, "Land owners do not need and do not want another government agency meddling in our affairs. . . . The people of our area are paying for more government than we want, more than we need and more than we can afford." Despite Ederer's views, which were typical of many park opponents, the Ozark National Scenic Rivers Bill became law in 1964.[23]

The Ozark National Scenic Rivers Bill set the stage for the broader National Wild and Scenic Rivers Act of 1968. Still, the Ozark bill showed once again that congressional delegations had to be united to create national parks because they normally faced organized opposition, either from homeowners or from a coalition of economic interests afraid to lose access or revenue. The Ozark hearings also demonstrated Bible's fundamental fairness in dealing with all sides of an issue. He was cautious and allowed everyone involved to be heard, but he never set out to deceive residents about the impact a national park might have on their lives.

While the Ozark National Scenic Rivers Bill proved to be a classic case of a dedicated congressional delegation working with local economic interests toward a common goal, the Indiana Dunes presented Bible and other park enthusiasts in Congress with the most controversial and hard-fought park issue of the decade. The Dunes stretched for twenty-five miles along Lake Michigan between East Chicago and Michigan City. The region's steel companies wanted the area for a deep-water port, but the Dunes provided an ideal site for an urban park along the lines the Outdoor Recreation Review Commission recommended, and the Senate report on the site was extremely favorable.[24]

When the Saint Lawrence Seaway was completed in 1957, however, Indiana moved quickly to capitalize on the anticipated economic boom caused by the construction of a deep-water port. The state issued revenue bonds to finance the $70 million project, but Paul Douglas of Illinois, one of the Senate's most liberal and respected members, moved to block it by creating the 3,800-acre Dunes National Monument. Thus, the issue of the Dunes was joined; as always, it pitted recreationists against developers. But Douglas had help: President Kennedy initially supported the park, as did Anderson and Bible.[25]

Yet the political road proved extremely bumpy. In February 1960 Bible's Public Lands Subcommittee held hearings on the Indiana Dunes National Lakeshore proposal, while Anderson worked toward a compromise between the Indiana delegation, which supported the steel interests, and Douglas, backed by environmental groups. Anderson's efforts only exacerbated the problem, and no further action was taken.

There matters stood until March 1964, when Bible scheduled another round of hearings on the Dunes controversy.[26] On March 5, 6, and 7 the

Public Lands Subcommittee held open hearings in Washington, D.C., on S. 2249, the Indiana Dunes National Lakeshore bill. Presenting a balanced approach between the desires of developers and recreationists, Congressman J. Edward Roush of Indiana's Fifth District emphasized that the Senate proposal would not interfere with industrial development or the deep-water port. Representative Charles Halleck of Indiana's Second District opposed the bill because it would, in his view, lock up future industrial development along the shore. That was exactly what Douglas and others wanted to accomplish—stop the steel companies, principally the Bethlehem Steel Company, from destroying the Dunes.[27]

More interested in the steel than the Dunes, Halleck wanted to ensure the area's industrial development. He claimed that the park site contained 2,000 acres of prime industrial property that would be required in the near future for economic growth. Senator Vance Hartke of Indiana was similarly concerned, but supported S. 2249 as an equitable compromise, as did his Indiana Senate colleague, Birch Bayh.[28] Bible and his subcommittee agreed and, on May 17, 1965, unanimously approved S. 2249 to be sent to the full Interior Committee. Afterward Douglas sent Bible a telegram: "God bless you, Alan. Many, many thanks. We are friends from the heart forever." In his memoirs, Douglas again paid tribute to Bible for the role he played in passing the Indiana Dunes bill.[29]

But passage was yet to come: in July the compromise collapsed when Halleck refused to go along. President Johnson continued to support S. 2249, but Roush's companion bill, H.R. 8927, died in committee. Not until June 21, 1966, with Bible's considerable support, did the Senate pass the Indiana Dunes bill, renumbered S. 360. On October 14, 1966, the House passed H.R. 51, a companion to the Senate bill, and President Johnson formally signed the Indiana Dunes National Lakeshore Act on November 5, 1966.[30]

The Indiana Dunes Lakeshore Park was a tribute to Douglas's dedication and perseverance. For years he had expended political capital in fighting developers, and his colleagues in the Senate ultimately followed his lead. In the House, Morris Udall and John Saylor led the fight against the Halleck coalition, and they prevailed. Presidents Kennedy and Johnson, Secretary Udall, and Park Service director Hartzog all sided with Douglas in his fight to preserve a part of the Dunes for public use. It took the efforts of key congressional leaders and committee chairmen and the administration's support to defeat the steel interests. The battle for the Dunes illustrates the extraordinary difficulty in creating national parks. As always, compromise and balance proved to be the only way to success, and in committees, where he did his best work, Bible played an important part in achieving that success.

The Assateague Island National Park was less controversial, but many of the same economic forces united to try to defeat it. Senators Joseph D. Tydings and Daniel Brewster of Maryland sponsored S. 20, which called for the government to buy significant portions of Assateague Island for a Washington-Baltimore urban park. Johnson supported the plan, as did Udall. After the Maryland Court of Appeals ruled in May 1965 that housing developers could install their own septic tanks, clearing the way for heavy construction along the beach front, Bible and Udall quickly met to discuss the bill.[31] Once Bible agreed to move it through the Parks Subcommittee by the end of May, Udall urged Bill Moyers, assistant to the president, to call Bible and ask him if Johnson could do anything to help. The reminder of Johnson's power over Bible was none too subtle, but Udall cautioned Moyers not to be critical because "Alan is our best work horse."[32]

What Moyers said to Bible is unknown, but the effect was immediate. Bible pushed the bill through his subcommittee. It quickly cleared the Senate and was ready for the president's signature on September 20, 1966. Afterward Senator Brewster offered his "deep gratitude" to Bible for his two years of work in creating the Assateague Island National Seashore.[33]

Bible also demonstrated initiative that extended beyond Congress. He had always expressed concern about the mounting cost of land purchases to create national parks (western national parks could be more easily carved out of the public domain) and the lack of citizen participation in the process. Consequently, in July 1966, Jackson, Kuchel, and Bible sent Udall a draft of S. 3676 to establish a National Park Foundation that would enable private philanthropy to help establish parks and historic sites. Udall enthusiastically supported the idea because "the preservation of natural beauty is a precept of President Johnson's Great Society." When Congress took no action, Bible reintroduced S. 3676 at the beginning of the 90th Congress.[34]

S. 814, co-sponsored by Jackson and Kuchel, was identical to S. 3676. It created an eight-member board of directors—including six private citizens—to join the interior secretary and the National Park Service director in receiving donations to be converted to Park Service use. In turn, the Park Service could use the proceeds to buy new lands for the park system. The bill easily passed through congressional committees, and President Johnson signed it on December 18, 1967. Unfortunately, the National Park Foundation has never realized its potential because many of the appointees have used their positions for political and ceremonial purposes rather than for the best interests of the Park Service.[35]

The Park Service needed all the money it could get. Bible's committee was considering legislation to make strands of northern California redwood groves a national park. The cost estimates were staggering—up to $92 million for 58,000 acres. Beginning in 1963, the Sierra Club launched a massive campaign to alert the public to the danger the great trees faced from the timber industry. Later it came out with *The Last Redwoods and the Parkland of Redwood Creek*, detailing the history of the trees with magnificent photographs and a generous dose of propaganda. No one could dispute that the trees were disappearing, victims of the logger's saw.[36]

Like the mining industry, the timber industry was its own worst enemy. It clear-cut redwoods along California's Highway 101 for all to see and reflect upon. The Sierra Club questioned why trees other than the majestic redwoods were not used and made Redwood National Park its top priority. In September 1964 the Park Service released a study that called for a 54,000-acre park at Redwood Creek. Environmental groups wanted a larger park, up to 90,000 acres, but accepted the Park Service's recommendation. Predictably, the lumber industry opposed the park, arguing that the three state parks in the area were enough since the trees were in no danger of disappearing. But the thrust of its case was the park's economic impact on the region: the lumber industry would be ruined. This attitude toward the California redwoods was typical of the industry as a whole. As one spokesman for lumber interests said in a similar case, "Locking up these trees in a park is like taking Miss America, with a luscious big bust and a solid flank, and making her a nun. It is a goddam waste of talent."[37]

Still, both sides were open to compromise. The industry wanted access to Redwood Creek, which had the best timber, while park supporters in Congress were willing to exchange the Redwood Creek site for Mill Creek in Del Norte County and keep the 54,000-acre park. On October 4, 1967, Senator Jackson called the White House and requested an appointment with President Johnson to discuss the compromise. The following Saturday Jackson, Bible, Kuchel, Laurence Rockefeller, and others presented the plan. Johnson agreed to it, and the next week Jackson introduced S. 2515, co-sponsored by Bible and Kuchel, to establish Redwood National Park.[38]

The bill contained the highly unusual provision of allowing federal land under Forest Service jurisdiction to be exchanged for land the lumber companies owned. Secretary of Agriculture Orville Freeman vehemently opposed the plan because it would set a bad precedent for future park proposals and give up land estimated to be worth $40 to 60 million. Despite Freeman's objection, the exchange provision remained because it helped hold down the staggering cost of land acquisition in northern California. Also, while not openly hostile to the Redwood Park bill, California governor Ronald Reagan was decidedly cool toward it. He demanded that the lumber interests get federal land to continue their logging operations and to prevent any economic dislocation in the area.[39]

The Jackson-Bible-Kuchel compromise had enough support in Congress, among the public, and with conservation groups to carry the day. Writing to Bible to thank him for his efforts, even Sierra Club president Dr. Edgar Wayburn said, "We feel the compromise plan worked out by the committee is basically a good one." Attempts in the House and Senate to amend the bill to increase the park's size failed, and both houses accepted the judgment and expertise of their committees. With the help of John Saylor and Morris Udall, the House accepted the compromise package, and the measure to create Redwood National Park became law on October 2, 1968.[40] In yet another important environmental battle, Bible had been one of the prime tacticians of the victory.

During the heady days of the New Frontier and the Great Society Alan Bible stood quietly yet effectively at the center of the debate over land-use policy in America. From the Cape Cod National Seashore bill in 1961 to the creation of Redwood National Park in 1968, he emphasized balance and accommodation to achieve results, a lesson he had learned from Lyndon Johnson. He also grew beyond the confines of narrow constituent interests to embrace national goals and objectives. Like other development-oriented western senators such as Clinton Anderson, Henry Jackson, Thomas Kuchel, and Carl Hayden, Bible deserves a large share of the credit for the expansion of the national park system and the preservation of millions of acres of pristine land. But for Bible, his major triumph in this field still lay ahead: Alaska.

Chapter Ten

Pork Problems and the Baring Burden,

1962–1968

While Bible found his work on the national level satisfying, he was mainly concerned with Nevada's interests. He expended a great deal of time and effort in behalf of mining and on water, land, and recreation measures. Bible's activities during his second full term did much to make him a primary architect of modern-day Nevada, dominated politically by Las Vegas and economically by tourism and recreational activities. The irony was that while Bible did much for Nevada, he encountered greater success in creating national parks in other states than he did in his home state.

While Bible lost on most fronts in his national campaign to revive the western mining industry, he did achieve some modest victories in Nevada. In March 1960 he pointed out to Senator Carl Hayden that the Bureau of Mines was forcing the titanium research facility in Boulder City to phase out its program, which a General Services Administration contract had funded. More importantly, the bureau had failed to include funding for Boulder City in its 1961 budget request, an omission that would eliminate forty jobs in that small community. It would be a blow to a fledgling town only recently transformed from a federal reservation to an independent city, due in part to Bible's efforts, and it would harm the community's economic development just as he was gearing up for a reelection campaign. Bible suggested to Hayden that the Bureau of Mines keep the operation open and initiate further research in new areas to aid western mining. He convinced Hayden that research on titanium was crucial because the Soviet Union was making rapid progress in this field while the United States lacked even a viable research facility. Bible asked for an additional $200,000 appropriation to keep the facility functioning.[1]

In May 1960, as a member of the joint conference committee on the Interior Department money bill, Bible won approval for the $200,000 appropriation to keep the Boulder City operation in business. Afterward he suggested to the Bureau of Mines that the plant should conduct additional research on high temperature metals and again noted that forty jobs would be lost if

145

the facility closed its doors.[2] The Bureau of Mines wanted to consolidate its Boulder City and Reno operations in the northern city. Although the actual number of employees would probably remain the same, most, if not all, of the Boulder City workers were unlikely to relocate to Reno. The Bureau of Mines also failed to appreciate the impact the closing would have on the community, a major factor in the senator's request for funding.

Bible's concern about the future of Nevada's mining industry seemed to be justified. In early 1962 he vigorously opposed President Kennedy's plan to barter surplus agricultural products for beryllium produced in foreign countries, particularly when the United States was reducing its research funding. To Bible this was yet another example of the federal government overlooking Nevada mining interests in deference to foreign competitors. He pointed out that Nevada had significant beryl ore deposits in White Pine and Lincoln counties that should be developed for use as heat shields and fuel containers ahead of any foreign markets. Finally, Bible asked the Bureau of Mines to expand its research capabilities and seek new domestic sources for mineral production.[3] Apparently, the Bureau of Mines heeded the senator and made no further attempts to curtail its Nevada operations until 1965.

But if the Bureau of Mines was suddenly quiet, it remained determined to press on with its consolidation plans. In early 1965 the agency again announced its desire to close the Boulder City facility for economic reasons. Bible was not about to let it close without a fight. Once more he used his influence and power in the Interior and Appropriations committees to block the Bureau's efforts. On April 29 the full Senate Appropriations Committee met; Bible secured language in the budget bill that directed the Bureau of Mines not to close its Boulder City research facility in fiscal year 1966 until an investigation could be completed. The Bureau of Mines was in no position to complain, considering the generous appropriation for Nevada of $1.9 million, $250,000 more than the appropriation over each of the next three years.[4] Even so, Bible was neither satisfied nor convinced that the Bureau of Mines had gotten his message, and he took steps to make sure that there was no misunderstanding.

Only four days after gaining the funding for the Boulder City facility Bible won chairman Hayden's approval for a staff investigation of the Boulder City laboratory. The study received the widest possible news coverage in Boulder City.[5] Unsurprisingly, the hand-picked team, headed by Bible's legislative assistant, Joseph T. McDonnell, concluded that the operation was indeed productive and should remain open. Hayden's committee agreed. The 1966 appropriation was safe.

Wanting to keep the facility going permanently, Bible followed up with a demonstration of raw senatorial power. In May 1966, in a Senate Interior

Committee meeting, Bible placed $1.6 million in the Interior Department money bill to operate the Bureau of Mines in Nevada, including the Boulder City plant. That month the Interior bill reached the Senate Appropriations Committee, of which Bible was also a member. The committee moved into executive session, chaired by Bible, and reported favorably on the Interior money bill, clearing the way for a floor vote. In executive session Bible had the following language inserted into the appropriation:

> It is the desire of the committee that operation of the Bureau's Boulder City, Nevada, metallurgical laboratory be continued indefinitely. Should closure again be proposed, the committee is to be notified at least one year in advance. This will afford the committee ample opportunity again to examine the advisability of such action.[6]

Clearly, Bible intended the Boulder City operation to continue as a research facility as long as he represented Nevada in Congress.

The Bureau of Mines made no further attempts to close the operation until 1971. This time, however, Bible and the bureau worked together to use the installation for research on metal recovery and new uses for sulphur. The Bureau of Mines was unable to close its southern Nevada research center until 1984, long after Bible's retirement, when it reassigned most of the center's employees to the Reno facility.

In October 1964 Bible turned his attention to protecting Nevada's titanium mining industry, specifically the Titanium Metals Corporation of America (TMCA), located in Henderson. TMCA was the nation's leading producer of the metal, and Bible was determined that it would stay that way. The cause for concern was the upcoming round of trade negotiations in Geneva, Switzerland, where the United States would submit a list of trade items that tariffs would protect from foreign competition. In 1964 titanium imports to the United States carried a 20 percent duty; Bible wanted to block any reduction, which would severely undercut the industry and harm southern Nevada's economy.

Titanium comes principally from rutile ore, which is then converted into what is called titanium sponge, and later processed into ingot metal. It is much lighter than steel and stronger than aluminum, which makes it desirable in the production of military hardware. The Henderson plant sold almost all of the titanium it produced to the government for use in jet engines, missiles, armor plates, helicopters, troop carriers, and helmets.[7] The titanium industry had invested large sums of money in research and development and was still hard-pressed to make ends meet, even with the 20 percent import duty to discourage shipments from Japan and Great Britain.

On October 15, 1964, Bible took the Senate floor to denounce the importation of cheap foreign products. He pointed out that foreign competitors capitalized on lower labor costs to make items that they sold in the United States at prices below what the same item could be produced for domestically. As a result, American-based businesses were unable to compete, prompting worker layoffs. In the case of titanium about 800 jobs were at stake in Henderson, to say nothing of related workers and businesses dependent upon the Henderson plant.[8]

Additionally, Bible was incensed at the Japanese government's trade policy, which he blamed for driving DuPont and Union Carbide out of titanium production. While the American list price for titanium sponge was $1.32 per pound, the Japanese offered it at $1.25 per pound, including the 20 percent duty. To compound the problem, despite American objections, Japan sold titanium to the Soviet Union, which American firms were barred from doing for national security reasons. Bible objected not only to the inequities in the trade arrangement, but also to an American ally selling a product that the Soviets could use to boost their military preparedness.[9]

Despite Bible's fears, tariffs on titanium imports remained unchanged. Still, the whole system of trade relations between the United States and the world seemed terribly unbalanced. The most graphic example occurred when the Soviets began to sell titanium to the United States—an inexplicable situation, given the high priority of the metal for military use. Bible was concerned: while the United States prohibited its firms from shipping to the USSR, it allowed Japan to do so. Then the Soviets could sell to American businesses, undercutting domestic producers—and sell they did: 27,000 pounds of titanium in June 1967 at 95 cents a pound, including the import duty, while the domestic price stayed at $1.32 per pound.[10]

On September 1 Bible officially complained to Secretary of the Treasury Henry H. Fowler and requested an investigation of Soviet "dumping" of titanium on the American market. He noted that Soviet sales exceeded their yearly production, at a cost far below their estimates. Fowler agreed to look into the matter, but by 1968 the Soviets apparently had disposed of their excess titanium and nothing more was heard about it.[11]

Bible's successes on behalf of mining were mixed. He won a small measure of protection for Nevada's mining industry, particularly the federal research facility in Boulder City. He was especially effective in the legislative arena, where he used his influence to gain appropriations. Still, he was far more influential in securing water projects for his constituents, due largely to the solid bloc of western senators who understood that water development was political capital and worked to help each other whenever possible—despite differences of opinion.

As noted earlier, to obtain the coveted Washoe Project, Nevada made a compact with California to determine rights to the unappropriated waters of the Truckee, Carson, and Walker rivers. Both states benefited because northern California needed water for its growing tourist industry in the Lake Tahoe area, while Nevada's western farmers wanted more water for agricultural and municipal purposes. At issue was the best use of unappropriated stream water: recreation in California or farming in Nevada.[12]

In 1960 California and Nevada agreed to divide 34,000 acre-feet of Lake Tahoe water that would affect downstream users. California received 23,000 acre-feet or 68 percent of the flow: the rest, 11,000 acre-feet or 32 percent, was Nevada's allotment. After years of haggling the two state commissions agreed to divide Truckee River water, with California getting 35,000 acre-feet and the right to share an additional 10,000 acre-feet a year. In the Walker River negotiations, completed in 1963, each state agreed to a split that gave Nevada 65 percent and California 35 percent. Meanwhile, Carson River water was so allocated as to enable Alpine County in California to exercise future rights to irrigate another 10,000 acres of farm and pasture land.[13]

After thirteen years of negotiation, bickering, and fierce fighting the two states signed the California-Nevada Compact on July 25, 1968. California's legislature ratified it on September 17, 1970, and Nevada's legislature on March 5, 1971. While Bible took no part in the negotiations, he was concerned because the Washoe Project's fate depended upon the water interests of the two states. As long as the negotiations continued, California's congressional delegation would support the Washoe Project. Not surprisingly, the Washoe Project proved to be more enduring than the compact.

Begun in 1964, construction continued on the Stampede Dam until June 1966, when Bible toured the site. At the time he wanted a $2 million appropriation for fiscal year 1967 to keep the project on schedule and to complete the Truckee Basin phase. In addition to the flood control benefits and increased municipal and agricultural use, Bible hoped that the reservoir would become a major recreational attraction in the Reno-Sparks area. Once finished, the dam created a seven-mile forest lake on the Little Truckee River above the Boca Reservoir for boating, swimming, and camping.[14] On November 3, 1966, Secretary Udall suddenly informed Bible that instead of the anticipated $2 million appropriation the department had allotted the Washoe Project a little over $9 million to finish the Stampede Dam almost a year ahead of schedule, with completion set for early 1970.[15]

While the Washoe Project stayed on course for completion, Bible turned his attention to other matters concerning water use in northern Nevada. On January 12, 1967, he introduced S. 266, which would revise the Newlands Reclamation Act of 1902 to allow the Bureau of Reclamation to consider climate and soil composition in calculating water delivery to family farms of

Bible (left) looking over the progress of construction at Stampede Dam, 1966.
(Alan Bible Collection)

more than 160 acres. The bureau had come under intense criticism for ignoring the 160-acre limitation, which it had done throughout its existence. The result was a massive water subsidy to the West's growing agribusiness empire. If enacted, Bible's bill in effect would have lifted the 160-acre limitation. The Senate took no action on his proposal; after Bible retired the government abolished the 160-acre limit, giving legal sanction to a decades-old fact—continued consolidation of western land ownership based on subsidized water.[16]

Water problems of a different kind faced southern Nevada. Until 1954 the Las Vegas Land and Water Company had controlled growth in Las Vegas while steadfastly refusing to expand its service beyond the city limits. As hotels and casinos proliferated, groundwater sources were depleted at an alarming rate. A crisis had developed: Las Vegas faced the prospect of limited growth unless alternate sources of water could be tapped to fuel the valley's expansion.

Las Vegas development interests wanted to capitalize on every possibility for expansion and profits, from real estate promotion to tourist dollars. The first breakthrough came in 1954, when the Las Vegas Land and Water Company sold its holdings to the Las Vegas Valley Water District, which moved at once to expand service. On October 10, 1960, a conference of federal, state, and local leaders met in Las Vegas to consider a project to bring water from Lake Mead to Las Vegas. The conference included Nevada's two senators, Bible and Howard Cannon, and Congressman Walter Baring. Bible led the delegation by agreeing to press the Senate for funds to study the project. His influence paid immediate dividends. One week later, on December 18, Bureau of Reclamation commissioner Floyd Dominy began preparing a report on the Las Vegas Valley's irrigation and domestic water requirements. In early 1961 Bible renewed his support for the project before a meeting of directors of the Las Vegas Water District.

But considerable difficulty in financing, responsibility, and jurisdiction lay ahead.[17] The next breakthrough for Las Vegas came in 1963, when the Supreme Court decided *Arizona* v. *California*. The decision guaranteed Nevada 300,000 acre-feet of water a year from the Colorado River, with the entire amount earmarked for use in the Las Vegas Valley. While one obstacle disappeared, another loomed: Udall's Pacific Southwest Water Plan. In 1963, to emphasize the need for a coordinated regional approach to western water issues, Udall noted:

> The problems of the lower Colorado, which we have studied and are continuing to study, have reached a highly critical stage and now can be solved only through a new breed of thinking . . . no one person, no one entity, no one dam or development pattern in any one state can erase those problems. Only regional action coordinated at every level will suffice.[18]

Although by no means novel, Udall's concept of regional water planning failed to solve the unending problem of greed. Each of the seven states of the upper and lower basin wanted every drop of water it could get from the river, which made compromise difficult and often impossible. More importantly, Udall's Pacific Southwest Water Plan had a tremendous price tag, well over $1 billion. As a result, many believed that it stood little chance of passing Congress, despite the secretary's insistence that hydroelectric power sales would finance the mammoth project. All sides expected challenges from environmentalists poised to follow up on their Echo Park Dam victory by opposing any further dams along the Colorado.

The question of how to finance the southern Nevada water plan was the major dilemma facing Nevada's congressional delegation, but the problem was at least as much political as financial. To have any chance of congressional approval, the plan needed the endorsement of Udall and Arizona's Senator Carl Hayden. Hayden's support was vital: he was chairman of the Senate Appropriations Committee and father of the Central Arizona Water Project. Both of these powerful Democrats wanted the Nevada plan included in the more ambitious regional concept, which Bible believed unlikely to pass Congress. He had to find a way to separate the Nevada project from the Udall and Hayden plans without alienating the two Arizonans.

Bible moved quickly to gain approval for a plan that would benefit Nevada alone. First, he approached Udall. On February 19, 1964, the secretary appeared as a witness before the Senate Appropriations Committee's Interior Subcommittee, which was conducting hearings on the Interior Department's fiscal 1965 budget. Pressed by Bible, Udall indicated that he would support a separate bill for the Nevada water plan, although he believed that the Pacific Southwest Water Project should move forward with everyone's support, including Bible's.[19] Udall was obviously reluctant to support a series of distinct water projects in the Colorado River basin, which would mean dismantling his regional concept. While Udall planned on a broad scale, Bible and others thought strictly in terms of state interest; Bible was adamant, preferring a separate bill to avoid tying up the Nevada project in Congress with the ambitious regional plan. Indeed, he told Udall that "the Southern Nevada Water Project must be built at the earliest possible date in order to insure one of the fastest growing counties in the United States an adequate and dependable water supply."[20]

Bible had forged ahead in charting southern Nevada's future. But the political stakes in Clark County were high for two related reasons: its population overwhelmed the rest of Nevada and it increasingly formed the basis for the senator's political support. Bluntly stated, if Bible failed to deliver this vital water project, his political career might be over.[21] With such great political risks involved, Bible asked to meet with President Johnson during the week of February 27, 1965, to gain his support for a separate water plan for southern Nevada. He wanted the president to alter the course his interior secretary had set.

Johnson proved willing to help his old friend. He assured Bible of his support despite the problems involved in building a municipal water supply pipeline from the existing federal reservoir, Lake Mead. Since the proposed extension was not a multipurpose project, there was no way to reallocate the costs so that the water company could repay the government. Apparently, Bible convinced Johnson that the details could be worked out: the president quickly moved the project ahead.[22] The sticky details involved in water transportation had never troubled Johnson anyway.

When the fight began in 1965, Bible still had little cause for optimism. The Nevada water bill remained tied to Udall's plan and stalled by the continuing battle between Arizona and California. True, the Supreme Court in 1963 had decided the suit in Arizona's favor, conceding the state's water rights to the Gila River and the 2,800,000 acre-feet the Pittman amendment guaranteed. The high court also had awarded Nevada its yearly allotment of 300,000 acre-feet while rejecting California's claim for additional water. But the angry members of California's delegation moved quickly to salvage through the legislative process what their state had lost in the courts: they blocked the passage of the Central Arizona Water Project and with it Nevada's water line. Senator Thomas H. Kuchel, the Republican minority whip, led his fellow Californians in holding Arizona's ambitious water plans hostage. Kuchel wanted a guarantee that prohibited Arizona from infringing on California's water rights while restricting Arizona to its annual allotment of 2,800,000 acre-feet.[23]

The situation could not have been more threatening for Nevada, and Bible knew it. California had the political clout to stall or ruin legislation adverse to its interests. Kuchel's strategy was to link the Arizona project to Udall's regional water plan. This tied the Southern Nevada Water Project to both plans and doomed it if Arizona and California failed to compromise.

To salvage Nevada interests from the Arizona-California fight, Bible had to find a way to pry the Nevada project loose from the Udall and Arizona plans while gaining the Senate Republican whip's support. Early in 1965 Bible pressed Hayden for a commitment to support a separate Southern Nevada Water Project. Hayden agreed that the political and economic differences between Arizona and California had caught Nevada in the middle. He promised to support Nevada's project as separate legislation.[24] With backing from Udall and now Hayden, Bible moved to win assurances from the deputy budget director, Elmer Stoats, that Johnson's administration would receive the project favorably. More importantly, he had Johnson's personal blessing for a separate bill authorizing the Southern Nevada Water Project.[25]

With the political groundwork laid, Bible was now ready to introduce legislation that would guarantee southern Nevada's growth well into the next century. On May 20, 1965, hearings began before the Committee on Interior and Insular Affairs on Senate Bill 32, which Bible introduced and Cannon co-sponsored. The measure would build a water delivery system that enabled Nevada to use its yearly allotment of 300,000 acre-feet of water from the Colorado. In addition to authorizing the secretary of the interior to construct, operate, and maintain the Southern Nevada Water Project, the bill provided for construction of six pumping plants, a regulatory reservoir, a four-mile tunnel, and 31.4 miles of pipeline to deliver water from Lake

Mead to existing and potential municipal and industrial developments in Las Vegas, North Las Vegas, Henderson, Boulder City, and Nellis Air Force Base. The estimated cost of the three-phase project was $72 million (later revised to $81 million), to be paid over 50 years at 3 percent interest. The bill further empowered the secretary of the interior to contract with the State of Nevada through the Colorado River Commission to repay the project's costs and transfer the authority to run the facilities.[26]

Besides chairing the committee hearings, Bible carefully orchestrated them. A parade of friendly witnesses, from Nevada's Democratic governor Grant Sawyer to Bureau of Reclamation commissioner Floyd Dominy, endorsed the project. Even Senator Kuchel, finding no advantage to California in blocking Nevada's plans, endorsed a separate Nevada water project.[27] The unanimous committee report was so overwhelmingly favorable that the Nevada water bill sailed through the Senate unopposed. Bible and his fellow Nevadan, Howard Cannon, had done their work well.

But the House of Representatives was another matter. A move calculated to bring Nevada's obstructionist congressman, Walter Baring, into the Democratic fold nearly scuttled S. 32. For years Baring had irritated the party leadership by refusing to support legislation vital to the Kennedy and Johnson administrations. When S. 32 finally reached the House, the membership balked at the 3 percent interest rate attached to the repayment schedule. Perhaps a few members were genuinely concerned about that provision, but their opposition clearly was due to Baring, since the Nevada delegation had always been flexible on the interest rate.[28] House Democrats had a unique opportunity to embarrass Baring by calling the attention of Nevada voters to their politically inept representative—and they took full advantage of it. Here was a rare sight, indeed, and one that should have delivered a clear message to Nevada voters.

Officially, Johnson remained neutral, but his intense dislike for Baring played a role in what happened. How many House members would be willing to oppose a piece of noncontroversial legislation sponsored by two popular Democratic senators in a Democratic-controlled Congress and endorsed by a Democratic president riding the crest of a landslide? Despite the animosity toward Baring, the Southern Nevada Water Project cleared the House with Democratic support, 239 to 134, on October 7, 1965, and went to the White House for the president's signature.

Despite Johnson's good relations with Bible and Cannon, his signature was slow in coming. Although the president privately supported the Southern Nevada Water Project, Baring's lack of reciprocal support for White House programs upset him. He signed the bill on October 25, 1965, just in time to avoid a pocket veto. He then telephoned Bible and Cannon—pointedly

The Nevada delegation meeting with the governor. (Left to right) Senator Howard Cannon, Senator Alan Bible, Representative Walter Baring, and Governor Grant Sawyer. (Alan Bible Collection)

ignoring Baring—and told them that he had signed the bill, but he would also seek legislation to clarify the language in section 6 relating to interstate water rights. Although section 6 needed clarification in light of the Supreme Court's ruling in *Arizona* v. *California*, the president was more concerned with politics than with grammar or semantics. According to Mike Manatos, a White House staff assistant, the plan had been to let Bible and Cannon "sweat a little" to teach Baring a lesson before signing the bill—a debatable tactic, since they already disliked Baring, who remained as contrary as ever. In fact, Johnson even considered vetoing the legislation out of disdain for Nevada's lone congressman. But as Jack Carpenter, Bible's longtime aide, pointed out, the president could not veto a bill vital to a state whose two Democratic senators gave the White House almost total support.[29]

Euphoria soon turned to gloom, which was often the case with events surrounding water projects. Politicians, unlike the general public, are well aware that the enactment of laws does not necessarily guarantee results, especially in the field of public works legislation. Congress must appropriate funds to implement the laws; in this case the Southern Nevada Water Project could be completed only by securing the necessary funds every year until the project was finished—a burden that fell heavily on Bible as a member of the Senate Appropriations Committee. The task was formidable, because the escalating war in Vietnam had cut deeply into Johnson's Great Society programs and public works proposals. Nevada also had to carry the Baring burden: the intractable congressman continued to antagonize House Democrats, who eagerly awaited any chance for retribution.

As expected, for a variety of reasons, it was difficult to fund public works projects in 1966. The Johnson administration moved to curb domestic spending to counter the mounting costs of the war in Vietnam. But for Nevada, Vietnam was only half the problem. On September 15, 1966, in another move targeting Baring, the House Appropriations Committee cut $1.4 million earmarked for completing the planning phase of the water project. Moving quickly to repair the damage, Bible announced that he would work to restore the funds when the bill reached the Senate Appropriations Committee. Meanwhile, Senator Cannon launched a letter-writing campaign pleading for support from his colleagues.[30] On September 27 Bible and Cannon hurriedly met with fellow senators in an effort to gather enough votes to restore the funds cut by the House. The life of the Southern Nevada Water Project was at stake. If the Bureau of Reclamation failed to complete its construction plans, the project would be dead for that year and easier to defeat the next year. More importantly, restoring the funds to the budget would commit the Johnson administration to continued support, despite House budget cuts.

Bible's efforts bore fruit. Two days later the Senate Appropriations Committee voted to restore the House funds in the Public Works Appropriations Bill. The Senate leadership immediately named Bible to the three-member Senate Conference Panel to iron out differences between the Senate and House versions of the public works bill. He succeeded again in the conference report, which included the funds originally cut by the House. The bill in final form passed both houses of Congress, and Johnson signed it. The Southern Nevada Water Project had once again been saved.[31]

These September triumphs pushed through the preconstruction work and allowed the Bureau of Reclamation to place a construction office in Henderson. Commissioner Floyd Dominy then requested $6,925,000 in building funds for the project in the Interior Appropriations Bill for fiscal year 1968. On July 20, 1967, the House Appropriations Committee approved the Bureau of Reclamation request, and the Senate followed suit, much to Bible's delight: "The House has now given full recognition to the importance and urgency of this undertaking."[32] The next month the Bureau of Reclamation and Colorado River Commission signed contracts to provide for delivery of 138,000 acre-feet of water a year from Lake Mead after completing the first stage of the project.

Still, spending on Vietnam constantly threatened the water project, especially in 1967, when the Johnson administration froze all public works projects, pending a review. Although Bible recognized that the impoundment probably was unconstitutional, he feared that a prolonged legal battle might

Senator Alan Bible (left) meeting with Floyd Dominy, commissioner of the Bureau of Reclamation, during Senate budget hearings on the Southern Nevada Water Project, May 18, 1965. (Alan Bible Collection)

harm not only Nevada's economy, but also his close relationship with the president. Knowing Johnson well, Bible decided that political lobbying, not court action, was the key to success.

In the summer of 1967 Bible received a telephone call from President Johnson, who invited him to the White House for an evening of drinks and conversation. Bible, frequent visitor to the White House, accepted the president's offer. He met with his top aide, Jack Carpenter, and they drew up a laundry list of Nevada's needs, with funds for the Southern Nevada Water Project at the top. When Bible arrived at the White House at about

President Lyndon Johnson and Senator Alan Bible meeting in the Oval Office.
(Bible family collection)

6:30 P.M., Johnson put his arm around the senator's shoulder as he escorted him through the door. Then, without warning, he assured Bible, "Don't worry, I told those budget people to give my good friend Alan the money for that water project—he is a friend of mine."[33]

Always the consummate politician, Johnson knew that Bible came to the White House armed with a list of requests. Having neither the time or the inclination to listen, he quickly disarmed his friend by unexpectedly offering what he knew Bible wanted most: funds to complete the single most important project in southern Nevada history, a politically important measure. Recalling the incident years later, Bible smiled while reporting that the laundry list never left his pocket.[34]

The president's decision to release the impounded funds for the Southern Nevada Water Project removed the last obstacle. Unquestionably, it was the most important executive decision affecting southern Nevada since President Harry Truman selected Nevada as the site for nuclear weapons tests. It was also personally important for the state's senior senator, who faced his toughest reelection battle. Indeed, 1968 was supposed to be a very difficult year for Democrats as closely aligned with the president as Bible was. During the campaign, however, Bible reminded southern Nevada voters that he had delivered on the water project and should be returned to the Senate to keep delivering.

And he did so. In 1969 and 1970, when further budget cuts might have adversely affected the project, Bible was able to restore the funds through supplemental Senate appropriations, allowing the work to be completed on

Ground-breaking ceremony, Southern Nevada Water Project, September 7, 1968.
(Courtesy of Bureau of Reclamation, U.S. Department of the Interior)

schedule. On June 2, 1971, stage one of the project was dedicated in ceremonies honoring the "Father of the Project," Senator Alan H. Bible.[35] Finally,
on November 1, 1971, the Bureau of Reclamation officially relinquished control of the plants and operating facilities to the Nevada Colorado River Commission and the Las Vegas Valley Water District. The completion of stage one
enabled Southern Nevada to receive a maximum of 132,200 acre-feet of water

a year from the Colorado. Construction of stage two of the project began in 1977 and was finished in 1982. Stage three was never built because the project's final planning and construction phases incorporated it into stage two. With stage two completed, southern Nevada had a water delivery system capable of providing 300,000 acre-feet of water a year from the Colorado River to the Las Vegas Valley.

The Southern Nevada Water Project was the key factor in triggering the Las Vegas Valley's growth and development over the last two decades. In 1970 Clark County's population was 273,288, and its consumption of water from the Colorado River at 38,256 acre-feet. A decade later the population had reached 463,087, and annual water consumption had jumped to 135,872 acre-feet. As the 1990s began the Las Vegas Valley was using 260,000 acre-feet of water a year from Colorado River sources.[36] Indeed, the population explosion and expansion of southern Nevada's tourist industry are both directly attributable to the completion of the vital public works project.

The Southern Nevada Water Project also strengthened the economic value of water, fueling expansion by widening the limits of the Las Vegas Valley's growth. It reinforced the perception that living in an arid environment imposed no limits. Hotels and casinos built glorious fountains and waterfalls, and real estate developers moved ahead with artificially created lakes surrounded by expensive landscaped homes for sale to newcomers assured that water was no problem in the desert.

The project also had unforeseen political consequences that changed Nevada's power relations. The Supreme Court's 1964 decision in *Reynolds* v. *Sims,* which implemented the principle of one-person, one-vote, one-value, coincided with the project's construction. When Nevada had to reapportion its legislature to meet the high court's demands, Clark County was the big winner; its tremendous population boom has enabled it to dominate the state's political life since the late 1960s. Today it controls a majority of Nevada's legislature. With this concentration of political power, gaming interests have wielded enormous influence as the largest employer in the state and the life-blood of the tourism on which the state depends for revenue.[37] As a result, Las Vegas became an extended company town because it lacked a diversified economy, although it has recently tried to move in that direction. The Southern Nevada Water Project helped gaming far more than it attracted new industry to the area.

Clearly, Bible was the spokesman on water issues in Nevada, and he built his political power base on his ability to deliver federally financed water projects for the state. He exhibited considerable political skill in maneuvering the Southern Nevada Water Project through Congress and to completion while avoiding the environmentalist concerns voiced against Udall's Southwest Water Plan and the Central Arizona Project. Had he not steered a course independent from Udall and Hayden, it is unlikely that the project ever would have been built. Also, by the end of the 1960s, with less discretionary money available for new public works programs, Congress began to take a different view of costly water projects. In 1986 Congress established a new federal policy that required beneficiaries to share in the costs by providing money in advance of construction.[38] The burden of building costs was no longer on the backs of the nation's taxpayers, but on those who benefited the most from the project.

While Bible and others had been unsuccessful in enticing the Pacific Northwest to part with its water resources, the region was more than willing to expand its hydroelectric facilities into the Southwest, which was almost as hungry for power sources as it was for water. The plan, the Pacific Northwest–Pacific Southwest Intertie, called for the expansion of the Bonneville Dam, the symbol of New Deal dam building in the West, into eleven western states, involving 251 electric utilities at a cost of $697 million. The electrical output would increase by 4,400,000 kilowatts. Nevada would receive about 200 megawatts a year and share about $724 million in benefits with Arizona over fifty years.[39]

Naturally, Bible threw his full support behind the project. The plan called for a 488-mile transmission line from the Nevada–Oregon border, through the middle of Nevada, to Hoover Dam. Not only would the power line add about $500,000 to local tax revenues, but it would create another 100 jobs to build the Lake Mead substation, estimated to cost about $48 million. On March 11, 1967, Bible was the featured speaker at ground-breaking ceremonies for the Lake Mead Power Substation in Boulder City. Linking the power project to his desire for Pacific Northwest water, he said, "Enlightened foresight and sensible hindsight . . . will someday be applied to a giant North-South water project benefitting Nevada. If these factors can work in the field of electrical power, they can work equally well in the field of water resources."[40]

While interbasin water transfers remained a dead issue in Congress, the power project linking the Pacific Northwest and Southwest sailed through the congressional budget process. Bible kept a sharp eye open from his seat on the Appropriations Committee to ensure the smooth flow of government money to the western states. Along with the interbasin transfer issue, Bible tried to revive the Great Basin National Park plan, which had stalled in Congress when Representative Baring did an abrupt, inexplicable turnabout in 1962 and came out against Bible's park bill, which had passed the Senate unanimously.

For two years neither side would yield. In March 1964 the Interior De-

Senator Alan Bible speaking at the ground-breaking ceremony for the Pacific Northwest-Pacific Southwest Intertie, Boulder City, Nevada, March 11, 1967. (Alan Bible Collection)

partment officially endorsed Bible's plan, pointing out that Baring's proposal failed to provide the features required in a national park. By limiting the size of the park, Baring's bill failed to ensure sufficient protection for the surrounding scenic attractions.[41] The department's support for Bible's bill was unsurprising, since he had become a leader in formulating national park legislation and, as chairman of the Interior Subcommittee on Public Lands, was directly responsible for the hearings on the major park bills. This was in stark contrast to Baring's inexperience, reflected in his proposal, which endangered not only the overall park plan but other legislation important to Nevada.

As noted, Baring constantly antagonized Presidents Kennedy and Johnson, upon whom Bible and Cannon relied to authorize military expenditures

President Lyndon Johnson campaigning in Nevada in 1964. (Left) Senator Howard Cannon and Governor Grant Sawyer; (right) Senator Alan Bible. (John Nulty photo; Bible family collection)

and vital water projects in Nevada. Baring voted against the Johnson administration's civil rights bills, mass transportation measures, urban renewal plans, food stamp program, and Medicare while denouncing eastern liberals as "egg-head atheists" and suggesting that "beatniks, pacifists, and draft-dodgers be sent to Moscow."[42] While on a campaign swing through Las Vegas in 1964, President Johnson praised the state's Democratic leaders but ignored Baring. Senator Cannon also chose not to mention Baring's name in his Reno address the following day, but he did praise other party officials.

In early 1965 Bible tried to gain acceptance of the park plan by introducing S. 499. Baring countered with H.R. 6122. Both bills were identical to the 1962 proposals, and the issue was again joined. But this time Bible placed the burden of holding hearings and passing legislation on Baring. Bible reasoned that the Senate had already looked at the matter, held two separate hearings, and passed a bill; now it was Baring's turn to move forward if he was sincere about the Great Basin National Park. It soon became apparent that Baring and his small group of supporters wanted to defeat any plan, using delay and inaction while appearing to support a park concept that would encompass mining and grazing.[43]

Petitions from the Ely Chamber of Commerce and Mines backing the park flooded Bible's office in July 1965.[44] He responded by outlining his position to the Ely National Park Committee, adding that public pressure might induce Baring to pass a "park bill, any bill, outlining any proposal." Then and only then could the Senate and House work together to iron out the differences between the two proposals.[45] This was an extraordinary public admission that Bible could not work with Baring and would rather work through a conference committee to create the Great Basin National Park.

By August the Bible and Baring positions and strategies were clear. Baring stressed that advocates of multiple-use—ranchers, miners, and sportsmen—had written his park bill and reflected the will of White Pine County land users. He refused to acknowledge that hikers, campers, nature lovers, or recreationists had a legitimate interest in land-use policy. Furthermore, the congressman declared he would call for hearings in the House only if Bible pledged his unqualified support in writing and proposed a similar bill in the Senate.[46] In short, a Great Basin National Park was possible only on Baring's terms or, more accurately, on the conditions specified by Ely ranchers and miners. Baring demanded that his Senate colleague ignore the 1960 multiple-use act and recreational needs. Bible could do neither and maintain credibility with his Senate colleagues on national issues affecting parks and recreation. While Bible usually was agreeable to compromises, Baring had gone too far.

Bible rejected Baring's terms, but the Ely Chamber of Commerce and Mines quickly accepted Baring's proposal and pleaded with the congressman to pass whatever parks bill he could obtain in the House. They asked Secretary Udall to support Baring's bill, hoping to pressure the congressman to move ahead as quickly as possible.[47] Bolstered by the support of Ely business leaders, Baring gave Nevada newspapers his correspondence on the issue, along with that of the Chamber of Commerce and Mines.

Bible and his press secretary, Dwight Dyer, were furious. Baring had never asked the senator to respond publicly to the congressman's proposal, and the news accounts made it appear that Bible, not Baring, had caused the long delay. A few days after the story appeared in the Nevada papers Baring wrote to Bible that the senator's written guarantee of support was unnecessary, but Wayne Aspinall, chairman of the House Interior and Insular Affairs Committee, would probably want some assurances before scheduling hearings.[48] Bible and Cannon refused to let Baring's efforts to shift responsibility, first to the Senate and then to Aspinall, intimidate them. On September 1 they issued a joint statement in which they refused to commit to the Baring plan because it failed to meet national park standards and faced a certain veto by President Johnson.[49]

For almost six years Baring maintained two positions. First, he contended that his bill was a true multiple-use plan although it excluded recreation from consideration, despite the clear intent of Congress to the contrary. Second, he blamed the delay in enacting a Great Basin National Park bill on others, principally Senators Bible and Cannon, Secretary Udall, and chairman Aspinall. In early 1966 he made clear in a letter to the Ely Chamber of Commerce and Mines that he would support park legislation only if it received the unqualified endorsement of Ely mining and cattle interests. In still another effort to deflect responsibility, he asked Udall to meet with his mining and cattle people to work out a compromise that would essentially be a capitulation. The secretary refused and remained steadfast behind Bible's bill. Pressure on Baring continued to mount when President Johnson endorsed Bible's plan on February 26, 1966.[50] Shortly afterward Baring tried again to shift blame from himself to others. He charged in the press that Udall had turned down his invitation to negotiate, as had Nevada's two senators, and it was now their duty to come forward with a Great Basin Park plan.[51]

Bible fought back. On March 27, 1966, he wrote a stern letter to Baring, requesting a meeting of the Nevada delegation to discuss the future of the Great Basin National Park. He told the congressman to be prepared to accept full responsibility for the park plan's demise, then released the letter to the press. It appeared on the front page of the *Ely Daily Times* the next day and prompted a subsequent editorial that blasted Baring:

> Baring has opposed creation of a park since its inception. He blocked the Senate bill of 1962 and then put together what he has attempted to call a compromise bill. Bible has listened long enough to Baring's endless line of excuses. . . . Now he must meet with Senator Bible who has proven he knows how to pass Nevada legislation in Washington.[52]

The day after the editorial appeared Baring informed Bible that a compromise bill should be drafted that "would not be opposed by the cattlemen, Fish and Wildlife, mining interests, labor interests, and others."[53]

To draft such legislation was clearly impossible, given the positions taken by the grazing and mining interests in the Ely area. However, the delay from the first hearings in 1959 to the stalemate in 1966 gave ample time to assess the park's importance to White Pine County's economy. Exploitation of the controversial beryllium discoveries, the main focus of the 1959 hearings, never materialized. No significant mining activity occurred in the area of the proposed park. One hundred head of cattle and nine hundred sheep were grazing in the area and could continue to do so under Bible's bill, which also recognized existing water rights. But the annual hunting and removal of several hundred deer would be banned, and, in all likelihood, one ranch running forty head of cattle would be put out of business.[54] With some sarcasm, Bible accurately summed up the situation: "As support of the Great Basin National Park developed, the region abruptly took on new value, almost overnight it was valuable mineral property. There was no commercial mining then or now, but the area is touted as an area of great potential."[55]

Finally, on April 19, 1966, Secretary of the Interior Udall and the Nevada delegation held their long-awaited meeting in Bible's office. Congressman Baring appeared uninformed. Initially, he blamed the 1962 park plan defeat on Congressman John Saylor of Pennsylvania, whom he charged with refusing to vote for legislation that included mining and grazing permits. This was startling information to everyone present and of questionable validity, since Saylor had recently supported park bills with mining and grazing provisions. Baring produced a letter from a woman who had written to him opposing the park on nonspecific grounds. The letter was relevant to none of the topics under discussion. Baring then recounted his travels in a four-wheel-drive vehicle to the area; he said he saw some mining there but supplied no specifics about its productivity. Later Bible and Cannon revealed that the area Baring had visited was outside the park's proposed boundaries. Undaunted, Baring again told Udall that various groups had written his park bill. "I have to report to these groups," he said, adding, "I would be deserting my interests and commitments if I took a stand at this minute. I have to speak to them."[56]

Baring's was unwavering: a few cattle raisers, miners, and hunters would decide the park's fate. At the end of the meeting he asked Udall to meet again with "his people" to work out a compromise. The secretary declined, while Bible and Cannon were dismayed by the congressman's reluctance to take a stand on the issue. Secretary Udall publicly rejected the Baring plan in October, killing any chance to create a Great Basin National Park.

Nevada's mining and grazing interests had won. They successfully defended their right to use and exploit two-tenths of 1 percent of the state's land base, an area that contained little mineral potential whose main utilitarian purpose was to supplement the food supply and income of a few ranchers who owned about 2,000 head of cattle and sheep. The same economic interests that had long dominated western land-use policy had thwarted the preservation of the region's scenic beauty.

Traditionally, the key to securing national park legislation was proof that the area under consideration was economically worthless. Well aware of this burden, Bible firmly believed that the Wheeler Peak region was as nearly devoid of potential for economic development as any place in the United States. By the late 1950s western mining clearly was declining, but he rallied to its aid with numerous proposals to restrict imports and develop regional production for defense and domestic consumption.[57] When mining and grazing interests opposed the Humphrey-Saylor wilderness proposal, Bible supported the key amendments to the Anderson plan to include mining exploration and development, along with grazing rights, which enabled the 1964 Wilderness Act to become law. He included similar provisions in his plan for the Great Basin National Park.

The greed of a few mine owners and stock raisers and the duplicity of their congressional spokesman defeated the Great Basin National Park plan and, in the process, further depressed White Pine County's economy. Bible and Cannon had correctly predicted the national park's impact on the entire region. In its absence, the county's economy and the land's condition continued to deteriorate. In 1974 the Bureau of Land Management made a study of Nevada's rangelands which showed a continuing process of degradation from overgrazing livestock.[58] In 1978 the Kennecott Copper Mines closed, shattering the last remnants of prosperity and causing a devastating population decline. By 1983 White Pine County officials were proposing power plant projects to ease the distress caused by a failed economy that a national park with its tourists and concessions probably would have relieved.[59]

Losing the Great Basin National Park was a personal blow to Bible, all the more so because of his success in legislating parks. He was unable to carry out a park plan for his home state, demonstrating anew the need for a united congressional delegation to fend off vested economic interests. Bible persisted, however, not in White Pine County, but in the Lake Tahoe basin, the subject of conflict between California and Nevada since before the turn of the century.

The controversy centered on the Reclamation Service's desire to use Lake Tahoe as a storage reservoir to feed the Truckee-Carson reclamation project in western Nevada. But reclamation officials had badly overestimated the annual flow of the Truckee River, the only available water source that could keep the project from failure, by implication saving the Reclamation Service's reputation in the process. But to gain control of Tahoe's waters the Reclamation Service had to come to terms with an electric power syndicate, California conservationists, and lakeside property owners who feared that the withdrawal of water would cause a deterioration of land values.[60]

The controversy had a long history. In 1909 the power combine and the Reclamation Service entered into negotiations that resulted in a tentative contract agreement. The power company received a virtual power monopoly over the Truckee River that would boost profits by about $500,000 a year, while the Reclamation Service gained ownership and control of the dam at the river outlet. When chief forester Gifford Pinchot reviewed the proposal, he immediately refused to approve the contract because it granted power rights in perpetuity. Afterward the issue became a rallying point for California conservationists and property owners, who saw the matter as one of protection versus development.[61]

A year later the State of California entered the dispute. It claimed ownership of all the surplus water from Lake Tahoe, contesting the claims of the federal government and the power companies. To make matters worse for reclamation officials, they had consulted neither California nor Tahoe property owners when they were planning reclamation projects for western Nevada. The federal government wanted control over the lake's water for future use to save a questionable project in Nevada at California's expense. The weight of the evidence and logic was on California's side. In 1911 President William Howard Taft killed the proposed contract between the power monopoly and the government.[62]

Still, California and Nevada continued to fight over the lake, which was about two-thirds in California and one-third in Nevada. California was determined to defend its recreational interests, while Nevada and the Reclamation Service were equally dedicated to using the water for agriculture. The issue reached crisis proportions in 1924 when the Truckee went dry and Nevada farmers threatened to blow up the dam to release millions of gallons of water into Nevada. Five years later drought again drove farmers to the lake, this time with a steam shovel. They threatened to cut a ditch at the outlet of the lake to release 75,000 acre-feet of water needed in Nevada. Law enforcement officials restored order, but the incident graphically illustrated the emotions on both sides of the border.[63]

Except for the 1944 court decree that adjudicated water rights to the Truckee, emotions and issues had not significantly changed when California and Nevada began negotiating to form an interstate compact to work out their water disputes. Water was not the only issue that divided Californians and Nevadans. Lakeshore development became a major issue in the 1960s, and Bible took an early and firm stand. He viewed the Tahoe shoreline much as he viewed the Cape Cod Seashore—it was in danger of disappearing through commercial and residential expansion, which, if not checked, would consume all the land available to the public for recreational use.[64] Thus, Bible wanted to protect what remained of a shoreline that loggers once had ravaged to shore up the Comstock's mines—the graveyard of forests.

What emerged was a dual strategy to save the Nevada side of Lake Tahoe, involving Bible, his longtime friend Joseph F. McDonald, Sr., and Governor Grant Sawyer. In late September 1961 Bible and Secretary Udall toured the Tahoe basin and met with Governor Sawyer, who had made a similar inspection two months before. Udall and Bible agreed to use money from the Land and Water Conservation Fund to acquire a large tract of shoreline property for inclusion in the national park system. Meanwhile, Sawyer took the lead in proposing the establishment of state parks to protect the disappearing lakeshore.[65]

With its provision for matching funds to states for the creation of parks and recreation facilities, the Land and Water Conservation Fund was the key to Bible's plan to help Sawyer establish state parks on the Nevada side of the lake. After being assured of President Johnson's full support by Udall, Bible issued a statement: "Most important to Nevada, it will make possible a state park to preserve much of the remaining unspoiled beauty of Lake Tahoe for this and future generations."[66] On February 11, 1965, he introduced S. 1116, co-sponsored by Senator Kuchel, to authorize $100,000 to study the idea of establishing a national parkway around the entire lake. Although Congress took no action, it marked Bible's initial attempt to involve the national government in the lake's protection.[67]

Bible moved on a parallel course to halt the decline in Lake Tahoe's water quality. The issues were no less complicated because the same factor that created the need for a national park to preserve the lakeshore contributed to the declining water quality—uncontrolled growth. Like the problems surrounding the Truckee, Carson, and Walker rivers, water pollution required the cooperation of two states and five counties, all of which shared jurisdiction over the lake.

The pollution problem resulted from seepage that found its way into the lake from septic tanks as well as raw sewage from illegal campers and other recreationists. Disposal plants were unable to keep pace with the area's growth, while runoff from building sites in the mountains only made matters worse. After numerous conferences and meetings over a two-year period, Bible introduced S. 3946 on July 30, 1968, to establish a bi-state compact to study water pollution problems and land development in the Tahoe basin. The bill had the support of California's Republican senators, Thomas Kuchel and George Murphy, along with Congressmen Baring and Harold T. "Bizz" Johnson, who introduced companion legislation in the House, H.R. 19032. The bill would have provided for an area-wide planning agency with the power to adopt and enforce a regional plan of resource conservation and orderly development. While the House and Senate took no action, it showed that water pollution was becoming a concern in California and Nevada. Bible remained in the forefront of the federal government's involvement at Lake Tahoe in the years to come.[68]

Bible was far more successful in expanding recreational facilities in southern Nevada, where issues of bi-state cooperation and conflicting county priorities were absent. The key was Lake Mead, the huge reservoir created when Hoover Dam backed up the Colorado River 115 miles to Bridge Canyon. About 255 square miles, with a shoreline extending nearly 550 miles, Lake Mead was formally established on October 13, 1936, when Secretary of the Interior Harold L. Ickes approved the operating agreement between the Bureau of Reclamation, which controlled the dam, and the Park Service, which administered the artificial lake. For almost thirty years Lake Mead had been the symbol of growth in recreational facilities that would have heartened Stephen Mather, the National Park Service's first director, and every director since the New Deal. Lake Mead was one of America's most popular playgrounds.[69]

But the operating agreement between the Park Service and the Bureau of Reclamation created funding problems, jurisdictional disputes between Arizona and Nevada, and fuzzy lines of authority and responsibility. Consequently, on February 4, 1963, Bible introduced S. 653 to make Lake Mead the nation's first congressionally designated recreational area under the National Park Service's exclusive jurisdiction and to provide for fixed boundaries between Arizona and Nevada. When President Johnson signed it on October 8, 1964, the result was more efficient administration for the nation's fourth-leading park attraction.[70]

Afterward Bible moved quickly to expand the lake's harbors, docks, roads, and visitor accommodations to keep pace with an influx of visitors that had soared to nearly four million a year in 1965. On December 30, 1964, Park Service director George Hartzog, Jr., gave Bible a list of projects under construction and those that had received congressional approval. The total appropriation needed was just over $2 million, and Hartzog assured the senator that the expansion of Lake Mead facilities was receiving his personal attention.[71]

Bible continued to press the initiative. In 1965 and 1966 he obtained funding through the Appropriations Committee for $118,000 to build access roads and parking lots and $465,000 for a new visitors' center, utility building, and seven comfort stations. Like Lake Tahoe, Nevada's other premier recreation area, Lake Mead began to suffer major pollution problems in early 1967, and for the same reason: overdevelopment. On December 14, 1967, Bible extracted a promise from Max Edwards, assistant secretary of the interior for water pollution control, to assign top priority to the problems at Lake Tahoe and Lake Mead. He told Edwards, "The federal government should be ready to provide all needed assistance." From Bible's perspective, the government had to do more than finance and construct massive water projects to accommodate growth beyond what the desert environment could tolerate. He believed that the government should also pay to clean up the mess caused by Nevada's development faction, and he remained one of the most influential spokesmen for this group.[72]

Overdevelopment caused pollution problems at Lake Mead because Las Vegans were dumping ten million gallons of sewage a day into the Las Vegas bay. The sewage, which contained high amounts of bacteria, phosphorous, and nitrogen, was then pumped back into Las Vegas's water. Valley residents were literally drinking their own sewage and polluting their most valuable recreation resource at the same time, prompting Vernon Bostick, the consulting ecologist, to comment, "The trouble with engineers is they can't leave nature alone."[73] But the solution proved to be more studies when Secretary Edwards followed up on his pledge to Bible to investigate the problem by awarding a $40,500 grant to Clark County under the Clean Water Restoration Act of 1966.[74] Apparently, no one, including Bible, stopped to consider that uncontrolled growth was the root cause of the Las Vegas Valley's pollution problem.

As Las Vegas grew, so did its desire for diversified recreation. Lake Mead remained the most popular playground, but skiing enthusiasts looked to Mount Charleston, high above the Las Vegas Valley, for winter recreation. Kyle and Lee canyons, along with Mount Charleston, standing 11,000 feet above sea level, had the potential to become a major winter tourist attraction in southern Nevada, where Californians could gamble and ski in the same weekend.

In early 1964 Bible encouraged the Forest Service to expand its facilities inside the Toiyabe National Forest and to improve recreational accommodations at Mount Charleston. The Forest Service immediately responded with an eight-year improvement plan requiring $1.2 million to maintain family camping and picnic sites, along with thirty-five new sites in Kyle Canyon and twenty-five at Lee Canyon. While camping and picnic areas would attract summertime users, the ski resort's potential created the largest need for federal expansion. As with Lake Mead, Bible forged ahead as the number one procurer of recreation resources in Nevada.[75]

By July 1965 Mount Charleston had moved closer to realizing its recreational potential. A ski lift with a capacity to move 500 people an hour was nearing completion. An additional lift with a 1,000-person capacity was planned for the following year. With the lodge's completion expected the same year, winter skiing promised to become a major recreational activity near a city best known for its high temperatures and high-stakes gambling.[76] Again, Bible had done much to encourage the process.

Indeed, during his second full term, Bible had built an impressive record of bringing federal dollars to Nevada to stimulate growth and development. He looked inward—first to the Senate, then to Nevada and the intermountain West—in building political capital to support the region's core interests: reclamation, mining, and the federal presence. But in 1968, as that term ended, the protests over the war in Vietnam, the Tet offensive, Johnson's decision not to seek reelection, urban riots, the assassinations of Martin Luther King and Robert Kennedy, and the rioting at the Democratic Convention in Chicago had left the party in disarray. Democrats like Bible, who were standing for reelection, were on the defensive on their foreign and domestic agenda.

Bible's close identification with President Johnson, which he had used to great advantage in 1956 and again in his 1962 reelection campaign, made him particularly vulnerable. While Bible had constantly argued against the American dollar drain abroad because it curtailed investment at home, he was conspicuously silent about American dollars rolling into Vietnam. In 1964 he voted for the Tonkin Gulf Resolution (he was not alone, of course: it passed the Senate with only two dissenting votes), and in 1965 his views remained unchanged. In a New Year's message to American soldiers in Vietnam, Bible said, "The overwhelming majority of your countrymen . . . fully support your efforts. I believe that you fight in a remote corner of Southeast Asia today so that you and millions more will not have to fight in a bigger, more tragic war closer to home."[77]

One year later Bible still supported the war effort. He endorsed President Johnson's state-of-the-union message calling for both guns and butter: "The President has eloquently stated our determination to keep our commitments while working for peace in Vietnam. I support this policy." In 1968, at the Democratic Convention in Chicago, he voted for Hubert Humphrey over Eugene McCarthy and against the peace plank in the party platform.[78]

Bible's support for Johnson's Vietnam policy was a function of personal loyalty, politics, and belief. He owed the president a great deal for his help in obtaining projects for Nevada. If he had broken with the president over Vietnam, Johnson surely would have taken a measure of revenge on Nevada and its senior senator. Bible had neither the desire nor the stomach to challenge Johnson, and certainly not on an issue so important to the president. Nor did he have influence on foreign policy, and he had risen in politics in an age of deference to presidential prerogative and congressional foreign policy experts. But after 1968 he grew increasingly critical of the Vietnam War and its management by President Nixon. He voted for the Mansfield amendment that called for a deadline for troop withdrawals, and he was distressed over Nixon's continued bombing of North Vietnam.[79] While personal and party politics largely explain Bible's position, he seems to have held some reservations about America's mission in Southeast Asia.

Bible shared a great many beliefs with his political mentors, McCarran and Johnson. The threat of internal subversion topped the list. Bible was shocked when the Supreme Court declared sections of the 1950 Subversives Activities Control Act unconstitutional in 1968. He said, "I know of no nation that can long survive if its sworn enemies are permitted access to its defense and security structure"—a position in which he believed and which would be politically popular in conservative Nevada. Afterward he voted with Senators Sam Ervin (D–North Carolina) and Everett Dirksen (R-Illinois) to keep the Subversive Activities Control Board in business. With only five senators present and voting, the Bible-Ervin-Dirksen view prevailed over those of William Proxmire (D-Wisconsin) and Albert Gore (D-Tennessee).[80]

Years later Bible felt that Vietnam was a tragic mistake. But in 1968 the war was a political liability in his reelection bid.[81] To compound matters, Republicans had captured control of Nevada in 1966 when Paul Laxalt unseated Grant Sawyer in the governor's race and Ed Fike defeated John Foley in the lieutenant governor's contest. A year later Fike, with Governor Laxalt's blessing, entered the Senate race against Bible.

Ed Fike was a tall, good-looking, and well-liked campaigner who began his assault on Bible early. He hired the polling firm of Merrill-Wirthlin and Associates to assess his strengths, weaknesses, and overall campaign strategy based on the issues of overriding importance to Nevadans. As might be expected, Johnson and his handling of the Vietnam War ranked first among Nevada voters. Both Republicans and Democrats were dissatisfied. The majority of Nevadans favored giving greater control of the war effort to military leaders to bring the conflict to a quick end. In Nevada the hawks significantly outnumbered the doves. While certainly a hawk, Bible was vulnerable on the war issue because Fike's supporters were more militant hawks than those who backed Bible.[82]

Fike quickly moved to attack Bible on the war issue. Addressing an audience of eighty-five women at a North Las Vegas casino, he declared that Bible was "either powerful and influential and therefore must share the blame, or he has no power and influence, in which case there is no need to send him back to Washington." This attempt to link Bible to Johnson caused only frustration; Fike later commented, "To hear the senator talk today you'd hardly think he knew Lyndon Johnson."[83]

Indeed, for the first time in his Senate career, Bible ran for reelection independent of Johnson's power and influence. He played to his strengths in

Fig. 10. "There, There, I Don't Think You're a Rubber Stamp."
(Las Vegas Review-Journal, *August 5, 1962*)

1968, and that meant emphasizing that he had delivered for Nevada because of his power and influence in the Senate, which resulted from his seniority. His campaign literature and theme, "Nevada is stronger with Bible," provided a laundry list of the projects he had secured for constituents. That was exactly what Nevadans most liked about Bible—he put Nevada first. Republican pollsters found the same feeling: "This strong identification of Bible's activities and interests with that of the state must be considered a valuable

Fig. 11. "Bible's Pork Barrel Projects, Inc." (Las Vegas Review-Journal,
October 31, 1968)

Bible asset. . . . Both supporters of Fike and Bible perceived Bible's strongest
attribute as being his activities in behalf of the state." [84]

For years Bible had correctly gauged what Nevada voters expected from
their elected officials. They wanted a senator who supported their interests
and brought prosperity to the state. In essence, Nevadans voted their pocket-
books and were more concerned with domestic issues than with foreign
policy. They perceived Bible as active and aggressive in working for their
interests, and this made his seniority in Washington valuable. Bible's campaign was geared to his strengths and calculated to maximize voter appeal.
But his weaknesses could be exploited, particularly his image of avoiding
positive stands and being easily influenced by Johnson and Senate leaders.
Those who saw Bible as weak and indecisive said, "That guy is strictly a
politician, not a statesman," or "He's just another New Dealer and he's
always apologizing for Johnson." Still another, reflecting a longtime criticism
of Bible, said, "He's a rubber stamp senator" (see fig. 10).[85] To some extent,
Nevada voters were aware of these negative factors; but overriding them all
was Bible's service to Nevada, which gave him a clear advantage in 1968. A
few days before the election the cartoonist for the *Las Vegas Review-Journal*
captured the tenor of the campaign in a cartoon that depicted Fike as hopelessly trying to catch Bible's "pork barrel" operation (fig. 11). Three days after
the cartoon appeared the *Review-Journal* endorsed Bible.[86]

While little quantitative evidence exists that pork-barrel projects translate into votes, the Nevada senatorial election of 1968 seems to have turned on Bible's record. He defeated Fike by 14,554 votes, 83,622 to 69,068. Again, Clark County, the home of the Southern Nevada Water Project, was the key to victory: Bible outpolled Fike there by 15,114 votes. The margin of his victory was impressive, but the results of the presidential election made it all the more so: Richard Nixon carried the state over Hubert Humphrey by 12,590 votes.[87] Fike was never able to convince voters that Bible was responsible for the malaise in Vietnam or the general state of chaos that seemed to grip the country.

Despite the criticisms of Bible's performance as senator, especially his rubber stamp image, he was a far better choice than Fike would have been. During the campaign Bible received evidence that Fike had benefited from questionable land deals concerning the Colorado River Commission. When he met with his key advisers, they urged him to go public with the information. Bible refused, saying, "If I have to destroy a man and his family to get reelected I would rather not be senator."[88] Two years later the information about Fike helped defeat him in the governor's race against Democrat Mike O'Callaghan. Eighteen years later Fike was indicted for obtaining $4.5 million in fraudulent bank loans.[89]

The election of 1968 proved that Bible's conception of his senatorial role squared with the views of his constituents and that he held a "safe seat" as far as Democrats were concerned. He had won by an impressive margin despite difficult circumstances. Although he had purposely distanced himself from Johnson during the campaign, the president understood the need to do so, and the two men remained close friends. On Bible's birthday Johnson sent him a routine congratulatory letter, adding a handwritten note at the bottom: "I am so happy the way you came through." Before leaving office Johnson wrote to Bible, "Your friendship and support will remain indelible in my mind. They've been wonderful years for me, made richer by the fact that you were at my side."[90] So Bible and Johnson parted company, the president in defeat, and the senator at the apex of his career.

Chapter Eleven

Something Saved, Something Lost,

1969–1974

While catastrophic to Lyndon Johnson's presidency, the Vietnam War was not the only reason to doubt his leadership. Civil unrest combined with the quagmire in Southeast Asia to produce a vague feeling that something had gone terribly wrong with American society. Federal programs to aid the poor and disadvantaged seemed costly and wasteful when money failed to solve domestic problems and additional troops produced only a stalemate in Vietnam. America appeared to be losing the war at home against poverty and discrimination, and overseas against communism.[1]

As Johnson's prestige declined, Bible and other longtime congressional allies ran for cover. With Richard Nixon's election, congressional opposition continued: first to the war in Vietnam, then to presidential impoundment of funds that Congress had appropriated for public works and social programs. Still, the president and Congress had to co-exist and share power to move forward with the legislative process.

Contrary to some perceptions of presidential power, the Nixon years were less than the high tide of the "Imperial Presidency." Indeed, there probably had never been such a presidency in American history except for brief and isolated periods when war seemed to dictate the extraordinary use of executive power, such as Lincoln's suspensions of the habeas corpus and Roosevelt's internment of Japanese Americans on the West Coast. Political scientist Robert A. Dahl wrote that during the 1960s Congress "both lost and acquired power."[2] After Johnson's departure Congress may in fact have gained far more than it lost with a president from a minority party.

Congress was far from ineffective in the 1970s. Nixon repeatedly bowed to the will of Congress over impoundments, the "secret" war in Cambodia, and his desire to increase executive powers and privileges. The Nixon years demonstrated what Richard E. Neustadt claimed in 1960: presidents have little power to command because of diverse and conflicting loyalties in institutions.[3] Consequently, Congress continued its role as policymaker as it had done under Kennedy and Johnson.

Lacking a clear electoral mandate, Nixon faced a Democratic Congress determined to set its own legislative agenda. From his perspective, Nixon confronted the momentum of liberal policies and programs enacted by a party entrenched in interlocking special interest commitments that produced escalating budget deficits. He responded with vetoes and the impoundment of appropriated funds to restore fiscal responsibility.[4] Compounding the problem was the congressional budgetary process, which the power of subcommittees and the resulting lack of coordinated leadership in Congress had made a shambles.

This condition of drift—or, as some would say, the greater exercise of democracy in Congress—allowed Bible and others to steer an independent course in pursuing their legislative agendas. To be sure, Congress was unsure of the direction it should follow because the budgetary process was out of control and its majority differed fundamentally with the president. For Bible, the general state of the economy and escalating government expenditures had to be brought under control, but not at the expense of western projects—especially water reclamation.

Land, water, and mining issues continued to dominate Bible's thinking in 1969. On September 9 the Senate finally passed a national minerals policy bill. Bible co-sponsored S. 719, which he believed would be a springboard to solve the nation's mining problems, the result of unprecedented consumption that forced increased reliance on foreign imports. S. 719 placed responsibility for planning and coordination squarely on the federal government by encouraging development and research. Although the source of funding for the program was vague, it showed that Congress and the president finally recognized the minerals problem. In 1970 the House passed similar legislation, which President Nixon signed on December 31, 1970.[5]

Although gratified, Bible felt that the measure was too late. He believed that economic catastrophe lay ahead because mineral development was tied to trade policies that hampered domestic development. For example, early in 1971, Nixon announced that he would cut spending and raise taxes to stimulate the economy and reduce inflation. But when Congress and the public rejected his remedy, Nixon opted to control the currency through the Federal Reserve Board by increasing interest rates and constricting the money supply. The plan failed to curb inflation. Between 1971 and 1973 the cost of living rose 15 percent, and the balance-of-trade deficit grew, producing "stagflation"—rising prices and economic stagnation.[6]

Bible's predictions of economic decline, based on America's overwhelming reliance on imported raw materials from silver to crude oil, proved correct. But broader foreign and trade policies were beyond his influence and expertise. Still, the new congressional outlook on domestic metal production provided an opportunity to force a change in the government's position on metal production. The Public Land Law Review Commission (PLLRC) was created in 1964 at Representative Wayne Aspinall's insistence, as his price for supporting Clinton Anderson's wilderness bill. Bible was initially cool to the idea of serving on the commission, but he later changed his mind when he saw that it would provide a forum to influence the future course of public land-use policy.[7]

Once on the commission, Bible insisted that the western mining industry have a strong voice in its deliberations. On November 20, 1964, he wrote to Lawrence O'Brien, special assistant to President Johnson, to recommend W. Howard Gray's appointment to the Advisory Council on Mining. Gray had a long association with Bible, with the Nevada Mining Association, and with the American Mining Congress as chairman of its Public Lands Committee. Gray's selection signaled that the commission would have the full influence of the mining industry on public land-use recommendations. With Senators Gordon Allott (R-Colorado) and Len B. Jordan (R-Idaho) on the commission, too, Bible had strong support from other western mining senators who shared his views.[8]

The Public Land Law Review Commission took six years to complete its work, at a cost of nearly $7 million. On June 23, 1970, it submitted to Congress and the president a 342-page report containing 18 statements of basic concepts, 137 specific recommendations, and nearly 200 supplemental recommendations. Declaring that public lands should be used to ensure maximum benefit to the general public, the commission recognized the right of all users of the public domain to be heard on all policy issues. But mining received an even stronger endorsement when the commission recommended that mineral exploration receive preference over most, if not all, other uses of the public lands.[9] This, coupled with the National Minerals Policy Act of 1970, set the stage for Bible to move ahead on a broad range of policy issues affecting the western mining industry.

He began on September 17, 1971, by introducing S. 2542, the Mineral Development Act of 1971, to execute the PLLRC's recommendations. Shortly afterward Bible outlined the provisions of his plan in testimony before the Minerals Subcommittee of the Interior and Insular Affairs Committee. He said his bill would repeal certain provisions of the 1872 mining law by substituting the recommendations in chapter 7 of the PLLRC report. Specifically, it affected unpatented mining claims that allowed exploration on public lands without first making a valuable discovery. Under Bible's proposal, miners could perfect unpatented claims if they discovered valuable minerals within three years from the date of the new law; otherwise, dormant claims would be wiped out.[10] For Bible, it was a happy medium: mineral exploration was possible, but so was preservation of the land for other uses.

While the bill included provisions favorable to the mining industry, the controversial sections related to royalties. Under the Bible plan, the Treasury Department would receive a 2 percent royalty with a ceiling of 4 percent of the operation's net income. It also required a $5-per-acre annual labor charge with an escalating clause up to $20 an acre after fifteen years. Unless work progressed and the fees were paid, the claim would be null and void.[11] These requirements seemed reasonable enough, but to Gray and the American Mining Congress, so long accustomed to free use of the public lands, any increase in operating costs prompted a negative reaction—even against their foremost advocate.[12]

Gray saw Bible's bill as a "road block" to exploration and inconsistent with the PLLRC's supposed support for mining. More importantly, he refused to accept the PLLRC's recommendations on environmental protection, such as land classification for environmental enhancement, which might restrict access for mining operators. Nor did he agree in concept that greater attention should be paid to environmental impact studies before using some public lands. Instead, Gray said only that "they are of sufficient importance that the mining industry should watch with particular care legislation dealing with this subject matter."[13]

Gray's attitude reflected the views of the majority of the industry, which contributed significantly to its poor public image. Recognition of this came grudgingly; on October 11, 1971, at a meeting of the American Mining Congress in Las Vegas, Gilbert E. Dwyer, the AMC's public relations executive, told the assemblage, "The mining industry is badly in need of a new public image in the area of environmental concern." Dwyer went to the heart of the matter when he said, "The mining industry has a credibility problem. . . . Unless our industry makes its point of view known and understood, decisions about our future will be made entirely by others."[14]

Bible heartily agreed. Addressing the same meeting, he called on the industry to work closely with environmentalists in shaping the future of mineral production in the United States. He said, "Mining needs to clean up its methods and clean up its image"—and he could very well have added the damage to the landscape caused by mining operations. Instead, Bible was kinder to his constituents: "An industry that takes from the Earth a non-renewable resource and leaves behind the inevitable scars of its work is a natural target for the environmentalist. . . . This is perhaps mining's biggest challenge in the 1970s."[15]

But the mining industry ignored its own protectionist organizations and political supporters. Reviewing Bible's bill, the National Wildlife Federation deemed it a significant improvement over the 1872 mining law. Although the federation agreed that Bible's plan followed many of the PLLRC's recommendations and still supported its overall thrust, it was concerned about some of the leasing provisions. But the American Mining Congress refused to compromise at all. It blocked enactment of S. 2542 with a variety of delaying tactics that prompted one critic to observe, "Congress turned to more pressing matters, and the hoary old 1872 law sailed into the 1980s, warts and all." [16]

Once again, greed prevented the western mining industry from supporting Bible's bill. For the first time in American history miners would have to pay the federal government for what they took from the public domain, and they resented it. Additionally, they failed to take seriously the concerns of environmental organizations, making a mockery of Bible's plea, "Mining must join the crusade for environmental quality controls." [17] Self-interest and disregard for the environment remained the twin pillars on which the western mining industry had been built, and it remained unchanged in the 1970s.

While the western mining industry continued to be its own worst enemy, American foreign policy only made matters worse. Bible had warned for years of the dire consequences of American dependence on foreign sources for raw materials; by the 1970s the situation had deteriorated still further. In 1973, in response to the Yom Kippur War, the Organization of Petroleum Exporting Countries (OPEC) announced that it would no longer ship oil to countries that supported Israel. The effects were immediate. Thrown into chaos due to its reliance on foreign sources of raw materials, the United States suffered from unprecedented inflation for the rest of the decade. It was no surprise to Bible that foreign producers were holding America hostage, but the magnitude of the problem he had forecast for almost two decades shocked him. [18]

The foreign policy Bible assailed struck him as unrealistic and dangerous, particularly when balanced against domestic demands. But the nation's overall energy policy most frustrated him. In 1968 he was appointed to the Joint Congressional Committee on Atomic Energy to succeed Senator Richard Russell (D-Georgia), who had died. Bible immediately used his new position for two purposes: to jettison the Committee on the District of Columbia, on which he had served for eleven years, and to develop an expanded commitment to peaceful uses of atomic energy. While a national minerals and fuel policy had never been established with a long-range commitment, atomic energy provided a one way to move America beyond its reliance on traditional fossil energy sources and foreign domination.

A policy on new energy sources proved as difficult to enact as one on minerals development. On March 24, 1971, Bible introduced S. 1349, the Nuclear Geothermal Power Research and Demonstration Act of 1971, to complement P.L. 91-581, which passed in 1970. The bill authorized the leasing of public lands for geothermal development. Bible argued that his measure was an important step along the path toward energy independence by providing alternate means for electrical power instead of continuing to rely on fossil fuels, which were nonrenewable and a major source of pollution. But the Senate failed to enact Bible's plan.[19]

In November 1971 President Nixon froze the $2.5 million that Congress had appropriated for alternative energy research. Bible was not only angry but confused, because the president's special message to Congress listed the energy crisis as his administration's top priority. As Bible said, "Actions speak louder than words."[20] The Nixon administration differed little from the previous Democratic administrations in this insensitivity to the issue of nonpolluting, clean-burning energy sources and the continued reliance on foreign energy. To be sure, the problem had become more acute and pressing. But in 1971 less money was available for discretionary domestic programs, and experimental energy development programs were yet another casualty of the Vietnam War.

Hence, the president and Congress continued to vacillate about energy and minerals, with no clear consensus. Legislators like Bible, who came face-to-face with the countervailing forces in the energy, minerals, and environmental protection fields, sought a balanced policy, but it proved elusive. The mining industry was far more intransigent than environmentalists, while energy producers continued to build power plants fueled by fossil sources. It was a vicious circle, with more than enough blame on all sides. The dilemma continued through the 1970s until the scare at Three Mile Island produced public rejection of nuclear power sources. The result was more reliance on finite fossil fuels and on foreign sources, particularly oil.

Moreover, mining and energy policy are land-use issues, and concerns about the environment had permeated all policy-making levels since the late 1950s. The failure to reach a consensus with land extractive industries contributed mightily to air and water pollution. Likewise, the western livestock business, which relied on the public domain to sustain its livelihood, came under attack from environmental groups more concerned with recreation than with cows. Overgrazing, no less than mining, destroys the natural landscape, causing erosion and polluting valuable watersheds. As with mining, Bible had to choose between his land-based constituents and the demands of environmentalists and recreationists—a replay of the conflicts over the Great Basin National Park.

But this problem went back much further. When the Taylor Grazing Act was enacted in 1934, it seemed like a major piece of conservationist legislation.[21] But as with the Reclamation Act of 1902, the results proved disappointing. The law did little to improve the condition of the public domain. Besides continuing to overgraze their cows and sheep, ranchers opposed every attempt by the Grazing Service, and later the Bureau of Land Management, to increase grazing fees and repair the damage caused by their abuse of the range. Like the Newlands Act, the Taylor Grazing Act made it possible for large livestock operators to consolidate their control over the public domain.

Livestock operators were the most powerful land-based interest group in Nevada, which forced Bible to defend them. While believing that they were the victims of unfair foreign competition and deserved a measure of protection, he defended their cause with considerably less enthusiasm than had his predecessor, Pat McCarran. Bible resented their dogged opposition to national parks, especially the Great Basin National Park. Almost without exception, his grazing constituents opposed what they considered unfair government regulation and increased grazing fees.

Indeed, grazing fees were at the core of the dispute between government regulators and the western livestock industry, with Bible caught squarely in the middle. Predictably, he rallied to the defense of his constituents and used his position as chairman of the Public Lands Subcommittee to press their interests. In 1962 he and other senators had succeeded in forcing a postponement of a 50 percent hike in the grazing fee schedule. After holding hearings in Reno in 1963, Bible repeated his request that Secretary Udall reconsider postponement of a fee increase because the cattle business was experiencing a serious depression. For Bible and other western senators, the tactic was always the same—another year of deference because the industry was depressed.[22] Bible ignored the reality that the Taylor Grazing Act was simply a subsidy to western cattle and sheep producers, who always seemed to want more federal dollars.

Despite pleas from Bible and others, Udall went ahead with the increase because it was needed and livestock raisers had been receiving a free ride for years. For example, the fee increased in 1951 from 8 cents to 12 cents AUM (Animal Unit per Month). In 1955 the price was set at 15 cents, and in 1958 it rose to 19 cents, based on a formula that pegged fees to livestock prices. In 1963 the fee jumped more than 50 percent, from 19 cents to 30 cents per AUM, with 10 cents of the new increase earmarked for range improvement. Yet the cost rose considerably more on lands not covered by the Taylor Grazing Act: Forest Service, 60 cents per AUM; Bureau of Indian Affairs, $1.25; and commercial rates, $3.00.[23]

In November 1965 the Department of the Interior began to study the procedures for establishing grazing fees. This prompted a strong reaction from Bible and Aspinall, chairman of the Public Land Law Review Commission. In a strongly worded letter to President Johnson, Aspinall asked him to defer the study until the PLLRC had completed its work and made its recommendations. Aspinall correctly asserted that new government regulations would only complicate his commission's work, but he also espoused the perspective of western representatives by opposing any hike in fees, no matter the circumstances. For whatever reason, the Johnson administration backed away from the issue.[24]

Meanwhile, on March 1, 1966, the State of Nevada, through its newly created Committee on Federal Land Laws, presented its preliminary case to the PLLRC. In a carefully worded statement, Nevada lawmakers said:

> Reformation of public land law practice should guarantee full and continuous state, local and private development or use of lands now in federal ownership for the maximum benefit of the state in which the lands are located with due regard for the needs of all the people.[25]

Nevada lawmakers wanted to liquidate the public domain. The committee later clarified its stand by emphasizing that "high priority to revenue production for state and counties by sale to private owners, grants to public agencies for use or sale, and by classification for disposition, be given by the PLLRC."[26] But thirteen years before Nevadans launched the much-heralded "Sagebrush Rebellion," they staked out a position opposing not only federal control, but public ownership of western lands.

Within a year the Nevada State Cattle Association followed the lead of the State Committee on Federal Lands. Like the state, the cattle association opposed both federal land ownership and outright private ownership. For example, the cattle association felt that those with grazing permits who purchased federal land should be allowed to deduct the permits' value from the land's appraised value because they had made "investments in the spirit of free enterprise in hopes of providing a family living and profit." However, if the permit holder chose not to buy the land on which the government had allowed grazing, the federal government or the new purchaser should provide compensation.[27] Apparently, the Nevada Cattle Association supported the free enterprise system when it came to compensation for permits, but not to the extent of paying $3 per AUM for commercial forage.

Little had changed as Bible began his third term, and the PLLRC report was still two years away. In the closing days of the Johnson administration the Interior Department again considered a plan to boost the fees charged to ranchers for using the public domain. Once more Bible rose to their defense, complaining that any increase would be "a tragic and unnecessary attempt to cripple the livestock industry in the West."[28] While the Johnson administration backed away, incoming Secretary of the Interior Walter Hickel approved the hike, incurring the wrath of western senators like Bible.

While the increase from 30 to 44 cents per AUM upset Bible, he was angrier at Hickel. He believed that the Nixon appointee had deceived him during confirmation hearings before the Senate Interior and Insular Affairs Committee, when Hickel agreed that any increase should await the PLLRC report. Nonetheless, the 1969 increase went into effect, but the Nixon administration canceled a similar proposal for 1970.[29]

In June 1970 the PLLRC finally issued its findings. To no one's surprise, it had something for everyone. But Nevada and its livestock raisers opposed federal ownership of public lands, so nothing in the commission's report supported their land liquidation plan.

Chapter 6 on range resources was encouraging because most of the recommendations for the public lands supported regional economic growth. While proposing more money for range improvement to aid the livestock industry, the commission recommended that "public grazing lands be retained in federal ownership to protect them against further deterioration and to rehabilitate them where possible."[30]

On a related front, Bible demonstrated his versatile land-use values. Wild horses and burros on the public domain needed protection from ranchers. On March 4, 1971, he co-sponsored S. 1116 to protect and manage the wild and free-roaming horses and burros in the West. The bill required all agencies concerned with land management to provide forage to sustain the animals, because livestock interests considered the horses and burros competitors for the sparse food supply. Bible quietly sidestepped his grazing constituents and supported preservationists to save part of Nevada's heritage.[31]

But in Bible's world of conflicting and competing constituent demands, schizophrenia, not consistency, was the rule. In the tug-of-war between grazing interests and other land users, he often supported opposing positions at the same time. On June 9, 1971, only three months after co-sponsoring the wild horse and burro act, he co-sponsored S. 2028 to amend the Taylor Grazing Act to give holders of grazing permits many of the rights and privileges of land ownership. Calling for a 20-year permit with nearly automatic renewal privileges, the proposal also gave the right to decide the range's carrying capacity to the owner, not the Bureau of Land Management or the Forest Service. Fortunately, the Senate took no action on the scheme to bestow possessory rights to grazing permit holders, and Bible dropped the matter.[32]

Thus, by 1974, as Bible was leaving the Senate, the essence of western regionalism had changed dramatically since the end of World War II. Mining and pastoral interests were no longer the dominant industries in the West. Now water—or, more accurately, water development—defined the nature of western culture. While the West as a region continued to support its land-based industries, as Bible's career demonstrates, water development made the new West an empire in agriculture, industry, and tourism. He completed his career much as he began it—as a dedicated reclamationist.

Bible stood squarely for the supremacy of state water rights and against the concept of federal reserve rights articulated in *Winters* v. *United States* and later in *Arizona* v. *California.* He was concerned about the secretary of the interior's growing power to determine the distribution of water from federally financed reclamation projects. These trends in western water law had practical meaning, especially in northern Nevada, where the perceived rights of Paiute Indians clashed with those of Anglo farmers over the Truckee River's waters. The fate of the California-Nevada Compact and the Washoe Project conceivably hung in the balance.

If the Washoe Project was to become an important source of water for irrigation, electric power, and municipal use, all sides had to agree on how much water could be used and by whom. In 1967 the TCID agreed to an annual delivery of 406,000 acre-feet a year from the Truckee and Carson rivers. On October 2, 1967, Secretary Udall approved the operating criteria for the Truckee-Carson river basins. The next year Bible secured $5 million for continued construction of the Stampede and Martis Creek dams, vital links in the Washoe Project.[33]

But the politics of western water development and the clash of economic interests over the years proved wasteful and inconsistent. The Pyramid Lake Paiutes opposed the Washoe Project until Secretary Udall assured them of another 60,000 acre-feet of water a year from the flow of the Truckee. Obviously, the Paiute water came from the amount available to the TCID. Then, on January 14, 1969, Udall, who was about to leave office, came out against the ratification of the California-Nevada Compact because it would bind Indian water claims to the terms of the compact, which the Interior Department considered unfair.[34]

Bible could not have disagreed more with his friend Udall. As always in water matters, he believed in state supremacy, which he saw the growing power of the federal government eroding. Worse yet, after thirteen years of negotiations and with a final solution in sight, Udall would reject the whole plan—the basis for the Washoe Project's future—because of theoretical Indian water rights. While the Supreme Court, in *Arizona* v. *California,* had given legal sanction to Indian water rights dating from the time the federal government established the reservations, the Paiutes of Pyramid Lake were unaffected because the *Orr Water Ditch* decree in 1944 had already determined their rights.[35]

But in the court of public opinion, the Paiutes were seen as victims in the struggle for a share of that precious and limited western resource—water. In a larger sense they were the victims, not only of a legal system that had ignored their rights for too long, but also of a reclamation mania that sought to redistribute every drop of water to someplace other than where it was located. By 1970 the whole reclamation system, originally envisioned as a step forward in democracy and self-sufficiency, had become an expensive and wasteful jumble of concrete that threatened the desert environment and the lives of those in it. There was not enough water to satisfy everyone's demands, including those of the Paiute Indians, but development interests and dam-builders, like Bible, refused to acknowledge this.

Meanwhile, conservation groups like the Sierra Club and popular magazines like *American Heritage* rallied around the Paiute cause, portraying Nevada ranchers, water companies, power users, and the federal government as villains in the alleged rape of Pyramid Lake.[36] But in the allocation of scarce resources like water, there were bound to be winners and losers, especially when the government refused to admit that the desert's resources were limited. By 1970 northern Nevada, the government, and reclamationists came face-to-face with the stark reality that there was not enough water to satisfy everyone's demands.

When Congress failed to approve the compact, it left California and Nevada much as they had been before negotiations began: uncertain as to their future rights and sources of water. Ironically, the Paiutes also lost because in 1983 the Supreme Court, in *Pyramid Paiute Tribe of Indians v. Truckee-Carson Irrigation District*, ruled that the 1944 decree in the *Orr Water Ditch* case had settled the question of Indian water claims to the Truckee.[37] In the end no one was satisfied with the outcome—the Indians, the states, the federal government, or Bible, who had labored for nearly twenty years in the cause of northern Nevada reclamation. But from a strictly legal position, ethics and morality notwithstanding, the compact provisions did not violate Indian water rights. Congress should have ratified the deal, as Bible wished.

Moreover, it is extremely unlikely that a bi-state compact could have been enacted after 1972. For a decade California had been moving in the opposite direction from Nevada in the area of water resource development. Earlier in the century, when the California Supreme Court upheld the rights of riparian users in *Herminghaus v. Southern California Edison Company* (1926), the public's reaction had been so violently opposed to the antigrowth opinion that lawmakers amended the state constitution to embrace the concept of water development for maximum economic benefit. From 1928 to 1971 water development was the state's avowed aim.[38]

But when preservationists defeated the Dos Rios Dam project, California entered a new era. In 1972 California passed a tough wild and scenic rivers act that severely limited the commercial development of its river system. Clearly, the state's water policy had changed significantly. A decade later California moved far ahead of Nevada by embracing the "public trust doctrine," which allowed preservationist groups to contest all water projects because of their potential impact on the environment.[39]

While any prospect for agreement on a bi-state compact appears impossible, California and Nevada have moved in lock-step on the concept of state water supremacy. Bible had long supported the idea articulated in section 8 of the 1902 Newlands Reclamation Act. As Bible read the act, it was a clear and unambiguous congressional expression of the supremacy of state water laws, and few, if any, western senators would have disagreed. After the 1963 Supreme Court decision in *Arizona* v. *California*, western senators moved ahead to change the court's direction of granting broader powers to the federal government through the Department of the Interior and its Bureau of Reclamation.

In 1965 and again in 1967 Bible joined with his friend from California, Thomas Kuchel, to roll back federal authority. They designed S. 2530, introduced on October 12, 1967, and known as the Water Rights Act of 1967, to implement section 8 of the 1902 Reclamation Act by requiring the federal government to follow state procedures and laws. The act would also have repudiated the doctrine of federal reserve rights to all state water by virtue of land withdrawals. While the Senate failed to act on the Kuchel-Bible proposal, the issue remained alive.[40] On February 10, 1970, Senator Clifford P. Hansen of Wyoming, a fellow member of the Interior and Insular Affairs Committee, wrote to ask Bible for his support and influence with the PLLRC to oppose the reserve rights doctrine, which the federal government was using to take over the administration of state waters. Western sentiment notwithstanding, the PLLRC recommended not that the reservation doctrine be repealed, but that Congress clarify and limit it for orderly planning.[41] Again, Congress failed to act, and the practical effect was federal dominance in the field of western water law.

When Bible left office in 1974, it appeared that his long-fought battle to uphold section 8, largely the handiwork of fellow Nevadan Francis Newlands, had been lost.

But in 1978 California took up the cause in *California* v. *United States*. The simple issue was whether the state, by virtue of section 8, had authority to regulate state water or the federal government had the power to do so as a result of a long line of court decisions following the Pelton Dam case. In *Ivanhoe Irrigation District* v. *MacCracken* (1958), the Supreme Court had ruled that section 8 did not permit states to regulate water use by the federal government. Still later, in *City of Fresno* v. *California* (1963), the court held that the Bureau of Reclamation could overrule state water rights to acquire water for federal dams.[42]

On July 3, 1978, speaking through Associate Justice William Rehnquist, the Supreme Court upheld section 8 and the supremacy of state water laws.[43] Once again the federal-state relationship in the West had taken a new and dramatic turn in the direction of states' rights—one that Bible had favored for so long. Yet, while the balance of power has shifted toward the states, the water problems are unchanged. The arid West lacks water; this will remain, as it always has been, the region's leading problem, made more acute by unprecedented population growth.

While western water law was evolving along the lines Bible advocated, he did change direction and move toward the views of environmental preservationists. To be sure, Bible was no John Muir, but neither was he the uncompromising, utilitarian-minded Nevadan who came to the Senate in 1955. Similarly, he was no longer the unabashed, uncritical apologist for the mining industry that he had been for most of his political career. Bible's attitude toward environmental issues changed slowly, but by 1968 they stood in stark contrast to the views of his mining friends such as Howard Gray, who, on November 25, 1968, telephoned Bible's office to say that he opposed the rumored appointment of Representative John Saylor to the post of interior secretary.[44] Bible also may have felt that the Nixon administration needed a westerner to head the Interior Department, but his view on parks and recreation was closer to Saylor's than to those of Gray and the American Mining Congress.

That became evident in Nevada between 1968 and 1974, when the development of the state's two key recreational areas, Lake Mead and Lake Tahoe, took center stage. Lake Mead was the most popular stop in the national park system, with 61 million tourists flocking to the dam and lake between 1936 and 1968. In 1968 alone tourism increased 10 percent over the previous year, and Bible kept pace by ensuring that facilities at Callville Bay, Echo Bay, Willow Beach, and Cottonwood Cove expanded to meet the recreational needs of southern Nevada and those who visited it.[45]

With the flood of new tourists each year came an increase in the cost of recreation, presenting Bible with the problem of getting larger appropriations while fending off Nixon's budget-conscious administration. Management costs rose from $527,000 in 1967 to $612,000 in 1970. The inevitable confrontation came in April 1970, when Bible lashed out at Nixon's budget for the National Park Service as "inadequate and unrealistic." It slashed nearly $2 million from the Lake Mead operation alone, inspiring Bible to predict a crisis in public recreation if "shortsighted economy were allowed to ignore established responsibilities and priorities."[46] Still, he had little room to complain: in August 1970 he obtained approval for an additional $809,000 for Lake Mead, which proved ample for its continuous operation.

While Bible struggled to maintain the status quo in southern Nevada, Lake Tahoe consumed far more of his energy and time. Lake Tahoe's economic development paralleled the area's environmental deterioration. The first large-scale exploitation of resources in the Tahoe Basin had been to fortify the deep silver mines of the Comstock: over a 20-year period 30 million board feet flowed from the basin to the mines each year. It cost more than $80 million in timber to remove about $400 million in minerals during the Comstock years.[47] Thus, by the end of the nineteenth century the forests around the lake had been decimated.

Adding to the problems were the battles between Lake Tahoe property owners and the Bureau of Reclamation in the early years of the twentieth century. At issue were water levels and planned outflows to service the irrigation needs of farmers in Fallon. Property owners feared that if water levels dropped, so would the recreational potential of their holdings. In the long run they were right; after 1945 the recreational value of lakefront property began to skyrocket.

Skiing led the way. The whole basin received a tremendous boost when the Squaw Valley resort hosted the 1960 Winter Olympic Games. The publicity and the avalanche of tourist dollars that the games generated led to further growth and urbanization on an unprecedented scale, both in seasonal tourism and in permanent residents.[48] This, coupled with casino construction on the Nevada side of the lake, brought California and Nevada into competition for every tourist dollar. During the boom period of the 1950s and 1960s neither state thought much about environmental deterioration until it threatened economic growth.

One of the early voices of concern was Bible's close friend and political ally Joseph F. McDonald, Sr. As editor of the *Nevada State Journal*, McDonald was the force behind the creation of the Nevada-California Lake Tahoe Association, which aimed to control growth in the Tahoe Basin. When the organization broke up amid conflicts over business profits, the Lake Tahoe Area Council was formed; by 1964 it had issued a regional development plan that sought to restrain the negative impact of unrestrained commercialism on the area. But it lacked the necessary enforcement machinery to compel the various counties (and the two states that controlled the land area around the lake) to follow its recommendations.[49]

Unfortunately, the federal government unintentionally magnified the basin's environmental problems. By supplying the money for pollution abatement and for a new sewage treatment system, the government generated more growth and development around the lake, adding to traffic congestion, smog, subdivisions, and commercial property expansion. Aware of the need for action, California and Nevada finally followed up on the Lake Tahoe Area Council idea and created a joint study committee to make recommendations for developing the basin. This, in turn, led in 1969 to the enactment of a bi-state compact, the Tahoe Regional Planning Agency (TRPA), dedicated to making proposals to both states. The TRPA was composed of representatives of identical state planning boards, the CTRPA in California and the NTRPA in Nevada.[50] The TRPA received the endorsement of Bible, Cannon, and Senator Alan Cranston (D-California).

But from the beginning the TRPA was hopelessly flawed. Its concern for tourist dollars and short-term profits meant continued environmental deterioration. Moreover, developers and commercial interests were snapping up the land around the lake, a situation similar to that of Cape Cod and the Indiana Dunes, which Bible had helped to halt in the early 1960s. Bible was worried about the pace of environmental destruction at the lake, which had been escalating since the end of World War II. So were Nevada lawmakers. Thus, on February 26, 1969, the Nevada legislature passed Joint Resolution No. 15, which called on Bible to introduce legislation to expand the Toiyabe National Forest to include as much lakefront property as possible and asked the Bureau of Outdoor Recreation to conduct a study and recommend land purchases by the federal government.[51]

On May 20, 1969, Bible introduced S. 2208 to authorize the study. On the Senate floor he remarked, "The lake is gravely threatened by the relentless march of commercial development. . . . We are in a race with the bulldozer of commercial development."[52] This was highly environmentalist rhetoric for Bible, and he was correct: California and Nevada growth interests had nearly destroyed one of the West's most beautiful areas in their relentless drive to build hot dog stands, condominiums, neon signs, and casinos. By 1969 Bible knew that he could save only a small portion of the Tahoe Basin for future public enjoyment.

Still, Bible opposed only crass commercial exploitation like resort development, not the commercializing of public recreation areas. Lake Tahoe prompted only the most recent expression of his thinking. To illustrate the point, on September 25, 1969, he wrote to Joseph F. McDonald, Sr., to inform him of the progress to expand the Toiyabe National Forest, telling him, "I share the goal of preserving much of the natural beauty that remains at Lake Tahoe." But on April 7, 1970, Bible succeeded in getting $379,000 from the land and water conservation fund to improve the facilities at Sand Harbor to "help finance utilities and boat launching facilities, roads and parking, eight comfort stations, and eighty picnic units."[53] As with federal assistance for sewage treatment, better recreation facilities just made matters worse by attracting more and more people to the area.

Although it seemed like a clash between preservation and prosperity, from Bible's perspective, it was far better to keep Lake Tahoe for public use than for private greed. On December 20, 1969, he introduced S. 3279 to extend the Toiyabe National Forest's boundaries to include about 12,920 acres, with six miles of undeveloped shoreline on the Nevada side of the lake. The cost was roughly $12.5 million, supplied by the Land and Water Conservation Fund. On April 9, 1970, J. Phil Campbell, undersecretary of agriculture, recommended enactment of S. 3279, which President Nixon signed on August 5, 1970.[54]

Trying to slow the commercialization of Lake Tahoe, Bible used the federal government's expanded presence to counter the TRPA. The issue came to a head in September 1971, when the Bureau of Outdoor Recreation recommended spending $70 million to buy land to protect the entire basin both from the TRPA and from uncoordinated federal expenditures that only exacerbated existing environmental problems. Unhappy with the report's conclusions, Secretary of the Interior Rogers C. B. Morton had the original BOR draft destroyed and a new report issued. In March 1973 he turned down a proposal for a national lakeshore in deference to local development interests and their spokesman on the TRPA.[55] He apparently gave in to development interests at the expense of the environment.

Despite Secretary Morton's reluctance to stand firm against local developers, Bible moved ahead to bring as much of the Tahoe shoreline as possible under federal protection. His target was the land held by the George Whittel estate. Originally purchased in 1936, the land, nearly 10,000 acres, stretched from Crystal Bay in the north to Zephyr Cove in the south. After nearly two years of negotiation with the Department of the Interior New York financier Jack J. Dreyfus bought the land from the Whittel estate before the government could act. Dreyfus planned to build a medical foundation on his lakefront property. In December 1971 Bible joined with the Forest Service to negotiate the purchase of the land from Dreyfus.[56]

Bible managed to wrest most of the land from Dreyfus, but not before agreeing that the financier could keep 141 acres of prime lakefront property—a necessary concession. Still, Bible faced the difficult task of juggling the Interior Department budget bill to pay the $11.8 million price tag. He took $8.1 million in land and water conservation funds from twenty-four other states to buy Dreyfus's land. From Nevada's standpoint, he had once again come through when it counted.[57]

Lake Tahoe's growth continued at an accelerated pace, triggered by the proliferation of gambling, which in turn contributed to increased traffic congestion, air pollution, and declining water standards. By 1970, 75 percent of the area's marshes, 50 percent of its meadows, and 15 percent of its forests had disappeared.[58] With political control firmly in the hands of local interests, it is a small miracle that any lakeshore was spared from commercial development. Bible deserves much of the credit for preserving the few hundred acres that were left for public use.

On the national front, environmentalists and their friends in Congress still had the momentum in the early 1970s. They pushed an impressive array of national parks, monuments, and historic sites through Bible's Parks and Recreation Subcommittee. Bible was committed to continuing the march of Johnson's Great Society into the Nixon years, despite budget cuts and the administration's clear lack of leadership and interest in the environmental field. Between 1969 and 1972 Bible's subcommittee helped add twenty-nine new areas to the National Park Service inventory (see table 9). The movement to protect America's scenic beauty had not yet run its course.

Yet, while Bible's Senate colleagues had long recognized his leadership in creating a vast assortment of parks and recreation areas, the public outside Nevada hardly knew his name. Ralph Nader's congressional study group correctly gauged Bible's national reputation when it described him as a candidate for "Senator Who."[59] He avoided national publicity while others like Henry Jackson, Hubert Humphrey, and the Udall brothers took the limelight. Preferring, because of his temperament, to be the invisible leader of his subcommittee, Bible remained the consummate Senate type: a work horse rewarded by the esteem of his colleagues, not the public. Unlike many who claimed credit for major accomplishments in the area of parks and recreation development, he had no need for publicity because he sought neither a higher office nor identification with a national cause.

Nonetheless, in the early 1970s Bible began to win acclaim outside his home state and the Senate. In 1970 he received the Special Medal Award from the American Scenic and Historic Preservation Society, a nonprofit organization dedicated to protecting America's scenic and historic treasures (conservation leader Horace M. Albright served as honorary president and trustee when the group honored Bible). Later he received the National Distinguished Service in Conservation Award from the National Wildlife Federation.[60]

But Bible's most significant contribution to the American public came after

TABLE 9

Major Legislation, Subcommittee on Parks and Recreation, 1969–1972 (Senator Alan Bible, Chairman)

1969–1970

Voyageurs National Park	Minnesota
Florissant Fossil Beds National Monument	Colorado
Chesapeake and Ohio Canal National Historic Park	Maryland
Apostle Islands National Lakeshore	Wisconsin
Sleeping Bear Dunes National Lakeshore	Michigan
Gulf Islands National Seashore	Mississippi and Florida
William Howard Taft National Historic Site	Ohio
Eisenhower National Historic Site	Pennsylvania
Lyndon B. Johnson National Historic Site	Texas
Fort Point National Historic Site	California
Andersonville National Historic Site	Georgia
Ford's Theatre National Historical Site	Washington, D.C.

1971–1972

Fossil Butte National Monument	Wyoming
Hohokam Pima National Monument	Arizona
Buffalo National River	Arkansas
Cumberland Island National Seashore	Georgia
Golden Gate National Recreation Area	California
Gateway National Recreation Area	New York and New Jersey
Glen Canyon National Recreation Area	Utah and Arizona
Lower Saint Croix National Scenic River	Wisconsin and Minnesota
Lincoln Home National Historic Site	Illinois
Puukohola Heiau National Historic Site	Hawaii
Grant-Kohrs Ranch National Historic Site	Montana
Longfellow National Historic Site	Massachusetts
Gulf Islands National Seashore	Florida
Mar-A-Lago National Historic Site	Florida
Thaddeus Kosciuszko Home National Memorial	Pennsylvania
Benjamin Franklin National Memorial	Pennsylvania
John D. Rockefeller, Jr., Memorial Parkway	Wyoming

Source: Wirth, *Parks, Politics, and the People,* 327.

he left office, and it has gone virtually unnoticed—his role in preserving Alaska's pristine lands. As George B. Hartzog, Jr., said, Bible was "a man who, more than any other in Congress, held the keys to life and death for the National Park System. . . . He controlled all of the legislation for the National Park System and all its appropriations to implement such legislation."[61] Without question, Bible played a crucial part in saving the Alaskan wilderness and was the one man the Park Service had to have in its corner if it had any chance of protecting large blocks of wilderness.

From the beginning in 1959 Bible had supported Alaska's statehood drive in the Interior and Insular Affairs Committee. But in the decade after it entered the union he had no contact with land issues in Alaska, and no legislation came before his Public Lands or Parks and Recreation subcommittees. This changed with a well-publicized oil discovery in 1968 on the north slope, prompting Secretary of the Interior Udall's order to freeze all land disposals. Thus, oil profits, the growing energy crisis, and the momentum of the environmental movement all came together to make Alaska the celebrated cause of the 1970s, just as the Echo Park Dam fight had been in the 1950s and ecology itself had been in the 1960s.[62]

Initially, it seemed safe to assume that Bible would support a balanced approach to protect development interests. After all, oil exploration might help alleviate the growing energy crisis. Equally importantly, Alaska's two senators, Ted Stevens and Mike Gravel, were dedicated to developing the state's rich storehouse of natural resources. Moreover, while environmental groups still maintained considerable clout in and out of Congress, the feeling was growing across the nation and on Capitol Hill, as part of a general backlash against the liberalism of the 1960s, that their objectives threatened American business productivity and should be tempered by the realities of the business world.[63]

This was the situation in 1969, when the House took up the Alaska Native Claims Settlement Act, whose provisions protected 76 million acres of pristine land for inclusion in national interest categories. The protectionist clause was defeated; John Saylor, the ranking minority member of the House Committee on Interior and Insular Affairs, told Hartzog that the fight could only be won in the Senate. Hartzog went to see "Scoop" Jackson of Washington, chairman of the Senate Interior and Insular Affairs Committee.[64]

While Jackson was supportive, he insisted that Hartzog see Bible, whose Subcommittee on Parks and Recreation had the primary responsibility for the Alaska native claims bill. Bible told Hartzog that he had never been to Alaska and was unfamiliar with the goals the National Park Service had set for the state. He said that the wishes of Alaska's two senators would guide him, and Hartzog knew all too well that they opposed any strong national park presence in their state. The cause, at least from Hartzog's perspective, might have seemed hopeless; he knew that Bible opposed any park plan that lacked the support of the local congressman and the state's two senators. But, always on the "sell," Hartzog invited Bible to vacation in Alaska. Though such a small matter, the fortunes of Alaska would be changed.[65]

Bible had visited many places in the United States and seen most of its scenic wonders. Comparisons with Nevada were inevitable: the gray-brown sagebrush landscape of the Great Basin provided a stark contrast to the wet, green, and wooded areas of many national parks. Other parks, particularly in the semiarid West, possessed spectacular scenic vistas that were largely missing from Nevada, except for Lake Tahoe and areas of White Pine County. Still, Bible never seemed to have been so captivated that his preservationist instincts commanded his full attention. Alaska changed that.

Hartzog did his work well. He guided the Bible party all over the state and explained the Park Service's goals for the area. Whether fishing, camping, or sightseeing, Bible was struck by the raw natural beauty, fabulously rich wildlife, and vast unspoiled wilderness of Alaska. All of those who were there agree that Bible's Alaska trip dramatically altered his perspective. After marveling at the land, wildlife, and undeveloped lakes and streams, Bible left the last frontier with a renewed dedication to preserving the area for the use and enjoyment of future generations.[66] To be sure, Bible only saw Alaska, unlike John Muir and Bob Marshall (author of the Forest Service's Regulations to Create Wilderness), who lived in the Alaskan wilderness. Nonetheless, the effect was the same on all three men.

Bible invited Hartzog to his home for a few days of rest and relaxation before returning to Washington, D.C. He asked Hartzog to draft language for the Alaska bill that would accomplish the Park Service's objectives. The result was section 17(d) (2), introduced by Bible at the mark-up session of the Alaska Native Claims Settlement Act (1971) before the Subcommittee on Parks and Recreation. The section withdrew 80 million acres of Alaskan state lands for inclusion in four national interest categories: national parks, forest service, fish and wildlife, and wild and scenic rivers. In addition, section 17(d) (2) provided that the secretary of the interior make recommendations for disposition of the land to Congress by December 1973; Congress had until December 1978 to act on the secretary's proposals.[67] Bible had given Hartzog 4 million more acres than he had originally requested and more than the House had provided for earlier.

Bible's action typified his approach to land-use issues. While section 17(d) (2) protected large areas of Alaska from exploitation, Bible also gave Congress time to study the matter and make sound decisions for the state's economic development. Like Hartzog, he knew that Alaska represented a chance for the nation to protect some of the most spectacular unspoiled land in the world. But while Congress had time to contemplate the future course of Alaska, so did the developers. They immediately focused on Secretary of the Interior Rogers C. B. Morton, who succeeded Udall in 1969. Their goal was to remove as much of the section 17(d) (2) land as possible from the protection of the National Park Service and have it placed under the Forest Service or Fish and Wildlife Management System, where it would be more accessible to them in the future.[68]

On December 17, 1973, Morton made his recommendations to Congress; as in the Tahoe matter, he demonstrated that the developers had lobbied well. Specifically, he recommended only 32 million of the 80 million acres that Bible had sought to protect through section 17(d) (2) for the National Park System, dividing the rest between the Forest Service (18,800,000) and the Wildlife Refuge System (31,590,000). Hartzog was hopping mad, particularly when Morton also recommended that sport hunting be allowed to continue in areas designated for national parks.[69] Again the battle lines were drawn. But this time, unlike the previous twenty years of upheaval over land-use policy, Bible was not present. He retired just before Congress began a new round of hearings and proposals on Alaska in January 1975.

Between 1973 and 1980 Congress struggled with land claims in Alaska. With Bible gone from the scene and Hartzog the victim of Nixon's politicizing of the National Park Service, the fight was left to others, principally Henry Jackson in the Senate and Morris Udall in the House, chairmen of their respective Interior and Insular Affairs committees. Jackson and Udall received support from a formidable array of environmental groups, and together they held off the development interests until a president more sympathetic to the cause occupied the White House—Jimmy Carter.[70]

Unlike Secretary Morton, Carter's secretary of the interior, Cecil D. Andrus, had a record of support for environmental causes, and Alaska proved no exception. In November 1978 he boldly withdrew 10 million acres of Alaskan lands for three years under the federal Land Protection and Management Act. A month later President Carter followed suit by proclaiming another 56 million acres protected from exploitation by the 1906 Antiquities Act.[71] Carter and Andrus had certainly saved the day, because time was running out: if Congress had failed to designate the use of section 17(d) (2) land by December 1978, it automatically would have become available to the State of Alaska for disposal (and no doubt the developers would have held the upper hand).

The actions of Carter and Andrus set the stage for the compromise achieved on December 2, 1980, when the president signed the Alaska National Interest Lands Conservation Act. As with all legislation, no one was

wholly satisfied, but on balance environmental organizations and their advocates in Congress did well, particularly considering the likely result had
President Ronald Reagan been allowed to make the final determination. The
act set aside 43.6 million acres for national parks, 53.8 for the Fish and Wildlife Service, and 3.4 for the National Forest Service, with 56.4 million acres
designated as wilderness (27 percent of the state).[72] A significant portion of
Alaska had been protected—and just in time. The environmental movement
that began in the 1950s with the fight over the Echo Park Dam had run its
course in Alaska; the 1980s belonged to developers and growth advocates.

In assessing what had been achieved in Alaska, George Hartzog, Jr.,
writes:

> Many people rightfully can claim credit for the great treasures that have
> been preserved for all generations in Alaska, and quite properly they
> should get that credit for many hands were on the oars. But the captains
> of the vessel that preserved the opportunity were Scoop Jackson and
> Alan Bible. Had it not been for them there would have been no work for
> the others in the years that followed the enactment of the Alaska Native
> Claims Settlement Act of 1971.[73]

Nor was Hartzog alone in his assessment of Bible's contributions to the
National Park System. On August 28, 1970, Senator Lee Metcalf of Montana
took the Senate floor to pay tribute to Bible during consideration of the Redwood National Park Bill in California. While institutional deference should
be taken into account, Metcalf's comments deserve to be quoted at length:

> When we are talking about conservation and the challenge of meeting
> the outdoor recreation demands of a growing nation, one man stands at
> the top in terms of accomplishment. I doubt that enough attention has
> ever been directed to the man and his work—the senior senator from
> Nevada, Alan Bible. During more than a decade in the U.S. Senate, Alan
> Bible has clearly established himself as a leading conservation figure.
> Certainly, his record in the area of parks and recreation is unmatched.
>
> As chairman of the Parks and Recreation Subcommittee and, before
> that, the Public Lands Subcommittee, Senator Bible has been instru-
> mental in passing legislation that has added no less than 47 new areas
> to the National Park System. And that record, I believe, is about to be
> greatly extended with the passage in the 90th Congress of bills creating
> two new landmark national parks—the Redwood National Park bill we
> are considering today and the North Cascades National Park and re-
> lated recreation and wilderness areas. This is a record unequaled by any
> other senator in his position in the history of Congress. I submit it as

a record that represents the greatest period of recreation development ever witnessed by our nation.

Senator Bible's calm guiding hand was largely responsible for solving the complex problems that had thwarted progress on the Redwood National Parks bill. It was the same effective capacity for overcoming obstacles that made his record of achievement possible.

Under Senator Bible's leadership we have seen the long overdue resurgence of national recreation areas, national seashores, and national lakeshores designed to provide for the badly neglected recreation needs of those in crowded urban areas. We have seen two new national parks— Canyonlands and Guadalupe Mountains. And we have seen many historical parks and national monuments established.[74]

Finally, Senator Jackson called Bible "the guiding force behind the greatest expansion and development of the National Park System in American history." As the key figure in the Senate, among his colleagues, "Alan Bible's name is synonymous with parks in federal and private lands all over the country." Jackson's conclusions serve as a well-deserved tribute:

A listing of legislation Senator Bible has piloted into enactment by Congress in the 1960s and 1970s reads like a roll call of the nation's national parks and historic treasures. He has earned the gratitude of the American people for his role in preserving their natural, scenic, recreation and historic heritage.[75]

Chapter Twelve

Conclusion

Whatever the merits and faults of his ideology—or lack of it—Alan Bible must be judged by his public policies and official acts, which were rooted in the bleak, sand and sagebrush of Nevada. He recognized that Nevada's economic development depended on traditional land-based industries and water reclamation projects. But the mineral and water resources available were often not enough to expand the state's economic base and relieve the chronic distress of boom and bust. So Bible looked to the federal government for aid in water resource development and subsidies to stabilize the mining industry. From his perspective, the flow of federal dollars into Nevada was federalism operating at its highest and best level. He deplored federal intervention except when it served his purpose, which it often did, as in the government's retention of western lands and the creation of national parks. Nevertheless, he paid close attention to those who made their living from the land, whether miners or ranchers.

Bible's career was grounded on the adage that "all politics is local." He always remembered his roots and the priorities of the people back home. Throughout his career jobs were a central issue and the key to his support for mining and reclamation causes in Nevada. He was a practical, realistic, and sober politician who faithfully focused on Nevada first while avoiding most of the controversial national issues of his day—including civil rights and the Vietnam War. For Bible, his job was simple: to represent the economic interests of his constituents and avoid conflict with those who could help him reach his objective.

Consequently, Bible fit well into the "get along, go along" Senate of the 1950s. He accepted its folkways and traditions. He was fond of his southern colleagues for their congeniality and their moderate to conservative view of public policy. He was at home among the small groups that controlled the Senate's inner club, because he was an agreeable man who enjoyed the company of others. There Bible came under the spell of Lyndon Johnson.

Johnson had an enormous impact on Bible's career and Nevada's development. From the beginning of their relationship in 1954 Johnson arranged Bible's committee assignments. In 1959 he maneuvered Bible onto the Appropriations Committee—a major reason for his power and influence. When

Johnson became president, Bible relied on his friend and mentor to secure passage of the Southern Nevada Water Project, which proved to be the most important piece of legislation for Nevada since the construction of Hoover Dam.

The Bible-Johnson relationship was based largely on mutual friendship and accommodation. Johnson could always rely on Bible's vote, and Bible could expect Johnson's help on projects vital to Nevada. But there was another dimension: loyalty. Johnson and Bible had learned from their mentors, Sam Rayburn and Pat McCarran, that loyalty in politics meant a great deal, and Bible was as loyal to his friends as Johnson was to his. Even decades after McCarran's death Bible never criticized or maligned him. He would acknowledge all of the "boss's" faults, but add that McCarran was his friend and he was not going to criticize him. It never seemed to bother him that others assailed McCarran and his methods, but he would not add his voice to the chorus.[1]

In 1968, when Johnson came under intense fire for his Vietnam policy, Bible was not among the critics. Although he avoided mentioning Johnson in his reelection campaign, he did not break with the president, as many other Democrats did—some for political reasons and others out of a sense of moral obligation. Bible cared little about foreign policy unless it affected Nevada economically, and his constituents felt similarly. But the reason he stood by the president's Vietnam policy was loyalty. Johnson had treated Bible well, and he could not bring himself to abandon the president after all that he and his state had received through the years.

The Bible-Johnson relationship reveals Bible's strengths and weaknesses. His loyalty to his friends, faithfulness to his committee work, reliability as a team player, and faith in the Senate institution were his major strengths. But he was not a risk-taker or idealist. Thus, he avoided taking a stand on civil rights publicly, although he voted for the Civil Rights Act of 1964. He never embraced the cause of civil rights because it was not a major issue in predominantly conservative Nevada, whose black population was small. Bible acted similarly when it came to Vietnam. If he had doubts about the war during the Johnson years, he kept them to himself, preferring instead for others to voice their concerns and objections.

But Bible's most glaring weakness was his excessive caution, sometimes to the point of inaction. He spent so much time studying all sides of an issue that he often became paralyzed when he had to decide on a course of action. He was prone to vacillate and frequently irritated close friends like Chester Smith with his indecisiveness.[2] Still, his strengths offset his shortcomings, particularly in the legislative arena.

Bible believed that his constituents would judge him by what he accomplished for them. That meant support for mining, livestock raising, and water development. In 1954 he asked for committee assignments that reflected Nevada's interests as well as his own, principally Appropriations. He ended up on the Interior Committee, where he stayed for twenty years. He became chairman of its Subcommittee on Public Lands and later Parks and Recreation, where he had a major impact on land-use policy throughout the nation. But the Appropriations Committee proved to be the key to his power. For fifteen years Bible sat on major subcommittees that distributed funds for vital water and public works projects throughout the West. During the 1960s he held all the important positions, from enacting legislation to authorizing appropriation, for the expansion of the national park system.

Bible was a work horse who combined expertise, fairness, and honesty with a low-key approach to legislative matters. He was publicity-shy, preferring to work behind the scenes, where he was at home with his colleagues. Bible liked almost everyone, regardless of ideology or partisanship, and never allowed policy preferences to cloud his personal feelings about another senator. In twenty years he could recall only three colleagues he disliked—Robert Kennedy (D–New York), John Tower (R–Texas), and Jacob Javits (R–New York)—and all for the same reason: each of them treated his colleagues in a distinctly unsenatorial manner, with arrogance and a disregard for expertise and personal feelings.[3]

None of these factors would have been nearly so important if the Democratic Party had not controlled the Senate for the twenty years that Bible served. As a member of the majority party, he was able to rise through the seniority system to become chairman of important subcommittees that were key in Nevada's economic development. Moreover, during the 1960s he benefited mightily from the proliferation and power of congressional subcommittees whose influence is still apparent today. Subcommittee chairmen, like Bible, are less powerful than chairmen of permanent standing committees, but they set their own agendas, have their own staff assistants, and are rarely challenged in their recommendations.

Bible's greatest legislative successes were in water and recreation development in Nevada. Here he received a boost from regional forces that combined after World War II to advance western economic development through water reclamation. Bible had an unwavering belief in reclamation as the heart of Nevada's economic future. From the Washoe Project in northern Nevada to the Southern Nevada Water Project, and a dozen other lesser plans, he labored for twenty years to expand Nevada's economic base. While northern Nevada's dependence on water from California complicated its development, southern Nevada had no such handicap. The Southern Nevada Water

Project was the key factor in the tremendous growth of the Las Vegas area from the 1960s through the 1980s.

As the spokesman on water issues in Nevada and the father of the project, Bible changed the political power base in the state. The proliferation and prosperity of casino gambling would have been impossible without the Southern Nevada Water Project. No doubt unintentionally, Bible did more than any other man to cause the shift in power from Reno to Las Vegas, thereby contributing substantially to the gaming industry's expanding control over state politics. After the United States Supreme Court's decision in *Reynolds* v. *Sims* (1964), which mandated the one-person, one-vote, one-value principle, the Nevada legislature had to reapportion itself to reflect the population growth in Clark County, giving more power to the southern section of the state at the expense of northern rural counties. This shift coincided with the completion of the Southern Nevada Water Project, which allowed Las Vegas to increase both in population and in political clout and made Clark County the most powerful political unit in the state. The insignificance of mining and livestock alongside gaming revenues has left no other countervailing economic force. Consequently, northern Nevada has been unable to keep pace because of its limited water development, which has curtailed economic expansion.

Bible's influence was felt in other ways, particularly his efforts to rebuild the Nevada Democratic Party. McCarran's red-baiting and high-handed political tactics to consolidate his personal power nearly ruined the state party. He was able to get along with only his most loyal supporters. Almost overnight Bible changed priorities, because he was more interested in advancing state interests than in accumulating personal power. Unlike McCarran, he shared personal victories with others in the Nevada delegation, which contributed to forging a more united front on Nevada's behalf. Also in contrast to McCarran, Bible formed a bond with the state's junior senator, Howard Cannon; together they served as a powerful combination because they could usually work together and use their clout in tandem. The Bible-Cannon team was as effective as any Senate delegation in the 1960s, with the possible exception of that from Washington, where Democratic Senators Henry "Scoop" Jackson and Warren Magnuson worked equally well as an effective legislative team.

While Bible's political and legislative legacy for Nevada was substantial, his contribution to the expansion of national parks and recreation areas transcended his parochial interests. Beginning in 1946, as Bible was starting his second term as state attorney general, the columnist and historian Bernard DeVoto began his prolonged assault on western land use—or, more appropriately, land abuse. In the 1950s his articles in *Harper's* magazine attacked cattle raisers, miners, and reclamation enthusiasts with equal vigor, and he continued to pound away effectively by portraying the West as a "plundered province." DeVoto was a conservationist who wanted more national parks created in the West, which earned him the hatred of western land users, particularly ranchers.[4] He and others with similar views desired a larger federal presence in the West to protect it from destruction by the region's extractive economic interests. While Bible was a most unlikely ally, his low-key approach achieved many of DeVoto's goals, despite his general support for mining and reclamation causes.

Bible was surprisingly successful in legislating DeVoto's program without fanfare or undue public notice. Privately, he even wished that the federal government could control all of his beloved Lake Tahoe to prevent the environmental damage and exploitation that had been occurring since the end of World War II.[5] More ironically, Bible, a native Nevadan, contributed substantially to igniting the "Sagebrush Rebellion" in his home state in 1979 by doing so much to keep western lands out of the hands of state and private developers. The avowed goal of the rebels was the political and economic control of western lands to prevent federal land-use management.

Bible's record of supporting and creating national parks, particularly in the West, is conclusive evidence that he was not of the rebel ilk and therefore could not have joined their cause.[6] Bible often spoke of states' rights in the West and paid homage to his grazing constituents. But underneath his words ran the strong belief that to turn over the federal lands in the West to the states, or to private developers, would constitute a national tragedy. His land-use record stands in stark contrast to his state's heritage of environmental neglect.

Still, Bible suffered legislative setbacks, most notably his failure to establish Nevada's Great Basin National Park in the early 1960s. He labored long in behalf of the park, but in the end a combination of mining and livestock interests led by their spokesman, Walter Baring, defeated him. It is ironic that Nevada was the only state without a national park when Bible left office, despite his contribution in creating parks throughout the country.

Another failure was Bible's inability to stabilize the western mining industry. His twenty-year struggle to revitalize the mining economy was unsuccessful because the forces behind an emerging global economy were beyond his influence and control. Still, the cause of western miners demonstrated Bible's dedication to advancing state and regional economic interests. He also realized that, by failing to aid and encourage domestic sources for mining and energy, the United States was falling into a trap of dependence from which it would be difficult, if not impossible, to extricate itself.

Nevertheless, Bible's support for mining interests had limits. He realized that in order to survive the industry had to change its tarnished image and become more environmentally conscious. Although still supportive, he had become increasingly irritated by the late 1960s with mining companies that constantly refused to consider the effects of their industry on the environment. Surprisingly, given his caution and his commitment to his constituents, Bible accepted changing public attitudes, which many Nevadans still refused even to acknowledge.

When Bible began his Senate career, he was a dedicated conservationist. He believed that natural resources should be used for economic development, as did Theodore Roosevelt and Gifford Pinchot before him. But with the defeat of the Echo Park Dam in 1956 preservationists claimed their first victory, and the struggle between conservation and preservation was joined. Initially, the political clout of environmentally conscious organizations like the Sierra Club and Wilderness Society impressed Bible. Still, like Stewart Udall, he remained committed to conservation practices as the Kennedy and Johnson administrations forged ahead with new and larger water projects in the western states.

With increased responsibility came increased awareness. In 1965 Bible became the chairman of the Senate Subcommittee on Parks and Recreation. Exposure to the very real prospect of vanishing wilderness and recreation sites convinced him of the need for balance in land use. Thereafter, his avowed public policy stand became one of balance between preservation and exploitation. He tried to maintain this balance of competing and conflicting interests throughout his tenure as chairman of the subcommittee. Because he understood that compromise was essential in the political process, he was largely successful.

Bible was one of the invisible leaders of the "Conservation Congress" (88th Congress, January 9, 1963–October 3, 1964), which created the Wilderness Act, the Land and Water Conservation Act, and a host of new parks and recreation sites.[7] He became one of the legislative leaders of the environmental movement for the remainder of the decade and beyond. Bible constantly stressed the theme of balance, which was difficult because environmentalism had become a major force in national political life.

Lyndon Johnson announced the transition from conservation to preservation and preservation to ecology in a special message to Congress on February 8, 1965: "Our conservation must not be the classic conservation of protection and development . . . but with the total relation between man and the world around him."[8] The consciousness of the country had been awakened, even among such dedicated dam builders as Johnson and Bible.

In 1969 the National Environmental Policy Act (NEPA) became law, and a year later the first Earth Day celebration ushered in what became known as the "environmental decade."

Bible contributed to the early momentum of the environmental decade by including section 17(d) (2) in the Alaska Native Claims Settlement Act. Again, the theme of balance appears, not only in 17(d) (2), but in Bible's general ideas about Alaska. Like many Alaskans, he did not believe that the whole state was a fragile ecosystem that needed federal protection, but that Alaska should be permitted to develop and prosper from its natural resources.[9] Thus, he provided the key vote in the Senate to pass the Alaskan pipeline bill, which earned him the gratitude of Alaska's Senator Ted Stevens, who came from Washington, D.C., to Nevada to attend Bible's funeral. From Bible's perspective, the pipeline provided the needed balance between preservation and development.

Bible's Senate career spanned twenty years, 1954–1974, in which the West grew into the nation's most powerful region, both economically and politically. His career offers a window through which to view and review the issues and concerns of western leaders at a time of tremendous change. In many ways Bible was typical of other mountain state senators. He was a practical man who did not concern himself with affairs that were not part of his legislative agenda or related to his state's economic interest. To some degree, this reflected his desert heritage, where survival dictated a preoccupation with the immediate issues of prosperity and security, which were often difficult to achieve in the sagebrush country.[10] It also was related to his understanding of the function of the Senate, where constituent demands took center stage. Logrolling and pork-barrel politics were the order of the day, and Bible was an eager participant.

Eventually, ill health forced that eagerness to wane. During most of Bible's third term he suffered from a complicated and prolonged spinal disorder that affected his balance and depth perception. As his condition worsened and his sixty-fifth birthday approached, he decided not to seek a fourth term. He announced in August 1973 that he would retire from the Senate when his term ended. He tried to persuade former governor Grant Sawyer and Governor Mike O'Callaghan to run for his Senate seat, but each declined because neither wanted to leave Nevada for Washington, D.C. Even Bible's friend and colleague Senator Lloyd Bentsen of Texas, the 1988 Democratic vice-presidential candidate and later secretary of the treasury, was unable to persuade the extremely popular O'Callaghan to enter the race.[11] Thus, with the two best-known and most popular Democrats out of the 1974 race, Lieutenant Governor Harry Reid challenged former Republican governor Paul

Laxalt. Reid put up a spirited campaign, but lost by 611 votes out of 158,000 cast.[12]

Bible resigned his Senate seat before his term expired so that Laxalt could advance in seniority over other members of the 1974 freshman class, gaining an advantage for Nevada.[13] This was vintage Bible, more concerned about his state's welfare than his political party. His sense of duty was the hallmark of his political career and characterized his labors in behalf of Nevada.

While few Americans knew Bible's name, the reverse was true in Nevada, where he had been in the public eye for nearly four decades. He had a profound influence on the lives of Nevadans because he affected the course of Nevada's economic and political life. Recognition of this importance came as he prepared to leave the Senate. The Democratic *Nevada State Journal* called his service "unusual." The *Nevada Appeal* called him a "winner who put his seniority to good use." The *Las Vegas Review-Journal* said, "Bible served Nevada well in Washington." Even the traditionally Republican *Reno Evening Gazette* said, "Retiring Senator Bible did a splendid job for Nevada in 20 years of service." Jack McCloskey, publisher of the *Mineral County Independent*, a keen observer of Nevada politics for more than half a century and a Republican who supported both McCarran and Bible, wrote, "Alan Bible exemplifies the epitome of integrity and strong character. . . . there is such a thing as an honest lawyer-politician."[14]

Alan Bible died on September 12, 1988, fourteen years after ending his Senate career. He left a many-sided legacy for Nevada and the nation. Accomplishments and failures may be forgotten, but Bible faithfully served his state. Perhaps the greatest compliment came from Hank Greenspun, his old nemesis from the 1952 Democratic Senate primary. In 1961 Bible had obtained a pardon from President Kennedy for Greenspun, who was convicted of violating the Neutrality Act for running guns to Israel in the late 1940s. Greenspun wrote a fitting epitaph for the life and career of Alan Bible:

> Alan Bible's legacy was to let every person know that despite petty, cheap, vicious politics, a man can rise to the highest positions and win the admiration and confidence of his constituents. The only advice we can give to those who would seek a career in public life is to pattern their character after Alan Bible. If they do they will become, as he did, a public official in whom trust was not betrayed.[15]

Notes

CHAPTER ONE. THE MAKING OF A POLITICAL PROTÉGÉ

1. Nevada, State Planning Coordinator's Office, *Nevada Statistical Abstract*, 1981; Russell R. Elliott and William D. Rowley, *History of Nevada*, 404, 405; U.S. Department of Commerce, Bureau of the Census, Population, *Thirteenth Census of the United States*, vol. 3, 78–80. For the purposes of this study, the West is defined in geopolitical terms: the thirteen states west of the hundredth meridian originally included in the Western Conference of Senators formed by Nevada's Senator Pat McCarran in 1947. Texas and Oklahoma were later added to the conference, bringing the total of western states to fifteen. Alaska and Hawaii were included when they were admitted to the Union. Throughout this study, the term "western states" refers to all of the above. The mountain West includes the states bounded by the Sierra Nevada and Cascade Ranges on the west and the front ranges of the Rocky Mountains on the east.

2. Alan Bible, "Recollections of a Nevada Native Son: The Law, Politics, the Nevada Attorney General's Office, and the United States Senate," 1–17. Bible's brother, Milton Jacob Bible, was five years younger and was severely injured in World War II. He never married and died prematurely as a result of his war-related injuries.

3. Alan Bible interview by author, September 5, 1986; Loucile Bible interview by author, August 22, 1989.

4. Bible, "Recollections," 11.

5. Elliott and Rowley, *History of Nevada*, 401. For the most part, mining was in decline from 1881 to 1905 and did not begin to recover until 1906.

6. *The Reclamation Act of 1902*, P.L. 161, 57th Congress, 2d Session, June 17, 1902, 32 Stat. 388, 43 USCA 431; Russell R. Elliott, *Servant of Power: A Political Biography of Senator William M. Stewart*, 111–117; Wallace Stegner, *Beyond the Hundredth Meridian: John Wesley Powell and the Opening of the West*; Samuel P. Hays, *Conservation and the Gospel of Efficiency: The Progressive Conservation Movement, 1890–1920*. Professor William D. Rowley, University of Nevada, Reno, is currently in the process of writing the first full-scale biography of Francis G. Newlands. For an overview of the political career of Senator Newlands, see William D. Rowley, "Francis G. Newlands and the Promises of American Life," *Nevada Historical Society Quarterly* 32, no. 3 (Fall 1989): 169–180.

7. Bible interview by author, September 6, 1986; Michael Malone and Richard

Etulain, *The American West: A Twentieth Century History*, 19. For a detailed account of the Newlands Project, see John M. Townley, *Turn This Water into Gold: The Story of the Newlands Project*.

8. Bible, "Recollections," 22; *Los Angeles Times*, May 14, 1926.

9. Churchill County High School, *Lahontan* (Fallon: Eagle Press, 1923), 24, 25, 26, Churchill County Museum and Archives, Fallon, Nevada. In addition to being freshman and senior class president, Bible was a member of the forum debating team for three years and vice-president of his junior class.

10. Bible, "Recollections," 31; Laurada Hannifan interview by author, November 8, 1989. Mrs. Hannifan is the daughter of Joseph Jarvis, partner of Jacob Bible, in Fallon Mercantile, 1928–1945.

11. Bible, "Recollections," 33; Bible interview by author, September 6, 1986; Loucile Bible interview by author, August 22, 1989.

12. *Sagebrush*, February 3, 1928, and February 22, 1929; Bible, "Recollections," 47–50.

13. Ibid.

14. University of Nevada, Reno, *Artemisia* (Reno: Associated Students of the University of Nevada, 1930), 28, 39, 51, 163, 231, 234, 235, 240, 243. Besides being ASU treasurer in 1930, Bible was a member of the executive committee governing the student body, the finance committee, Coffin and Keys Service Fraternity, Blue Key Service Fraternity, Nu-Phi Nu Pre-Legal Society, and Clionia, a University of Nevada in Reno service fraternity (*Sagebrush*, February 15, 1926, 1).

15. Bible interview by author, September 6, 1986.

16. Hays, *Conservation and the Gospel of Efficiency*, 127; Malone and Etulain, *The American West*, 69–71. The only available biography of a Nevada political leader during the Progressive period is Loren B. Chan's *Sagebrush Statesman: Tasker L. Oddie of Nevada*. The most complete and balanced account of the Los Angeles–Owens Valley water dispute is William Kahrl's *Water and Power*.

17. Bible, "Recollections," 59, 60; interview by author, September 6, 1986.

18. Ibid.

19. Jerome E. Edwards, *Pat McCarran: Political Boss of Nevada*. This is a well-written and lively account of McCarran's rise to power in Nevada and his control of the political machinery through fear, intimidation, and patronage. There is no other book-length treatment of McCarran's political career in Nevada or in the U.S. Senate. Historians and political scientists have tended to concentrate more on the career of Key Pittman, probably because of his role as chairman of the Foreign Relations Committee during the battles over neutrality in the late 1930s. See Fred L. Israel, *Nevada's Key Pittman*. A more recent treatment is provided by Betty Glad, *Key Pittman: The Tragedy of a Senate Insider*.

20. Alan N. Holcombe, *Our More Perfect Union*, 207–209.

21. Political scientist Richard Fenno, Jr., uses the term "home style" to describe representatives' view of their constituency in *Home Style: House Members in Their Districts*. The concept is equally applicable to the Senate.

22. Bible, "Recollections," 65–90; interview by author, September 6, 1986.

23. Smith interview by author, August 30, 1989. Smith, Bible's campaign manager for all of his successful Senate races, agrees that he was not comfortable campaigning among large crowds and much preferred small groups or one-on-one contacts. As a result, Bible's campaign effectiveness was limited.

24. Bible, "Recollections," 61–63.

25. Jack Carpenter interview by author, October 27, 1987. Mr. Carpenter was press secretary and administrative assistant to Senator Bible for eighteen years.

26. Edwards, *Pat McCarran*, 131.

27. Gordon Rice interview by author, August 22, 1989; Bible, "Recollections," 94.

28. Bible, "Recollections," 95–127.

29. Ibid.

30. Russell R. Elliott, *Nevada's Twentieth-Century Mining Boom: Tonopah, Goldfield, Ely*, 242–245.

31. Bible interview by author, September 6, 1986.

32. Bible, "Recollections," 124–127.

33. Stephen Kemp Bailey, *Congress Makes a Law: The Story behind the Employment Act of 1946*, xi. See also Tip O'Neill and William Novak, *Man of the House: The Life and Political Memoirs of Speaker Tip O'Neill*, 26, 245; and Claude Denson Pepper and Hays Gorey, *Pepper: Eyewitness to a Century*, 47.

34. Chester Smith is extremely well informed on national and state issues from 1940 to 1970 and served in many capacities at the federal and state level. He was a staff assistant to Senator E. P. Carville in 1946 and legislative clerk and press secretary to Senator McCarran, 1947–1950 and 1953–1954. He was assistant and state budget director for Nevada from 1951 to 1953 under Governor Charles Russell; executive secretary to Senator Bible, 1954–1956; member of the Nevada Democratic Central Committee, 1957–1959; chief clerk for the U.S. Senate Committee on the District of Columbia, 1959–1960; and staff director and counsel, 1960–1968. Additionally, he served as staff director and general counsel for the U.S. Senate Committee on Small Business, 1969–1974, and chief counsel for the U.S. Senate Committee on Rules and Administration, 1974–1979.

Smith recalls attending a speech by Senator Pittman in Battle Mountain, Nevada, in 1940 when Pittman showed up an hour later and clearly had been drinking. After taking the platform he "upchucked" on his suit lapel. Chester Smith interview with author, October 19, 1993.

35. *Nevada State Journal*, October 22, 1938; Bible, "Recollections," 85. Bible remembered the cartoon and McCarran's reaction almost fifty years after the incident. Likewise, Gordon Rice never forgot McCarran's response. In fact, Rice has a 16 × 20 inch poster of the famous cartoon hanging in his law office in Reno. Interview by author, August 22, 1989.

CHAPTER TWO. DEFINING THE NEW EMPIRE:
THE ATTORNEY GENERAL YEARS, 1938–1950

1. Earl Pomeroy, *The Pacific Slope: A History of California, Oregon, Washington, Idaho, Utah, and Nevada*, 83–89; Richard Lillard, *Desert Challenge: An Interpretation of Nevada*, 29. Lillard's comment was cited in Jerome E. Edwards, "Nevada: Gambling and the Federal-State Relationship," *Halcyon: Journal of the Humanities* (1989): 237–254. See also Robert G. Athearn, "Colonialism: The Enduring Dilemma," in *Major Problems in the History of the American West*, ed. Clyde A. Milner II, 573–588.

2. Malcolm J. Rohrbough, *Aspen: The History of a Silver Mining Town, 1879–1893*.

3. Malone and Etulain, *The American West*, 97, 98, 106. Every county and city in Nevada benefited from New Deal expenditures. Las Vegas was a major beneficiary of programs and public works that provided a solid foundation for future growth. The best scholarly analysis of New Deal expenditures in Las Vegas is Eugene P. Moehring, "Public Works and the New Deal in Las Vegas, 1933–1940," *Nevada Historical Society Quarterly* 24, no. 2 (Summer 1981): 107–129. See also Office of Government Reports, Statistical Section, Report No. 10, *Nevada* (Washington, D.C.: GPO, 1940), vol. 2, 1–3.

4. Richard Lowitt, *The New Deal and the West*.

5. Elliott and Rowley, *History of Nevada*, 406. In addition to maneuvering the Silver Purchase Act through Congress, Pittman tried to control the administration of relief efforts in Nevada through the appointment of administrators. See Harold T. Smith, "Pittman, Creel, and New Deal Politics," *Nevada Historical Society Quarterly* 22, no. 4 (Winter 1979): 254–270.

6. Lowitt, *The New Deal and the West*, 64–80; Phillip O. Foss, *Politics and Grass: The Administration of Grazing on the Public Domain*, 120, 173–176, 202; Paul W. Gates and Robert W. Swenson, *History of Public Land Law Development*, 632.

7. Nevada, State Division of Archives and Records, Attorney General Case and Client Files, 1940–1950; Nevada, *Report of the Attorney General*, July 1, 1938, to June 30, 1940, 1941 Index of Opinions. Between 1938 and 1942 sixty-seven extradition cases were reviewed.

8. Jeanne Elizabeth Wier, "The Mystery of Nevada," in *Rocky Mountain Politics*, ed. Thomas C. Donnelly, 88–114; also Mary Ellen Glass, *Silver and Politics in Nevada, 1892–1902*.

9. Bible, "Recollections," 136; Nevada, *Political History of Nevada*, 275, 306; Bible interview by author, September 5, 1986.

10. *Boulder Canyon Project Act of 1928*, P.L. 642, 70th Congress, 1st Session, December 12, 1928, 45 Stat. 1057, 1064, 4 USCA 617; *Statutes of Nevada*, chapter 141, 341. See also *Statute 54*, 775, which authorized the State of Nevada as well as Arizona to tax the Boulder Canyon project.

11. Nevada, *Report of the Attorney General*, Opinion 339 July 1, 1940, to June 30, 1942.

12. Nevada, *Report of the Attorney General*, Opinion 18, July 1, 1943 to June 30,

1944. See also *City of Reno* v. *McGowan*, 84 Nev. 291 at 293, 439 P2d 895 (1968); and *State* v. *Lincoln County Power District*, 60 Nev. 401, 111 P2d 528 (1941).

13. E. P. Carville to Alan Bible, June 14, 1943; Robert W. Kenny to Alan Bible, December 29, 1943; Alan Bible to Robert W. Kenny, May 31, 1943 (Kenny solicited Bible's help in bringing to Senator McCarran's attention the urgent need to continue government contracts after the war to sustain western prosperity); Alan Bible to Senator Patrick McCarran, June 25, 1943; Nevada, State Division of Archives and Records, Attorney General Case and Client Files, 1940–1950.

14. Gerald D. Nash, *The American West Transformed: The Impact of the Second World War*.

15. Peter Wiley and Robert Gottlieb, *Empires in the Sun: The Rise of the New American West*; Malone and Etulain, *The American West*, 109; Carl Abbott, "The Metropolitan Region: Western Cities in the New Urban Era," in *The Twentieth Century West: Historical Interpretations*, ed. Gerald D. Nash and Richard W. Etulain, 71–98. For a detailed analysis of the growth of western cities, see Carl Abbott, *The New Urban America: Growth and Politics in Sunbelt Cities*. In the last few years regional and local studies have contributed to understanding the impact of World War II on western development. See Bradford Luckingham, *The Urban Southwest: A Profile History of Albuquerque–El Paso–Phoenix–Tucson*; Eugene P. Moehring, *Resort City in the Sunbelt: Las Vegas, 1930–1970*.

16. Abbott, "The Metropolitan Region," 80.

17. Elliott and Rowley, *History of Nevada*, 312.

18. Eugene P. Moehring, "Las Vegas and the Second World War," *Nevada Historical Society Quarterly* 29, no. 1 (Spring 1986): 1–30.

19. Paul Kleppner, "Politics without Parties: The Western States, 1900–1984," in *The Twentieth Century West*, ed. Nash and Etulain, 295–338. During most of the postwar period Nevada voted for Democratic Party candidates. Still, voters were highly influenced by personalities despite a heavy Democratic registration. For an analysis of Nevada voting patterns, see Elmer R. Rusco, *Voting Behavior in Nevada*, 71.

20. Nash, *The American West Transformed*, 205, 206, 210; Senator Howard Cannon interview by author, October 25, 1988.

21. Bible, "Recollections," 202; Elliott and Rowley, *History of Nevada*, 320, n. 7.

22. Eric N. Moody, *Southern Gentleman of Nevada Politics: Vail M. Pittman*, 54, 55.

23. Jack Carpenter to author, September 13, 1990. Bible, like House Speaker Sam Rayburn, was criticized for being too cautious and slow to move throughout his political career. Like another speaker of the house, Tip O'Neill, Bible hated to say no to people, which a governor is constantly called upon to do. See D. B. Hardeman and Donald C. Bacon, *Rayburn: A Biography*, 207; and O'Neill and Novak, *Man of the House*, 22.

24. Edwards, *Pat McCarran*, 95, 136.

25. Elliott and Rowley, *History of Nevada*, 319.

26. In 1958 Dr. Fred Anderson, a longtime friend of Bible, entered the Demo-

cratic Party primary against Howard Cannon, who was then Las Vegas city attorney. Bible refused to endorse Anderson over Cannon, who won by 1,468 votes. Bible's endorsement might well have convinced enough voters to support Anderson, thereby swinging the election to his old friend. For years it was alleged that Anderson was bitter over the incident, which no doubt strained their relations. But there is no indication that Anderson remained upset (he did not mention the 1958 primary to the author). The two men resumed their cordial relationship. Some viewed Bible's actions in 1958 as evidence of his unwillingness to take chances. More to the point, he wanted to avoid making enemies. There is some truth in this analysis of his personality, but not in relation to the 1958 primary. His decision not to endorse Anderson was firmly rooted in his 1942 primary experience, when Democratic leaders remained silent, and in the Democratic debacle of 1946. Dr. Fred Anderson interview by author, August 22, 1989; and Gordon Rice interview by author, August 22, 1989. Rice, who resigned from his position as district court judge to work full time for Dr. Anderson, was very critical of Bible's decision not to support Anderson. See *Las Vegas Sun*, July 12, 1953; Nevada, *Political History of Nevada*, 308; and Hardeman and Bacon, *Rayburn*, 283.

27. 1929 N.C.L. 1941 Supp., Sec 3302.20 added Stats., 1945. The license fee was paid monthly and varied depending on the size of the operation. For example, there was a $25 assessment for each card table, $10 per slot machine, and $50 each for other devices.

28. The most authoritative source on the legislative changes and the reasons motivating revision is Robbins Cahill, "Recollections of Work in State Politics, Government, Taxation, Gaming Control, Clark County Administrator and the Nevada Resort Association," 280–290. For an overall discussion of gaming regulations and economics, see William R. Eadington, ed., "The Evolution of Corporate Gambling in Nevada," Proceedings of the Fifth National Conference on Gambling and Risk Taking, Reno, 1982.

29. Moody, *Southern Gentleman of Nevada Politics*, 66, 67.

30. Nevada, *Reports and Official Opinions of the Attorney General, Opinion 528*, July 1, 1946, to June 30, 1948, 273.

31. Nevada, *Reports and Official Opinions of the Attorney General, Opinion 628*, July 1, 1946, to June 30, 1948, 412–414.

32. Nevada, *Reports and Official Opinions of the Attorney General, Opinion 689*, July 1, 1948, to June 30, 1950.

33. Eric F. Goldman, *The Crucial Decade and After: America 1945–1960*, 53, 54, 126.

34. John Patrick Diggins, *The Proud Decades: America in War and Peace, 1941–1960*, 165, 166.

35. Ibid., 167.

36. Goldman, *The Crucial Decade and After*, 198.

37. *Las Vegas Evening Review-Journal*, November 20, 1941.

38. John M. Findley, *People of Chance: Gambling in American Society from James-town to Las Vegas*, 122–124, 139.

39. Ibid., 171; *Las Vegas Evening Review-Journal*, November 15, 1950. See also U.S. Congress, Senate, 82d Congress, 1st Session, 1951, *Third Interim Report of the Special Committee to Investigate Organized Crime in Interstate Commerce*, S.R. 202, 90. Kefauver, because of his crime committee hearings and publicity grabbing, became extremely unpopular with his Senate colleagues. In effect, he was telling the states how to solve their crime problem in a questionable manner. See William S. White, *Citadel: The Story of the U.S. Senate*, 78.

40. The author's review of correspondence files from 1938 to 1950 failed to disclose a single instance of communication between a law enforcement agency and Bible concerning organized crime in Nevada; Nevada, State Division of Archives and Records, Attorney General correspondence file, 1938–1950.

41. Moehring, *Resort City in the Sunbelt*, 140–172.

42. For a different perspective on Nevada and gambling, see Edwards, "Nevada: Gambling and the Federal-State Relationship." Nevada historian James Hulse believes the federal government should intervene in Nevada to clean up gambling because the state has been unwilling to do so. See James Hulse, *Forty Years in the Wilderness: Impressions of Nevada, 1940–1980*, 114. For a current overview of gaming regulation, statutes, and case law, see Michael W. Bowers, "Federalism and Gaming Regulation in Nevada: The Case of Spilotro v. State," in *Battle Born: Federal-State Conflict in Nevada during the Twentieth Century*, ed. A. Costandina Titus, 183–195.

43. Mary Ellen Glass, *Nevada's Turbulent '50s: Decade of Political and Economic Change*, 40–43; Joseph F. McDonald, "The Life of a Newsboy in Nevada," 125, 126.

44. Bible, "Recollections," 203.

45. Moody, *Southern Gentlemen of Nevada Politics*, 85–87.

46. Elliott and Rowley, *History of Nevada*, 408.

CHAPTER THREE. TWISTS AND TURNS, 1951–1954

1. Bob McDonald interview by author, June 11, 1990. Mr. McDonald could not recall the exact dates of the hunting and fishing trips, but both occurred in the early 1960s.

2. Bob McDonald interview by author, August 23, 1989; O'Neill and Novak, *Man of the House*, 121, (quote).

3. McDonald interview, August 23, 1989.

4. Bible interview by author, September 6, 1986. Almost certainly, Senator McCarran played a key role in the Bible-McDonald law firm securing the Stauffer Chemical legal contract. McCarran was involved in establishing the BMI plant in Henderson and worked on the negotiations to have the facility purchased

by Nevada to expand industrial development in southern Nevada. For a good analysis of BMI's role in the development of industry in southern Nevada, see Moehring, *Resort City in the Sunbelt*, 63–65.

5. James Gilbert, *Another Chance: Postwar America, 1945–1985*, 133–135.

6. For a detailed account of Greenspun's battles with McCarran and McCarthy, see Gary E. Elliott and Candace C. Kant, "Hank Greenspun Meets Joseph McCarthy: The *Las Vegas Sun* Challenges First Amendment Violations," in *Battle Born*, ed. A. Costandina Titus, 196–205.

7. Hank Greenspun and Alex Pelle, *Where I Stand: The Record of a Reckless Man*, 198–203. See also Michael S. Green, "The Las Vegas Newspaper War of the 1950s," *Nevada Historical Society Quarterly* 31, no. 3 (Fall 1988): 155–182.

8. Greenspun and Pelle, *Where I Stand*, 227.

9. Eva Adams, "Windows of Washington: Nevada Education, the United States Senate, the U.S. Mint," 184; Joseph F. McDonald, Sr., "The Life of a Newsboy in Nevada," 173.

10. Bible interview with author, November 1, 1986.

11. Ibid.

12. John F. Cahlan, "Reminiscences of a Reno and Las Vegas Newspaperman, University Regent and Public Spirited Citizen," 255–256.

13. Nevada, *Political History of Nevada*, 308; Elmer R. Rusco, *Voting Behavior in Nevada*, 63. See also Claude C. Smith, "The 1952 Election in Nevada," *Western Political Quarterly* 6, no. 1 (March 1953): 117–120.

14. Nevada, State Planning Coordinator's Office, *Nevada Statistical Abstract*, 4.

15. Bible interview with author, September 6, 1986.

16. Edwards, *Pat McCarran*, 170–178.

17. Ibid.

18. Edwards, *Pat McCarran*, 170–178.

19. Stephen E. Ambrose, *Nixon: The Education of a Politician, 1913–1962*, 610. In 1953 the Senate was equally divided: 48 Democrats and 48 Republicans. Thus, Richard Nixon as vice-president and presiding officer of the Senate broke the tie and voted with the Republicans, which enabled them to organize and control the Senate.

20. Edwards, *Pat McCarran*, 170–178.

21. *Arizona* v. *California*, motion on behalf of the State of Nevada for leave to intervene, October 1953, 53–55. For a brief explanation of Nevada's legal position, see *Nevada State Journal*, November 8, 1953, and December 1, 1953.

22. *Arizona* v. *California*, motion on behalf of the State of Nevada, 56.

23. Ibid., 12. Actually, Bible drastically underestimated southern Nevada's water needs in the year 2000.

24. Edwards, *Pat McCarran*, 193–195.

25. Ibid., 198, 199.

26. Chester Smith interview with author, October 3, 1988.

27. Ibid. Also Bob McDonald interview with author, August 23, 1989; and

Grant Sawyer interview with author, May 22, 1991. Sawyer, who was then district attorney of Elko County, was a strong Bible supporter.

28. Ibid.

29. Adams, "Windows of Washington," 250–254.

30. Bible interview with author, November 1, 1986.

31. Edwards, *Pat McCarran*, 183. Edwards provides an excellent summary of the backgrounds of Norman Biltz and John Mueller. Years later Biltz confirmed Bible's fears and suspicions about his alliance with Eva Adams when he said that Adams could always sneak a favor through. See Norman Biltz, "Memories of the Duke of Nevada: Development of Lake Tahoe, California and Nevada: Reminiscences of Nevada Political and Financial Life," 134.

32. Nevada, *Report of the Attorney General, Opinion 350*, July 1, 1954, to June 30, 1956, 20–31.

33. *Brown* v. *Georgetta*, 40 Nev. 500 (1954).

34. Nevada, *Official Returns of the General Election of 1954*, 76, 77.

35. Claude C. Smith, "The 1954 Election in Nevada," *Western Political Quarterly* 7, no. 4 (December 1954): 614–616; James L. Sundquist, *Politics and Policy: The Eisenhower, Kennedy, and Johnson Years*, 15, 20.

36. Ibid.

37. Edwards, *Pat McCarran*, 200.

38. Ambrose, *Nixon*, 267.

39. U.S. Senate, *Manual on Rules, Regulations, and Procedures* (Washington, D.C.: GPO, 1975), 853. Contrary to popular belief, Ernest Brown did not resign his Senate seat in order for Bible to be sworn in early and thus gain seniority over other freshman senators entering in January 1955. Governor Russell signed the official certificate of election on December 1, 1954, the same day the Nevada Supreme Court sitting as the official state board of vote canvassers certified to the Nevada secretary of state the ballot's statewide vote tallies and Bible's election. He was sworn into office the following day in Washington, D.C. If Bible had not been sworn in on December 2 the Senate would have adjourned after the McCarthy vote, thereby denying Bible seniority over other freshman senators. Also, it is likely that the republicans could have blocked the election of Lyndon Johnson as majority leader if Brown had retained his seat until January 1, 1955. The author is indebted to Chester Smith for correcting this often-stated misconception. However, it is true that Bible resigned from the Senate early in order that newly elected senator Paul Laxalt could advance his seniority over those freshmen entering the Senate in 1975. Laxalt was elected to succeed the retiring Bible on November 2, 1975. Bible resigned on December 17, 1974, and Laxalt was appointed to fill Bible's unexpired term, which ended on January 2, 1975, the day Laxalt began his six-year term (Smith to author, October 19, 1993).

CHAPTER FOUR. SIGNS OF THINGS TO COME:
THE QUEST FOR LAND, WATER, AND METALS, 1955–1956

1. Alan Bible Papers, Special Collections, Getchell Library, University of Nevada, Reno, Box 294, Index Citation 1/11/30, Press Releases 1954 to 1959 (hereafter cited as AB Papers).

2. Marc Reisner, *Cadillac Desert: The American West and Its Disappearing Water*, 139–142.

3. Elmo Richardson, *Dams, Parks, and Politics: Resource Development and Preservation in the Truman-Eisenhower Era*, 81.

4. Ibid., 86.

5. Ibid., 87.

6. Ibid., 102–104.

7. Phillip O. Foss, *Politics and Grass: The Administration of Grazing on the Public Domain*, 120, 173–176, 202; Paul W. Gates and Robert W. Swenson, *History of Public Land Law Development*, 618–622.

8. Bible interview by author, October 3, 1987. The much-heralded Sagebrush Rebellion, born in Nevada in 1979, simply restated the position of President Hoover, Senators McCarran and Barrett, and President Eisenhower on the issue of public lands in the West. In 1980 Ronald Reagan, in his drive for the presidency, would again call for western lands to be turned over to the states and private developers.

9. Richardson, *Dams, Parks, and Politics*, 119.

10. Ibid.

11. Ibid., 124.

12. Arthur M. Schlesinger, Jr., *The Cycles of American History*, 23–48.

13. Quoted in William E. Leuchtenburg, *In the Shadow of FDR: From Harry Truman to Ronald Reagan*, 131; Robert A. Caro, *The Years of Lyndon Johnson*, vol. 1, *The Path to Power*, 369–385 (Marshall Ford Dam), 469.

14. Richard Allan Baker, *Conservation Politics: The Senate Career of Clinton P. Anderson*.

15. Ibid., 53 (quote)–58.

16. Ibid., 65.

17. Ibid., 64.

18. Statement from the office of Senator Bible, February 25, 1955, AB Papers, Box 258.

19. Horace M. Albright to Alan Bible, January 23, 1955, AB Papers, Box 49.

20. Alan Bible to Charles Russell, March 8, 1955, AB Papers, Box 49.

21. Statement from the office of Senator Bible, April 10, 1956, AB Papers, Box 49.

22. Statement from the office of Senator Bible, June 22, 1956, AB Papers, Box 49.

23. Philip L. Fradkin, *A River No More: The Colorado River and the West*.

24. Baker, *Conservation Politics*, 65.

25. Donald J. Pisani, "The Polluted Truckee: A Study in Interstate Water Quality," *Nevada Historical Society Quarterly* 20, no. 3 (Fall 1977): 151–166.

26. U.S. Department of the Interior, Bureau of Reclamation, *Action Program for Resource Development, Truckee and Carson River Basins, California and Nevada,* October 1964, 7. See also Donald J. Pisani, "Western Nevada's Water Crisis, 1915–1935," *Nevada Historical Society Quarterly* 22, no. 1 (Spring 1979): 3–20.

27. Ibid. For flood control reports and recommendations, see U.S. Army Corps of Engineers, *Water Resource Development in Nevada,* January 1, 1959.

28. U.S. Congress, Senate, *A Bill to Provide for the Conveyance of the Newlands Project,* S. 2218, 84th Congress, 1st Session, 1955. See also statement from the office of Senator Bible, June 14, 1955, AB Papers, Box 101. The Senate took no action on S. 2218.

29. P.L. 858 (70 Stat. 777) and *U.S. Statutes at Large,* 69, 693 (1955).

30. Statement from the office of Senator Bible, April 26, 1956, AB Papers, Box 101.

31. Ibid. See also U.S. Congress, Senate, *A Bill to Amend the Act Authorizing the Washoe Reclamation Project, Nevada and California in Order to Increase the Amount Authorized to be Appropriated for Such Project,* S. 4009, 85th Congress, 2d Session, 1958.

32. Statement from the office of Senator Bible, April 26, 1956, AB Papers, Box 101. Dunbar, *Forging New Rights in Western Waters,* 199–201.

33. Donald J. Pisani, "State v. Nation: Federal Reclamation and Water Rights in the Progressive Era," *Pacific Historical Review* (August 1981): 265–283.

34. *United States* v. *Rio Grande Dam and Irrigation Company,* 174 U.S. 690 (1899).

35. Quoted in Pisani, "State v. Nation," 273.

36. *Kansas* v. *Colorado,* 206 U.S. 46 (1907).

37. Pisani, "State v. Nation," 274.

38. Donald J. Pisani, "Federal Reclamation and Water Rights in Nevada," *Agricultural History* (July 1977): 540–558.

39. U.S. Congress, Senate, *A Bill to Govern the Control, Appropriation, Use, and Distribution of Water,* S. 863, 84th Congress, 2d Session, 1956, section 2, 3 and 4. For an excellent short treatment of Federal Reserve Rights, see Pisani, "State v. Nation," 274–280.

40. S. 863, section 6, 5.

41. Co-sponsors of the Barrett bill included Bible, Malone, Henry C. Dworshak, Gordon Allott, Barry Goldwater, Herman Welker, Carl T. Curtis, Joseph C. O'Mahoney, Eugene D. Millikin, Clinton P. Anderson, Arthur V. Watkins, William Knowland, William Langer, Dennis Chavez, Wallace F. Bennett, Karl E. Mundt, Roman L. Hruska, Milton R. Young, and Francis Case.

42. S. 863, section 9, 7.

43. Percy Rappaport to James A. Murray, March 15, 1956, AB Papers, Box 101.

44. U.S. Congress, Senate, *A Bill Giving Congressional Consent for California and Nevada to Negotiate and Enter into a Compact with Respect to the Distribution and Use*

of the Waters of the Truckee, Carson, Walker Rivers, Lake Tahoe and the Tributaries, S. 1391, 84th Congress, 1st Session, 1955; P.L. 353.

45. Donald J. Pisani, "The Strange Death of the California-Nevada Compact: A Study in Interstate Water Negotiations," *Pacific Historical Review* (November 1978): 637–658. For an excellent discussion of the complex issues involving water rights at Lake Tahoe during the Progressive period, see Donald J. Pisani, "Conflict over Conservation: The Reclamation Service and the Tahoe Contract," *Western Historical Quarterly* (April 1979): 167–190.

46. Pisani, "The Strange Death of the California-Nevada Compact," 640.

47. Ibid., 641.

48. Martha C. Knack, "Federal Jurisdiction over Indian Water Rights in Nevada," in *Battle Born*, ed. A. Costandina Titus, 121–135.

49. *Winters v. United States*, 207 U.S. 567 (1908).

50. Norris Hundley, Jr., "The Dark and Bloody Ground of Indian Water Rights: Confusion Elevated to Principle," *Western Historical Quarterly* (October 1978): 455–481.

51. Ibid., 467, 468.

52. Ibid.; Donald J. Pisani, "Enterprise and Equity: A Critique of Western Water Law in the Nineteenth Century," *Western Historical Quarterly* 23, no. 1 (January 1978): 15–37.

53. *U.S. v. Orr Water Ditch Co., et al.* (U.S. Dist. Court, D. Nev, Equity No. A3, 1944); Knack, "Federal Jurisdiction Over Indian Water Rights in Nevada," 129.

54. Bible interview by author, October 3, 1987. Bible sponsored many pieces of legislation to aid Nevada's Indians. For example, on June 2, 1961, he introduced S. 2016 to give Walker River Paiutes the right to minerals on or under reservation land (P.L. 87–229 enacted September 14, 1961).

55. Glass, *Nevada's Turbulent 50s*, 88, 93.

56. Ibid., 91.

57. Bob Redwine to Alan Bible, February 27, 1957, AB Papers, Box 45. Nevada's population was about 285,000 in 1960, a little less in 1957.

58. U.S. Congress, Senate, *A Bill to Encourage the Discovery, Development, and Production of Certain Domestic Minerals*, S. 1583, 84th Congress, 1st Session, 1955.

59. U.S. Congress, Senate, *A Bill to Encourage the Discovery, Development, and Production of Certain Domestic Minerals*, S. 922, 84th Congress, 1st Session, 1955. Co-sponsors of the bill included Carl Hayden (D-Arizona), James Murray (D-Montana), Mike Mansfield (D-Montana), and Kerr Scott (D–North Carolina).

60. Statement from the office of Senator Bible, April 17, 1955, AB Papers, Box 45.

61. *Washington Daily News*, June 27, 1955; Also see *Evening Star*, June 27, 1955, for a more detailed treatment of the issue.

62. *Washington Daily News*, June 27, 1955.

63. U.S. House, *Memorandum of Disapproval of H.R. 6373 by Dwight D. Eisenhower*, August 14, 1955, AB Papers, Box 45.

64. U.S. Congress, Senate, *A Bill to Provide for the Maintenance of Essential Pro-*

duction of Tungsten Ores, S. 3379, 84th Congress, 2d Session, 1956. Co-sponsors of the bill were Bible, Malone, Goldwater, Ervin, and Scott.

65. Statement from the office of Senator Bible, April 6, 1956, AB Papers, Box 45.

66. Jack Carpenter interview by author, August 22, 1989.

67. Fred Seaton to James Murray, May 24, 1956, AB Papers, Box 45.

68. Ibid., 2.

69. P.L. 733, 67 Stat. 417.

70. *Nevada State Journal*, August 15, 1956.

CHAPTER FIVE. HOME FOLKS AND FOLKWAYS:
THE SENATE OF THE 1950S

1. Hardeman and Bacon, *Rayburn*, 428. See also O'Neill and Novak, *Man of the House*, 140.

2. Bible, "Recollections," 268–279.

3. Bible, "Recollections," 275; Smith to author, October 19, 1993. See also Eric F. Goldman, *The Tragedy of Lyndon Johnson*, 74–76; and Ralph K. Huitt, "Democratic Party Leadership in the Senate," *American Political Science Review* 55 (June 1961): 331–344.

4. *Nevada State Journal*, August 30, 1955.

5. Alan Bible to Lyndon Johnson, December 15, 1954; Eva B. Adams to Lyndon Johnson, September 13, 1955; Lyndon Johnson to Eva B. Adams, September 16, 1955: Senate Papers, Alan Bible, Box 365, LBJ Library.

6. Alan Bible to Lyndon Johnson, October 11, 1955; Lyndon Johnson to Alan Bible, October 17, 1955: Senate Papers, Alan Bible, Box 365, LBJ Library.

7. Bible, "Recollections," 272–275.

8. Nevada, *Political History of Nevada*, 308.

9. Bible, "Recollections," 272–275; Smith to author, October 19, 1993.

10. John R. McCloskey, "Seventy Years of Griping: Newspapers, Politics, Government," 543.

11. U.S. Congress, Senate, *A Bill to Dispose of Federal Property and Establish the Municipality of Boulder City*, S. 514, 84th Congress, 1st Session, 1955 (the bill passed the Senate on July 27, 1955; no immediate action was taken by the House); U.S. Congress, Senate, *A Bill to Prescribe Minimum Acre Allotments for Cotton Production*, S. 3671, 84th Congress, 2d Session, 1956. The bill was introduced by Senator John Stennis (D-Mississippi) on April 9, 1956. See also *Ely Record*, May 24, 1956.

12. *Battle Mountain Scout*, November 1, 1956; Austin E. Hutchenson and Don W. Driggs, "The 1956 Election in Nevada," *Western Political Quarterly* (November 1956): 132–134. See also Bible, "Recollections," 274.

13. Nevada, *Political History of Nevada*, 280, Official Vote Record: Eisenhower 56,049 to Stevenson's 40,640; Bible 50,677 to Young's 45,712; Baring 51,100 to Horton's 43,154. See also Elmer R. Rusco, *Voting Behavior in Nevada*, 46.

14. Hutchenson and Driggs, "The 1956 Election in Nevada," 133; Richard F. Fenno, Jr., *The Making of a Senator: Dan Quayle*, 165.

15. Governor Grant Sawyer interview by author, May 4, 1988; Jack Carpenter interview by author, August 22, 1989; Senator Howard Cannon interview by author, November 3, 1988; Governor Mike O'Callaghan interview by author, September 8, 1988; Loucile Bible interview by author, August 22, 1989.

16. Senator Howard Cannon interview by author, October 25, 1988.

17. Frank Chelf to Alan Bible, June 16, 1964, AB Papers, Box 264.

18. Cannon interview by author, October 25, 1988; Donald R. Matthews, *U.S. Senators and Their World*, 42–44.

19. Leuchtenburg, *In the Shadow of FDR*, 121, 122, 127, 128.

20. Bible, "Recollections," 279; Alan Bible to Lyndon B. Johnson, September 28, 1957; and Lyndon B. Johnson to Alan Bible, November 20, 1958: Congressional File, Box 39, LBJ Library. For a different perspective on Johnson, see Caro, *The Path to Power*. Caro argues that Johnson was not a committed New Dealer and was not an FDR supporter in terms of ideological commitment. Rather, Caro sees LBJ as a politician interested only in his personal advancement.

21. William S. White, *Citadel: The Story of the U.S. Senate*, 102.

22. Ibid., 182; Lyndon B. Johnson to Alan Bible, February 4, 1957, Congressional File, Box 39, LBJ Library.

23. Chester Smith to author, March 23, 1989; Bible, "Recollections," 261, 262.

24. AB Papers, Box 292; Bruce Covill and Beverly Wexler Weinberg, "Alan Bible: Democratic Senator from Nevada," 10.

25. Stephen Horn, *Unused Power: The Work of the Senate Committee on Appropriations*, 1, 11, 13, 14, 33; Paul H. Douglas, *In the Fullness of Time: The Memoirs of Paul H. Douglas*, 207.

26. Smith to author, March 23, 1989; Lyndon B. Johnson to Alan Bible, November 8, 1958, Congressional File, Box 39, LBJ Library.

27. Clayton Fritchey, "Who Belongs to the Senate Inner Club," *Harper's* 234 (May 1967): 104–110. Besides Bible, Harry F. Byrd, Allen Ellender, Hayden, Lester Hill, Hruska, Magnuson, Mansfield, John L. McClellan, John O. Pastore, Russell, Stennis, A. Willis Robertson, and Leverett Saltonstall were credited with inner club status. See also Douglas, *In the Fullness of Time*, 207.

28. White, *Citadel*, 21, 60, 65.

29. Ibid., 68–70; Douglas, *In the Fullness of Time*, 222; Bible interview by author, February 20, 1988.

30. Bible interview by author, February 20, 1988; Lyndon B. Johnson to Alan Bible, September 13, 1956, Senate Master File, Box 8, LBJ Library (quote). See also Alan Bible Tribute to Lyndon B. Johnson, *Congressional Record* (hereafter cited as *CR*), Senate, March 25, 1959, A2675; and Lyndon B. Johnson to Alan Bible, March 29, 1959, Senate Papers, Box 365, LBJ Library.

31. White, *Citadel*, 91, 129.

32. Matthews, *U.S. Senators and Their World*, 92–99.

33. Bible interview by author, February 20, 1988.

34. Matthews, *U.S. Senators and Their World*, 92–99.

35. Ibid.

36. Jack Carpenter interview by author, October 27, 1987; Bible interview by author, February 20, 1988.

37. Bible interview by author, February 20, 1988.

38. George E. Reedy, *The U.S. Senate*, 28.

39. Matthews, *U.S. Senators and Their World*, 113, 114. For a critique of the Senate, see Joseph S. Clark, *The Senate Establishment*.

40. James L. Sundquist, *Politics and Policy: The Eisenhower, Kennedy, and Johnson Years*, 156–180, 231–258. See also Michael Foley, *The New Senate: Liberal Influence on a Conservative Institution, 1959–1972*, 27. For a perspective on a Nevada senator from the class of 1958, see A. Costandina Titus, "Senator Howard Cannon and Civil Rights Legislation, 1959–1968," *Nevada Historical Society Quarterly* 33, no. 4 (Winter 1990): 13–29.

41. Edwards, *Pat McCarran*, 122.

42. Randall B. Ripley, *Power in the Senate*, 189; Matthews, *U.S. Senators and Their World*, 82–87; Bible interviewed by author, January 9, 1987.

43. Covill and Weinberg, "Alan Bible: Democratic Senator from Nevada," 4.

44. Bible, "Recollections," 331.

45. Matthews, *U.S. Senators and Their World*, 82–87. Also, Adams tried to pressure Bible by having her business associates in her office and trying to run every aspect of the senator's office (Smith to author, October 19, 1993).

46. Bible interview by author, February 20, 1988. Bible met frequently with mine owners and may well have considered their interest in supporting Adams's appointment. But it was clearly his desire to remove Adams from his office without alienating her. It is also possible that in later years Bible was mistaken about the origin of the Adams appointment. He probably asked President Kennedy for the favor (Smith to author, October 19, 1993).

47. Bible interview by author, February 20, 1988; Chester Smith interview by author, August 18, 1989; statement from the office of Senator Bible, September 23, 1961, AB Papers, Box 210; Drew Pearson, "The Washington Merry-Go-Round," *Washington Post*, September 21, 1961. Adams graduated in 1928 from the University of Nevada, Reno. In 1936 she received an M.A. degree in English from Columbia University. In 1950 she was awarded an LL.B. degree from American University and a master's of law degree from George Washington University. By the time Adams was nominated for director of the Mint, she had twenty years of government service and had been the administrative assistant to three Nevada senators.

48. Jack Carpenter interview by author, October 27, 1987.

49. Ibid.

50. Ibid. Chester Smith agrees with Carpenter's general statement, but in 1966 Bible blocked his appointment to a White House staff position and after the 1968

election refused to authorize a salary increase for Smith, saying, "The staff person hasn't been born that is worth $30,000 a year" (Smith to author, October 19, 1993).

CHAPTER SIX. ROLLING OUT THE PORK BARREL, 1957–1962

1. Richard Jensen, "On Modernizing Frederick Jackson Turner: The Historiography of Regionalism," *Western Historical Quarterly* (July 1980): 307–322. See also Michael C. Steiner, "The Significance of Turner's Sectional Thesis," *Western Historical Quarterly* (October 1979): 437–466; and Donald Worster, "New West, True West: Interpreting the Region's History," *Western Historical Quarterly* (April 1987): 141–156.

2. Donald K. Pickens, "Western Expansion and the End of American Exceptionalism: Sumner, Turner, and Webb," *Western Historical Quarterly* (October 1981): 409–418. In 1977, when President Carter issued his list of western water projects to be slashed from the budget, he failed to see that he was striking at the heart of western regionalism and the one issue that binds the region together regardless of political party.

3. Neal A. Maxwell, *Regionalism in the United States Senate*, 9, 10.

4. Ibid., 30, 31.

5. Ibid., 33.

6. Ibid., 49, 53.

7. Ibid., 54.

8. Ibid., 41, 44. See also Neal A. Maxwell, "The West on Capitol Hill," in *Western Politics*, ed. Frank H. Jonas, 357–359; and Neal A. Maxwell, "The Conference of Western Senators," *Western Political Quarterly* (December 1957): 902–910.

9. Gregory Jackson, *Regional Diversity: Growth in the United States, 1960–1990*, 3, 109, 127.

10. *Battle Mountain Scout*, November 1, 1956.

11. Nevada, *Political History of Nevada*, 280.

12. *CR*, Senate, February 11, 1956, D68; statement from the office of Senator Bible, February 19, 1957, AB Papers, Box 45.

13. *CR*, Senate, March 1, 1957, 2511–2512; statement of Senator Bible before the Senate Appropriations Committee, April 1, 1957. See also press release from the office of Senator Bible, April 1, 1957, AB Papers, Box 45.

14. Alan Bible to Lyndon B. Johnson, April 9, 1957, AB Papers, Box 45.

15. *Pioche Record*, April 26, 1957; and *Humboldt Star*, May 27, 1957 (both editorials place the responsibility for Nevada's mining decline squarely on Congress because of its failure to provide funds to implement P.L. 733; *CR*, Senate, August 7, 1957, 13655 (report of state mining inspector Mervin J. Gallagher on the loss of jobs in Nevada caused by the failure of Congress to provide funds to implement P.L. 733); *CR*, Senate, August 30, 1957, 45110 (article from the *Nevada State Jour-*

nal, August 25, 1957, criticizing the U.S. government for supporting mining in the Far East while American miners were losing their jobs).

16. Matthews, *U.S. Senators and Their World*, 72–74.

17. Henry Nash Smith, *The Virgin Land: The American West as Symbol and Myth*, 15, 20, 21. For a good general background on America's westward expansion, see Norman A. Graebner, *Empire on the Pacific: A Study in American Continental Expansion*. See also Hugh DeSantis, "The Imperialist and American Innocence, 1865–1900," in *American Foreign Relations: A Historiographical Review*, ed. Gerald K. Haines and Samuel J. Walker, 67–78. Two other excellent articles in the same collection that explore the relationship between economic interests and foreign policy are Mark A. Stoler, "World War II Diplomacy in Historical Writing: Prelude to Cold War"; and Samuel J. Walker, "Historians and the Cold War."

18. Robert J. McMahon, "The Cold War in Asia: Toward a New Synthesis," *Diplomatic History* 12, no. 3 (Summer 1988): 307–327.

19. John T. Rourke, "Congress and the Cold War," *World Affairs* 139, no. 4 (Spring 1977): 260, 265, 273; Robert Dahl, *Pluralist Democracy in the United States: Conflict and Consent*, 406; Robert A. Pastor, *Congress and the Politics of U.S. Foreign Economic Policy, 1929–1976*, 36, 37.

20. John Agnew, *The United States and the World Economy: A Regional Geography*, 72, 76; Pastor, *Congress and the Politics of U.S. Foreign Economic Policy, 1929–1976*, 205; Wiley and Gottlieb, *Empires in the Sun*, 36.

21. Agnew, *The United States and the World Economy*, 126, 127.

22. Ibid., 142, 153, 154; Michael P. Malone, "Beyond the Last Frontier: Toward a New Approach to Western American History," *Western Historical Quarterly* 20, no. 4 (November 1989): 409–427; Wiley and Gottlieb, *Empires in the Sun*, 23.

23. Michael P. Malone, "The Collapse of Western Metal Mining: An Historical Epitaph," *Pacific Historical Review* 55 (August 1986): 455–464. See also Peter Drucker, "The Changed World Economy," *Foreign Affairs* 64 (Spring 1986): 768–770.

24. Harry Magdoff, *The Age of Imperialism: The Economics of U.S. Foreign Policy*, 49.

25. Gabriel Kolko, "To Master the Third World," in *Major Problems in American Foreign Policy since 1914*, ed. Thomas G. Paterson, vol. 2, 620–624; Richard E. Feinberg, *The Intemperate Zone: The Third World Challenge to U.S. Foreign Policy*, 117, 118. For an excellent article supporting American mineral policy, see Michael Shafer, "Mineral Myths," *Foreign Affairs* 47 (Summer 1982): 154–171.

26. Alan Bible to Edgar Brossard, March 31, 1958, AB Papers, Box 124.

27. Statement from the office of Senator Bible, March 24, 1960, Box 124; Cannon interview by author, December 28, 1988. For example, the Bureau of Land Management planned to spend $1,800,000 in Nevada in 1962. The largest amount, $493,000, was for grazing lands and another $179,000 for soil conservation. A year later, BLM's budget for Nevada increased by $1,000,000, with $622,000 earmarked for grazing lands and $933,000 for soil conservation. In 1963 Bible supported an amendment to the Interior Department appropriation bill spon-

sored by Senator Wayne Morse to add another $250,000 to BLM's budget to reseed the Winnemucca grazing district. See statements from the office of Senator Bible, February 28, 1961, January 18, 1962, and June 11, 1962, AB Papers, Box 45, 77, 91.

28. U.S. Congress, Senate, *A Bill to Stabilize the Mining of Lead and Zinc*, S. 115, 87th Congress, 1st Session, 1961; Alan Bible to John F. Kennedy, June 23, 1961; Lawrence F. O'Brien to Alan Bible, June 27, 1961: John Fitzgerald Kennedy Library, White House Name File, Box 221.

29. Statement from the office of Senator Bible, August 8, 1961, AB Papers, Box 124 (quote); P.L. 87-347, October 3, 1961; statements from the office of Senator Bible, January 9, 1962, and April 17, 1962, AB Papers, Box 124.

30. Alan Bible to John F. Kennedy, January 25, 1962, John Fitzgerald Kennedy Library, White House Name File, Box 221.

31. U.S. Congress, Senate, *A Bill to Provide for the Conveyance of the Newlands Project to the Truckee-Carson Irrigation District, Fallon, Nevada*, S. 414, 85th Congress, 1st Session, 1957; Bible interview by author, January 22, 1987.

32. Statement from the office of Senator Bible, January 3, 1957; Department of the Interior News Release, June 11, 1958; statement from the office of Senator Bible, August 12, 1958; Department of the Interior News Release, August 26, 1958: AB Papers, Box 103.

33. Statement from the office of Senator Bible, August 11, 1959, AB Papers, Box 118.

34. U.S. Congress, Senate, *A Bill to Provide for the Allocation of Portions of the Cost of Davis Dam and Reservoir to Servicing the Mexican Water Treaty*, S. 3331, 86th Congress, 2d Session, 1960; *CR*, Senate, April 5, 1960, 6779.

35. U.S. Congress, Senate, *A Bill to Expand the Saline Water Conversion Program*, S. 3557, 86th Congress, 2d Session, 1960.

36. John F. Kennedy to Alan Bible, October 18, 1960, AB Papers, Box 115.

37. U.S. Congress, Senate, S. R. 48, 86th Congress, 2d Session, 1959; U.S. Congress, Senate, *Report of the Senate Select Committee on National Water Resources*, Report 29, January 30, 1961, V, VI.

38. Senate, *Report of the Senate Select Committee*, 11, 17–19.

39. Fred Powledge, *Water: The Nature, Uses, and Future of Our Most Precious and Abused Resource*, 286, 287. For an excellent overall treatment of western reclamation, see Lawrence B. Lee, "100 Years of Reclamation Historiography," *Pacific Historical Review* 47, no. 4 (November 1978): 507–563.

40. Anne Hodges Morgan, *Robert S. Kerr: The Senate Years*, 10, 26, 42, 43, 48, 241. For a utilitarian view of natural resources, see Robert S. Kerr, *Land, Water, and Wood*.

41. U.S. Congress, Senate, *A Bill to Expand and Extend the Saline Water Conversion Program Being Conducted by the Secretary of Interior*, S. 2156, 87th Congress, 1st Session, 1961; U.S. Congress, House, H.R. 7916, 8th Congress, 1st Session, 1961.

42. Statement from the office of Senator Bible, August 31, 1961; and Alan Bible

to Henry M. Jackson, August 12, 1963: AB Papers, Box 90; P.L. 87-295, September 22, 1961.

43. Florence Lee Jones, *Water: A History of Las Vegas,* vol. 2, 67, 78. See also Florence Lee Jones and John F. Cahlan, *Water: A History of Las Vegas,* vol. 1., for a good overall evaluation of the impact of water development on city growth.

44. Statement from the office of Senator Bible, September 20, 1961, AB Papers, Box 118. See also *Nevada State Journal,* October 30, 1962.

45. U.S. Congress, Senate, *A Bill to Provide for Research into and Development of Practical Means for the Utilization of Solar Energy,* S. 2318, 86th Congress, 1st Session, 1959; *Las Vegas Sun,* July 7, 1959; Marv Bennett to James E. Murray, September 24, 1959, AB Papers, Box 89.

CHAPTER SEVEN. DOLLARS FOR THE ENVIRONMENT, 1957–1962

1. Leopold cited in Donald Worster, *Nature's Economy: A History of Ecological Ideas,* 284–290. For the causes of the dust bowl disaster, see Donald Worster, *Dust Bowl: The Southern Plains in the 1930s.*

2. Samuel P. Hays, *Beauty, Health, and Permanence: Environmental Politics in the United States, 1955–1985,* 3, 13, 431, 436.

3. Conrad L. Wirth, *Parks, Politics, and the People,* 59, 126, 256.

4. Statements from the office of Senator Bible, February 5, 1957 (quote), and May 17, 1957, AB Papers, Box 47, 99. On February 16, 1959, Bible continued his drive to expand the Lake Mead recreation facilities when he introduced S. 1060, designed to streamline the park administration and at the same time to assure that the scenic and recreation values were protected. No action was taken by Congress, but S. 1060 did provide the basis for later reforms in park management. On June 5, 1959, Bible obtained another $311,400 for construction projects at the lake because of the enormous growth in the number of tourists. Between 1960 and 1963 only the Great Smoky Mountains logged more visitors than did Lake Mead.

5. Malcolm J. Rohrbough, *Aspen: The History of a Silver Mining Town, 1879–1893,* 14, 119; Duane A. Smith, *Mining America: The Industry and the Environment, 1800–1980,* 25.

6. Patricia Nelson Limerick, *The Legacy of Conquest: The Unbroken Past of the American West* 46, 61, 82, 157 (quotes). See also Gary E. Elliott, "Whose Land Is It: The Battle for the Great Basin National Park, 1957–1967," *Nevada Historical Society Quarterly* 34, no. 1 (Spring 1991): 241–256.

7. Gary E. Elliott, "A Legacy of Support: Senator Alan Bible and the Nevada Mining Industry," *Nevada Historical Society Quarterly* 31, no. 3 (Fall 1988): 183–197.

8. U.S. Congress, Senate, *A Bill to Establish the Great Basin National Park in Nevada,* S. 2664, 86th Congress, 1st Session, 1959; U.S. Congress, House, *A Bill*

to Establish the Great Basin National Park in Nevada, H.R. 9156, 86th Congress, 1st Session, 1959.

9. U.S. Congress, Senate, Subcommittee on Public Lands of the Interior and Insular Affairs Committee, *Hearing on Senate 2664,* 8th Congress, 1st Session, 1959, 220–221.

10. Ibid., 222.

11. Ibid., 228, 230.

12. Alfred Runte, *National Parks: The American Experience,* 48.

13. Gates and Swenson, *History of Public Land Law Development,* 631; P.L. 86-516, June 12, 1960, 74 Stat. 21S, 16 USCA 528–531.

14. U.S. Congress, Senate, Subcommittee on Public Lands of the Interior and Insular Affairs Committee, *Hearings on Senate 1760,* 87th Congress, 1st Session, 1961.

15. Ibid., 39–40.

16. William D. Rowley, *U.S. Forest Service Grazing and Rangelands: A History,* 233.

17. *Las Vegas Review-Journal,* April 10, 1964. See also transcript of meeting of Bible, Cannon, Baring, and Udall on April 19, 1966, 22, AB Papers, Box 258.

18. U.S. Congress, Senate, *A Bill to Preserve and Develop Shoreline Areas,* S. 2460, 86th Congress, 1st Session, 1959.

19. Ronald J. Engel, *Sacred Sands: The Struggle for Community in the Indiana Dunes,* 265.

20. U.S. Congress, Senate, Subcommittee on Public Lands of the Committee on Interior and Insular Affairs to Establish the Cape Cod National Seashore Park, *Hearing on S. 857,* March 9, 1961, 13.

21. Quoted in *CR,* Senate, June 27, 1961, 11391.

22. Ibid.; Wirth, *Parks, Politics, and the People,* 198. See also Aubrey Graves, "Fights on to Save Shore Areas," *Washington Post,* June 27, 1961.

23. U.S. Congress, Senate, Subcommittee on Public Lands of the Committee on Interior and Insular Affairs, to Establish the Ozark Rivers National Monument, *Hearings on S. 1381,* July 6, 1961, 7–11, 17.

24. Ibid., 28, 29.

25. U.S. Congress, Senate, Subcommittee on Public Lands of the Committee on Interior and Insular Affairs, to Establish the Sleeping Bear Dunes Recreational Area, *Hearings on S. 2153,* November 13, 1961, 17–20.

26. Point Reyes National Seashore was authorized on September 13, 1962, with 64,500 acres. Padre Island National Seashore was authorized on September 28, 1962, with 133,900 acres. See *The National Parks: Index 1985* (Washington, D.C.: GPO), 27, 70.

CHAPTER EIGHT. WINNERS AND LOSERS, 1963–1968

1. Foley, *The New Senate*, 27.

2. Ibid., 31. See also Alan Rosenthal, *Toward a Majority Rule in the United States Senate*.

3. Lawrence C. Dodd and Bruce I. Oppenheimer, *Congress Reconsidered*, 5–8, 15. For a good analysis of the changes in the Senate in the twentieth century and the impact of the 1946 reorganization and subcommittee government, see Lawrence C. Dodd and Richard L. Schott, *Congress and the Administrative State;* and Aage R. Clausen, *How Congressmen Decide: A Policy Focus.*

4. Foley, *The New Senate*, 32, 33.

5. Theodore C. Sorensen, *Kennedy*, 160.

6. Foley, *The New Senate*, 36, 37.

7. Ripley, *Power in the Senate*, 9, 12, 31, 66.

8. Bible interview by author, October 4, 1987; campaign material given to author by Bible; *The Making of a Senator: Dan Quayle*, 119. Fenno argues that a senator's governing experience in Washington directly affects his reelection campaign because legislative accomplishments are indispensable to success at home. Neil A. Maxwell makes the same argument in his study of western senators, *Regionalism in the United States Senate*, 81, 82.

9. Nevada, *Political History of Nevada*, 309.

10. Nevada, *Official Returns of the General Election of 1962*, 6.

11. Foley, *The New Senate*, 242, 243. Bible always took an eighteenth-century view of his and the Senate's role in the process of governance. He believed that he was an ambassador from Nevada and his primary obligation was to represent the interest of his constituents. See Bruce Ackerman, *We the People: Foundations*, 69, 271.

12. Dodd and Oppenheimer, *Congress Reconsidered*, 124–128.

13. Bible interview by author, January 22, 1987.

14. Foley, *The New Senate*, 36–56.

15. Bible interview by author, January 22, 1987.

16. Mike Manatos to Marvin Watson, January 11, 1966, White House Central File, Name File, Box 248, LBJ Library.

17. Lyndon B. Johnson to Charles Springer, May 7, 1964, White House Central File, Name File, Box 248, LBJ Library.

18. O'Neill and Novak, *Man of the House*, 317.

19. *Humboldt Bulletin*, November 2, 1961.

20. Ibid.

21. Statement from the office of Senator Bible, November 28, 1961, AB Papers, Box 42 and Box 109.

22. Statements from the office of Senator Bible, January 31, 1962, and March 15, 1962, AB Papers, Box 42 and Box 109.

23. *Barron's*, March 18, 1963; U.S. Congress, Senate, Banking and Currency

Committee, *Hearings on Repeal of the 1934 Silver Purchase Act*, April 29, 1963, 88th Congress, 1st Session, 11–26, 27–42.

24. Ibid.

25. U.S. Congress, House, *A Bill to Repeal Certain Legislation Relating to the Purchase of Silver and Other Purposes*, H.R. 5398, 88th Congress, 2d Session, 1963; U.S. Congress, House, *A Bill to Repeal Certain Legislation Relating to the Purchase of Silver and Other Purposes*, Report 183, April 3, 1963.

26. U.S. Congress, Senate, Committee on Banking and Currency, *Hearings on the Repeal of the 1934 Silver Purchase Act*, 73.

27. U.S. Congress, Senate, *A Bill to Repeal Certain Legislation Relating to the Purchase of Silver and Other Purposes*, Report 175, May 13, 1963; P.L. 88-36, June 4, 1963.

28. U.S. Congress, Senate, Committee on Banking and Currency, *Hearings on Repeal of the 1934 Silver Purchase Act*, 23, 24.

29. *Las Vegas Review-Journal*, March 24, 1964.

30. Ibid.; *San Francisco Chronicle*, February 21, 1964. It was erroneously reported that cartwheels were necessary in the operation of the gambling business. Equally erroneous was the belief that gamblers did not see silver dollars in the same terms as greenbacks.

31. Mike Manatos to Larry O'Brien, May 25, 1964, White House Central File, Name File, Box 248, LBJ Library. See also Mike Manatos to Jim Jones, July 30, 1968, Box 248, LBJ Library. Contrary to the opinion expressed by Denton L. Watson, Bible was not an archreactionary. Moreover, those who believed that Bible would support cloture because President Johnson needed all the votes he could get were likewise mistaken. Bible's loyalty began with protecting Nevada's economic interests, which meant casino gambling in 1964. Rule 22 protected minority interests like legalized gaming, and Bible fully appreciated the usefulness a filibuster could have in the future. See Denton L. Watson, *Lion in the Lobby: Clarence Mitchell, Jr.'s Struggle for the Passage of Civil Rights Laws*, 326, 598. For a humorous and interesting account of the pressure applied by the Johnson administration to secure votes for cloture, see Robert A. Burt, *The Constitution in Conflict*, 304–305.

32. U.S. Department of the Interior, Bureau of Mines, *Silver*, Bulletin 630, 8–9.

33. U.S. Department of Interior, Bureau of Mines, *Silver: Facts, Estimates and Projections*, Information Circular 8257, 9.

34. Statement from the office of Senator Bible, August 13, 1963; statement before the minerals subcommittee of the Interior and Insular Affairs Committee: AB Papers, Box 252.

35. *Silver: Facts, Estimates and Projections*, 11, 12.

36. *American Legion*, October 1964, 14–18.

37. *Washington Daily News*, February 8, 1965; *Las Vegas Sun*, January 13, 1964, and March 20, 1964; Las Vegas Chamber of Commerce resolution recommending the unlimited coinage of silver dollars, AB Papers, Box 252.

38. *Silver: Facts, Estimates and Projections*, 12.

39. Arlen J. Large, "Coin's Silver Content Sparks a New Debate in Congress, Industry," *Wall Street Journal*, April 2, 1964.

40. Ibid.

41. *Washington Evening Star*, May 19, 1965; *Wall Street Journal*, May 17, 1965; *Las Vegas Review-Journal*, May 17, 1965, and May 21, 1965.

42. U.S. Congress, Senate, *A Bill to Prohibit Certain Practices Creating Artificial Shortages in the Supply of Coins in the United States*, S. 2036, 86th Congress, 1st Session, 1965.

43. *CR*, Senate, May 25, 1965, 11052–11055. See also *American Metal Market*, May 26, 1965.

44. *Message of the President of the United States Relative to Silver Coinage*, Document No. 199, House, 89th Congress, 1st Session, 1965.

45. U.S. Congress, House, Banking and Currency Committee, *Hearings on the Coinage Act*, 89th Congress, 1st Session, June 4, 7, and 8, 1965, 12, 13–20; U.S. Congress, House, *Coinage Act of 1965*, H.R. 8746, Report 509, 1965.

46. House, *Hearings on the Coinage Act*, 130, 131.

47. U.S. Congress, Senate, Banking and Currency Committee, *Hearings on the Coinage Act*, 89th Congress, 1st Session, June 9, 1965, 27; U.S. Congress, Senate, *Coinage Act of 1965*, S. 2036, Report 317, 1965.

48. Senate, *Hearings on the Coinage Act*.

49. Ibid. The statement of Senator Simpson can be found on 32, Kennedy on 36, Pastore on 37.

50. Ibid., 43.

51. *Washington Evening Star*, June 15, 1965. The Coinage Act of 1965 passed the Senate on June 24, 1965, with only nine votes recorded against the measure (*CR*, Senate D570-1). Senator Howard Cannon, who opposed S. 2080, voted with the administration in hopes of retaining the 40 percent content of silver in half dollars. For a concise statement on Bible's role in the struggle to defeat the coinage act, see the *Nevada Register*, July 2, 1965, and July 23, 1965, editorial titled "Where Has All the Silver Gone: The Story of One Man's Fight in Washington."

52. Lyndon B. Johnson to Alan Bible, November 3, 1965, White House Central File, Name File, Box 248, LBJ Library.

53. *Economic News* 6, no. 2 (February 1963).

54. U.S. Congress, Senate, *A Bill to Revitalize the American Gold Mining Industry*, S. 2125, 88th Congress, 1st Session, 1963.

55. Ernest Gruening to Alan Bible, January 11, 1965; and Ernest Gruening to Lyndon B. Johnson, August 19, 1965: AB Papers, Box 109.

56. U.S. Congress, Senate, *The Gold Miners Assistance Act*, S. 2562, 89th Congress, 1st Session, 1964 (co-sponsors Bartlett, Bible, Cannon, Dominick, Metcalf, Montoya, and Mundt). See also S. 2596, *A Bill to Amend the Internal Revenue Code to Increase the Depletion Allowance*, 89th Congress, 1st Session, 1965 (co-sponsors included Anderson, Bartlett, Bennett, Dominick, Gruening, McGee, McGovern, Montoya, Mundt); *CR*, October 1, 1965; S. 24905, 24906; statements from the office of Senator Bible, October 1, 1965, and May 4, 1966, AB Papers, Box 109.

57. U.S. Congress, House, *A Bill to Preserve the Domestic Gold Mining Industry and Increase the Domestic Production of Gold*, Report 1923–1966, 7–8.

58. Ibid., 9–10.

59. *Washington Post*, March 6, 1967.

CHAPTER NINE. THE TRIUMPH OF RECREATION, 1963–1968

1. Baker, *Conservation Politics*, 257–259.

2. Ibid.

3. P.L. 89-80. For a detailed account of Senator Anderson's efforts to enact the WRPA, see Baker's *Conservation Politics*, 261–272. The evaluation of the act's importance is contained in Helen Ingram, *Water Politics: Continuity and Change*, 13, 14.

4. *Arizona* v. *California*, 373 U.S. 587 (1963); Norris Hundley, Jr., *Water and the West: The Colorado River Compact and the Politics of Water in the American West*, 304; *Boulder Canyon Protection Act of 1928*, P.L. 642, 70th Congress, 1st Session, December 21, 1928, 45 Stat. 1057, 1064, 43 USCA 617.

5. Hundley, *Water and the West*, 305, 306.

6. Ibid., 303.

7. Statement from the office of Senator Bible, April 20, 1964, AB Papers, Box 49.

8. Ibid.

9. Ibid.

10. U.S. Congress, Senate, *A Bill to Provide a Comprehensive Review of National Water Resources*, S. 3107, 89th Congress, 2d Session, 1966; U.S. Congress, Senate, Committee on Interior and Insular Affairs, *National Water Resources Act*, S. 3107, Report 1212, 1966, P.L. 90-515.

11. Statement from the office of Senator Bible, May 17, 1966, AB Papers, Box 118; U.S. Congress, Senate, *A Bill to Provide for an Investigation and Study to Recommend a General Plan to Meet the Future Water Needs of the Western States*, S. 1429, 90th Congress, 1st Session, 1967.

12. U.S. Final Report to the President and to Congress by the National Water Commission, *Water Policies for the Future*, 331. See also Ingram, *Water Politics*, 130.

13. Tim Palmer, *Endangered Rivers and the Conservation Movement*, 218, 228.

14. Covill and Weinberg, "Alan Bible: Democratic Senator from Nevada"; George B. Hartzog, Jr., *Battling for the National Parks*, 115.

15. Baker, *Conservation Politics*, 102, 103.

16. Ibid. (Bible's position on mining is stated on 139; see also 191–220 for details on Anderson's attempts to move the wilderness bill through Congress); *The Wilderness Act of 1964*, 16 USC 1131–1136, 78 Stat 890–896.

17. Hartzog, *Battling for the National Parks*, 88, 89; *Multiple Use-Sustained Yield Act*, 1960, 74 Stat L15.

18. Michael McCloskey, "The Wilderness Act of 1964: Its Background and

Meaning," *Oregon Law Review* 45 (June 1966): 288–321; *The Land and Water Conservation Fund*, P.L. 88-578, H.R. 3846.

19. Peter J. Ognibene, *Scoop: The Life and Politics of Henry M. Jackson*, 25, 26, 38, 51, 70–73, 224.

20. Stewart L. Udall, *The Quiet Crisis*, 182; Edward Abbey, *Desert Solitaire*, 192.

21. Palmer, *Endangered Rivers and the Conservation Movement*, 143, 144.

22. U.S. Congress, Senate, Committee on Interior and Insular Affairs, *Hearings on the Ozark National Rivers Bill*, S. 16, 88th Congress, 1st Session, April 8 and 9, 1963, and May 22, 1963, 14, 15.

23. Ibid., 26, 27, 112.

24. Baker, *Conservation Politics*, 222.

25. Ibid., 223.

26. Engel, *Sacred Sands*, 276, 277. See also Kay Franklin and Norma Schaeffer, *Duel for the Dunes: Land Use Conflict on the Shores of Lake Michigan*.

27. U.S. Congress, Senate, Committee on Interior and Insular Affairs, *Hearings on the Indiana Dunes National Lakeshore*, S. 2249, 88th Congress, 1st Session, March 5, 6, and 7, 1964, 10, 11, 13.

28. Ibid., 17, 34, 180.

29. Paul Douglas to Alan Bible, May 17, 1965, AB Papers, Box 47; Douglas, *In the Fullness of Time*, 541.

30. Lee C. White to Lyndon B. Johnson, July 30, 1964, White House Central File, Name File, Box 248, LBJ Library; Engel, *Sacred Sands*, 276, 277–281; P.L. 89-761.

31. *Washington Post*, May 5, 1966.

32. Stewart Udall to Bill Moyers, May 6, 1966, White House Central File, Name File, Box 248, LBJ Library.

33. Daniel B. Brewster to Alan Bible, September 22, 1965, AB Papers, Box 47.

34. U.S. Congress, Senate, *A Bill to Establish the National Park Foundation*, S. 3676, 89th Congress, 2d Session, 1966; Stewart Udall to Hubert Humphrey, July 25, 1966, AB Papers, Box 47.

35. U.S. Congress, Senate, *A Bill to Establish the National Park Foundation*, S. 814, 90th Congress, 1st Session, 1967; P.L. 90-209; George B. Hartzog, Jr., interview by author, July 30, 1990.

36. François Leydet, *The Last Redwoods and the Parkland of Redwood Creek*.

37. Quoted in John Ise, *Our National Park Policy: A Critical History*, 655.

38. Marvin Watson to Lyndon B. Johnson, October 4, 1967, White House Central File, Name File, Box 248, LBJ Library; U.S. Congress, Senate, *A Bill to Establish the Redwood National Park in California*, S. 2515, 90th Congress, 1st Session, 1967.

39. Orville Freeman to Alan Bible, October 20, 1967, AB Papers, Box 47.

40. The overall support for the Redwood Park compromise was reflected in the following news accounts: *Kansas City Times*, October 11, 1967; *San Francisco Chronicle*, October 15 and 20, 1967; *New York Times*, October 18, 1967; Edgar Wayburn to Alan Bible, October 18, 1967, AB Papers, Box 47; CR, Senate, October 31,

1967, 15588, 15589 (of particular interest are the comments of Senator Metcalf); P.L. 90-545.

CHAPTER TEN. PORK PROBLEMS AND THE BARING BURDEN, 1962–1968

1. Alan Bible to Carl Hayden, March 9, 1960, AB Papers, Box 45. Jack Carpenter to Gary Elliott, September 11, 1987.

2. Statement from the office of Senator Alan Bible, May 3, 1960, AB Papers, Box 45.

3. Statement from the office of Senator Alan Bible, January 26, 1962, AB Papers, Box 45.

4. Statement from the office of Senator Alan Bible, April 29, 1965, AB Papers, Box 45.

5. Alan Bible to Carl Hayden, May 7, 1965. See also *Boulder City News*, November 4, 1965, AB Papers, Box 46.

6. Statement from the office of Senator Alan Bible, May 10, 1966, AB Papers, Box 46. See also Tom Carnahan interview by author, September 14, 1987 (Mr. Carnahan is the research director of the Bureau of Mines in Reno); and *Boulder City News*, April 28, 1966, and February 2, 1967.

7. *Las Vegas Review-Journal*, January 5, 1966; *Washington Daily News*, August 16, 1967.

8. *CR*, Senate, October 15, 1964, A5320–321.

9. Ibid.

10. *Wall Street Journal*, August 18, 1967.

11. Alan Bible to Henry H. Fowler, September 1, 1967, AB Papers, Box 118.

12. Pisani, "The Strange Death of the California-Nevada Compact," 644.

13. Ibid., 644, 653. See also Christine Chairsell, "The California-Nevada Compact: Battling for Water in the North," in *Battle Born*, ed. A. Costandina Titus, 107–120.

14. Statement from the office of Senator Bible, June 1966, AB Papers, Box 118; *Nevada State Journal*, September 26, 1966.

15. Statement from the office of Senator Bible, November 4, 1966, AB Papers, Box 118.

16. For an analysis of the 1982 Reclamation Reform Act, which abolished the 160-acre limitation set by the Reclamation Act of 1902 (Newlands Act) and imposed a new limit of 960 acres, see U.S. Congress, House, Committee on Interior and Insular Affairs, *Water Subsidies: Basic Changes Needed to Avoid Abuse of the 960-Acre Limit*, GAO/RCED-90-6 (Washington, D.C.: GAO, 1989).

17. Jones, *Water*, vol. 2, 67, 78. In 1961 the State of Nevada commissioned a report on the water supply problems in the Las Vegas Valley. The report indicated that groundwater was being consumed at an alarming rate and recommended various conservation measures to preserve water-table levels. The study con-

cluded that only a water delivery system from Lake Mead to the valley would solve the problem. See Nevada, Director of Conservation and Natural Resources, *Report on Water Supply for the Las Vegas Valley*, 14–16, 18, 21.

18. U.S. Department of the Interior News Bulletin, January 22, 1963, 3. See also statement of Stewart L. Udall before the Senate Subcommittee on Irrigation and Reclamation concerning S. 1658, March 1964. On April 4, 1964, Udall forwarded his Pacific Southwest Water Plan to Henry Jackson, chairman of the Senate Committee on Interior and Insular Affairs. The estimated cost for the first phase was projected at $1,387,000,000. Consequently, Bible concluded that only a separate water bill similar to S. 2388, which he had introduced in 1963, would guarantee the Southern Nevada Water Project. See AB Papers, Box 154.

19. Statement from the office of Senator Alan Bible, February 19, 1964, AB Papers, Box 90.

20. Ibid.

21. In 1950 the population of Clark County stood at 48,289, and by the mid-1960s it was well over 200,000 people. Moreover, Clark County's heavy Democratic registration held the balance of state power, which had, by the 1960s, shifted from Reno to Las Vegas. See Nevada, State Planning Coordinator's Office, *Nevada Statistical Abstract*, 1981, 5.

22. Unsigned memos to President Johnson, February 4, 1965, and February 10, 1965, White House Central File, Name File, Box 248, LBJ Library.

23. Senator Kuchel's views were clearly expressed on the floor of the Senate in a speech delivered in opposition to the Central Arizona Water Project, S. 1658, sponsored by Carl Hayden and Barry Goldwater. See *CR*, April 25, 1964, 8824–8831. Kuchel took the position that the Central Arizona Water Project could not infringe on California's guaranteed allotment of 4.4 million acre-feet and wanted assurances from the two Arizonans that all water needed for the Arizona project would be subject to California's guarantee. Kuchel was also concerned about the powers of the secretary of the interior in the absence of congressional action to allocate Colorado River water following the Supreme Court decision in *Arizona* v. *California*. In 1965 he moved to assure congressional action that would protect state water laws with the introduction of S. 1636. When it failed to pass, Kuchel introduced the same legislation in the 90th Congress, S. 2530, which likewise failed to pass the measure. For support of the Kuchel position, see statement of Northcutt Ely, April 1964, before the Senate Committee on Interior and Insular Affairs on S. 1658, contained in the AB Papers, Box 154. Ely represented the six-agency committee of water users in southern California. See *Nevada State Journal*, January 7, 1965, section D.

24. Bible interview by author, October 3, 1987. It should be noted that Bible did not object to regional water projects. He simply wanted southern Nevada's project to be the first in time; otherwise, growth and development could not continue at the record-setting pace of the later 1950s. After Congress passed S. 32, Bible supported the National Water Commission and S. 3107 in the 89th Congress.

25. *Las Vegas Review-Journal*, April 11, 1965.

26. U.S. Congress, Senate, *A Bill to Authorize the Secretary of the Interior to Construct, Operate, and Maintain the Southern Nevada Water Project, Nevada, and for Other Purposes*, S. 32, 89th Congress, 1st Session, 1965, 1–5; U.S. Congress, Senate, Committee on Interior and Insular Affairs, Southern Nevada Water Project, *Hearings before the Subcommittee on Irrigation and Reclamation*, S. 32, 89th Congress, 2d Session, 1965. See also *Nevada Revised Statutes*, section 538:220.

27. Senate, *Hearings*, 23.

28. Ibid., 14. See also *Las Vegas Review-Journal*, September 27, 1965; and the *Nevada State Journal*, October 8, 1965. For example, Congressman Baring voted against the administration's Medicare, civil rights, and food stamp programs, which upset Congressman Fogarty to the point of voting against the Southern Nevada Water Project (*Las Vegas Review-Journal*, August 2, 1964). Moreover, Baring did not participate in the House debate and did not vote on the Southern Nevada Water Project. He was joined in a general pair with Congressman Duncan of Oregon, which, under the House rules, does not reflect how either congressman would have voted. See memorandum from Joe T. McDonnell to Alan Bible, October 21, 1965, in AB Papers, Box 258. For an explanation of House voting rules, see Lewis A. Froman, Jr., *The Congressional Process: Strategies, Rules, and Procedures*, 126.

29. Mike Manatos to Marvin Watson, January 11, 1966, White House Central File, Box 248. See also *Las Vegas Review-Journal*, October 24, 1965; and P.L. 89-292. Section 6 of S. 32 would have conflicted with the Supreme Court ruling in *Arizona* v. *California*, which gave the secretary of the interior broad powers in water allocation. Westerners have constantly asked for government assistance without federal influence or controls, all in the name of states' rights. Some took the view that deletion of section 6 was further evidence of the erosion of Nevada's rights in relation to Colorado River water. Luckily, Senators Bible and Cannon took no such position and moved quickly to remove section 6 by sponsoring S. 2999. See *CR*, June 24, 1966, 13631–13633; and *House Congressional Record*, vol. 112, no. 107, 13951. For an extreme position on Nevada's rights, see *Las Vegas Review-Journal*, April 17, 1966, editorial viewpoint by Tom Wilson. After signing the Southern Nevada Water Project bill, President Johnson wrote in a personal note to Bible that he hoped passage of the bill would help the senator because it was the least he could do for a man who had rendered so many past favors. See AB Papers, Box 258.

30. *Las Vegas Review-Journal*, July 24, 1966, and September 16, 1966.

31. *Las Vegas Sun*, March 28, 1966, April 30, 1966, and October 13, 1966. The October 13, 1966, editorial is extremely flattering in praising the contributions of Senator Bible in the success of the Southern Nevada Water Project. This is an interesting reversal of position for the *Sun*'s owner and publisher, Hank Greenspun, who for so long had been at political odds with Bible, an opposition that went back to the days when the senator was aligned with Nevada's political boss, Pat McCarran. But in 1961 Bible had urged President Kennedy to pardon Green-

spun for his violation of the Neutrality Act, restoring his rights, and Greenspun appreciated it.

32. Statement from the office of Senator Alan Bible, July 20, 1967, AB Papers, Box 89. See also U.S. Department of the Interior News Bulletin, March 18, 1967.

33. Bible interview by author, October 3, 1987; Carpenter interview by author, October 27, 1987. Neither man could remember the exact date of the meeting. The presidential diary cards show an evening meeting between Bible and President Johnson on July 25, 1967. See LBJ Library, Diary Cards for Senator Bible.

34. Ibid.

35. Jones, *Water*, vol. 2, 167. Also, Oran Gragson interview by author, October 27, 1987. Mr. Gragson, a Republican, was mayor of Las Vegas from 1959 to 1975; he agrees that without Alan Bible in the United States Senate, the southern Nevada Water Project would never have been completed. On April 30, 1969, Bible wrote a letter to President Richard M. Nixon expressing his concern over the administration's plans to cut more than $18 million from the budget that had been appropriated for the Southern Nevada Water Project. His plea was successful; Nixon notified Bible on January 31, 1970, that the funds would be restored in the budget. See Alan Bible to President Richard M. Nixon, April 30, 1969; and statement from the office of Senator Bible, January 31, 1970: AB Papers, Box 258.

36. *Nevada Statistical Abstract*, 1981, 4. The author wishes to thank Michael Wallen of the Las Vegas Valley Water District for supplying historic records on water consumption in the Las Vegas Valley. For a complete report on water conditions in southern Nevada, see Nevada, Division of Water and Planning, *Water Supply Report: Water for Southern Nevada*, 1982. See also Milton N. Nathanson, *Updating the Hoover Dam Documents* (Washington, D.C.: U.S. Department of Interior, 1978).

37. Edwards, "Nevada: Gambling and the Federal-State Relationship," 252.

38. Ingram, *Water Politics*, vi, vii.

39. Statement from the office of Senator Bible, May 4, 1964, AB Papers, Box 76.

40. Department of the Interior News Release, July 26, 1967, AB Papers, Box 76; statement from the office of Senator Bible, March 11, 1967, AB Papers, Box 76.

41. U.S. Department of the Interior, National Park Service, *News Release, Great Basin National Park*, 27 March 1964.

42. *Nevada State Journal*, August 2, 1964; *Ely Daily Times*, November 10, 1964.

43. U.S. Congress, Senate, *A Bill to Establish the Great Basin National Park in Nevada*, S. 499, 89th Congress, 1st Session, 1965. See also U.S. Congress, House, *A Bill to Establish the Great Basin National Park in Nevada*, H.R. 6122, 89th Congress, 1st Session, 1965; *Las Vegas Review-Journal*, May 9, 1965.

44. *Ely Daily Times*, July 7, 1965; *Las Vegas Sun*, July 9, 1965.

45. Alan Bible to M. Burrell Bybee, Chairman, National Park Committee, White Pine Chamber of Commerce and Mines, July 28, 1965, AB Papers, Box 258. See also the vertical file for correspondence of the Great Basin Range National Park Association, Special Collections Department, University of Nevada, Reno, Library. Additionally, the Richard C. Sill Papers maintained in the Special Col-

lections Department, University of Nevada, Reno, Library, contain many of the position papers of the Sierra Club. Both the Sierra Club and the Great Basin Range National Park Association supported the park along the lines of the various Bible bills and the Department of the Interior.

46. Walter S. Baring to M. Burrell Bybee, August 6, 1965, AB Papers, Box 258.

47. J. R. Deveraux to Walter S. Baring, August 10, 1965; Burrell Bybee to Secretary of Interior Stewart Udall, August 13, 1965: AB Papers, Box 258.

48. Walter S. Baring to Alan Bible, August 13, 1965, AB Papers, Box 258; *Elko Free Press*, August 18, 1965; *Battle Mountain News*, August 12, 1965; *Tonopah Times*, August 13, 1965; *Carson Nevada Appeal*, August 11, 1965.

49. Joint statement from the offices of Senators Alan Bible and Howard Cannon, September 1, 1965, AB Papers, Box 258.

50. Walter S. Baring to Nate E. Bayless, President, White Pine Chamber of Commerce and Mines, January 6, 1966; Stewart Udall to Walter S. Baring, February 5, 1966; statement from the office of Senator Alan Bible, February 26, 1966: AB Papers, Box 258.

51. *Nevada State Journal*, March 1, 1966.

52. Alan Bible to Walter S. Baring, March 27, 1966, AB Papers, Box 258, *Ely Daily Times*, March 28, 1966, and March 29, 1966.

53. Walter S. Baring to Alan Bible, March 30, 1966, AB Papers, Box 258.

54. Department of the Interior, National Park Service, to Alan Bible, April 1, 1966, AB Papers, Box 258.

55. Statement from the office of Senator Bible, *Washington Round-up*, April 1966, AB Papers, Box 99.

56. Transcript of meeting between Alan Bible, Howard Cannon, Walter S. Baring, and Secretary of the Interior Stewart Udall, 5, 6, 9, 15, 16, 18, 22, 25, 31, 33, AB Papers, Box 258.

57. Michael P. Malone, "The Collapse of Western Metal Mining: An Historical Epitaph," *Pacific Historical Review* 55 (August 1986): 455–464. See also Elliott, "A Legacy of Support," 183–97.

58. U.S. Department of the Interior, Bureau of Land Management, *Effects of Livestock Grazing on Wildlife, Watershed, Recreation and Other Resource Values in Nevada*, 21, 22, 38, 46, 49, 50–53, 55, 61. For a report on the continued deterioration of rangeland and riparian areas, see U.S. Congress, House, Committee on Interior and Insular Affairs, *Rangeland Management: More Emphasis Needed on Declining and Overstocked Grazing Allotments and Public Rangelands: Some Riparian Areas Restored But Widespread Improvement Will Be Slow*, (Washington, D.C.: Government Accounting Office, 1988).

59. Steve Oulman, "Copper, Cows, and Crown Jewels"; U.S. Department of the Interior, Bureau of Land Mangement, *White Pine Power Project: Draft Environmental Impact Statement, Summary*, October 1983, 3, 7, 10. For example, employment in the White Pine County mining industry dropped from 1,090 to 340 persons between 1971 and 1980 and overall employment dropped from 3,660 in

1971 to 3,280 in 1980. Moreover, adjusted per capita personal income in 1959 was $3,109 as compared to $3,078 in 1970. See Nevada State Planning Coordinator's Office, *Nevada Statistical Abstract*, 53, 55, 63, 147.

60. Donald J. Pisani, "Conflict over Conservation: The Reclamation Service and the Tahoe Contract," *Western Historical Quarterly* 10, no. 2 (April 1979): 167–190.

61. Ibid., 178, 179.

62. Ibid., 184, 185.

63. Douglas H. Strong, *Tahoe: An Environmental History*, 104, 105.

64. Ibid., 158.

65. Ibid., 91, 93; Stewart L. Udall to Grant Sawyer, November 3, 1961; statement from the office of Senator Bible, September 21, 1961; Stewart L. Udall to Alan Bible, August 6, 1964: AB Papers, Box 248.

66. Statements from the office of Senator Bible, August 12 and 21, 1964, AB Papers, Box 248.

67. U.S. Congress, Senate, *A Bill to Provide for a National Parkway at Lake Tahoe*, S. 1116, 89th Congress, 2d Session, 1965; *CR*, Senate, February 11, 1965, 2547.

68. Strong, *Tahoe*, 111–115; U.S. Congress, Senate, *A Bill to Provide for the Bi-State Tahoe Regional Planning Compact*, S. 3946, 90th Congress, 2d Session, 1968.

69. Department of the Interior News Release, October 12, 1966, AB Papers, Box 99.

70. U.S. Congress, Senate, *A Bill to Provide for the Administration of Lake Mead Recreation Area*, S. 653, 88th Congress, 1st Session, 1963; P.L. 88-639. See also Department of the Interior News Release, October 12, 1966, AB Papers, Box 99.

71. George B. Hartzog, Jr., to Alan Bible, December 30, 1964, AB Papers, Box 99.

72. Statements from the office of Senator Bible, June 27, 1965, December 14, 1967, and December 29, 1967; Department of the Interior News Release, June 9, 1966: AB Papers, Box 90.

73. Vernon Bostick, "Can We Stop Polluting Lake Mead Now," *Nevadan, Las Vegas-Review Journal*, June 23, 1968.

74. Murray G. Hoyt to Alan Bible, May 22, 1968; Alan Bible to Murray G. Hoyt, June 5, 1968; and Department of the Interior News Release, October 28, 1968: AB Papers, Box 90.

75. Statements from the office of Senator Bible, March 20, 1964, April 6, 1964, and June 26, 1964; Floyd Iverson to Alan Bible, July 27, 1965: AB Papers, Box 99.

76. Ibid.

77. Statement from the office of Senator Bible, undated, AB Papers, Box 125.

78. *Washington Round-up*, from the office of Senator Bible, January 1966, March 1967, AB Papers, Box 294. For details of the battle over the peace plank at the 1968 Democratic Convention, see Charles Kaiser, *1968 in America*, 238–240.

79. Alan Bible to Andy Ulrich, April 28, 1972, AB Papers, Box 125.

80. Statement from the office of Senator Bible, December 30, 1967, AB Papers, Box 108, 114; *Nevada State Journal*, January 1, 1968.

81. Bible, "Recollections," 320, 321.

82. Merrill-Wirthlin and Associates, *1968 Election in Nevada* (undated, 1968), 44A, 46A.

83. *Las Vegas Review-Journal*, October 27, 1968.

84. *1968 Election in Nevada*, 76A; *Las Vegas Sun*, November 3, 1968; *Nevada State Journal*, November 5, 1968.

85. *1968 Election in Nevada*, 77A, 78A, 79A.

86. *Las Vegas Review-Journal*, October 31, 1968, and November 3, 1968.

87. Nevada, *Official Returns of the General Election of 1968*, 6.

88. Carpenter interview by author, August 22, 1989; and Bob McDonald interview by author, June 11, 1991.

89. *Las Vegas Sun*, November 4, 1988.

90. Lyndon B. Johnson to Alan Bible, November 20, 1968; Lyndon B. Johnson to Alan Bible, January 17, 1969: White House Central File, Name File, Box 248, LBJ Library.

CHAPTER ELEVEN. SOMETHING SAVED, SOMETHING LOST, 1969–1974

1. Foley, *The New Senate*, 65.

2. Arthur M. Schlesinger, Jr., *The Imperial Presidency*; Dahl, *Pluralist Democracy in the United States*, 142.

3. Richard E. Neustadt, *Presidential Power: The Politics of Leadership*; Louis W. Koenig, "Reassessing the Imperial Presidency," in *The American Presidency: A Policy Perspective from Readings and Documents*, ed. David C. Kozak and Kenneth N. Cibroski, 568–577. For a good general treatment of the American presidency up to 1968, see Louis W. Koenig, *The Chief Executive*. See also Robert E. DiClerico, *The American Presidency*, 89–105, which details the conflict between the president and Congress over the impoundment issue.

4. Foley, *The New Senate*, 66–77. See also Lester M. Salaman, "The Presidency and Domestic Policy Formulation," in *Analyzing the Presidency*, ed. Robert E. DiClerico, 208–229.

5. P.L. 91-631.

6. Richard Current, T. Harry Williams, Frank Freidel, and Alan Brinkley, *American History—A Survey*, 912.

7. *The Public Land Law Review Commission*, P.L. 88-606, Stat 982, 42 USC 1391–1400. Representative Wayne Aspinall was concerned with land withdrawals by executive departments without the approval of Congress. He saw the commission as a way to reverse the trend in executive action. Aspinall wanted a greater role for congressional committees having jurisdiction over land-use policy in the decision-making process. The commission included Senators Gordon Allott, Clinton Anderson, Alan Bible, Henry Jackson, Len B. Jordan, and Thomas Kuchel; and Representatives Wayne Aspinall, Walter Baring, Lawrence Burton, John Kyl, John Saylor, Roy Taylor, and Morris Udall.

8. Alan Bible to Lawrence F. O'Brien, November 24, 1964; office files of John Macey, Box 852, LBJ Library. W. Howard Gray was appointed to the Public Land Law Review Commission on August 19, 1965.

9. U.S. Report to the President and the Congress by the Public Land Law Review Commission, *One Third of the Nation's Land*, 12.

10. U.S. Congress, Senate, *Mineral Development Act of 1971*, S. 2542, 92d Congress, 1st Session, 1971.

11. Statement from the office of Senator Bible, October 1971, AB Papers, Index Citation 1/2/3 through 1/2/5.

12. Ibid.

13. Nevada Mining Association, *Newsletter*, July 15, 1970.

14. *Reno Evening Gazette*, October 12, 1971.

15. Statement from the office of Senator Bible, October 15, 1971, AB Papers, Index Citation 1/2/3 through 1/2/5.

16. William K. Wyant, *Westward in Eden: The Public Conservation Movement*, 141–149. See also Thomas L. Kimball to Alan Bible, September 30, 1971, AB Papers, Index Citation 1/2/3 through 1/2/5.

17. Statement from the office of Senator Bible, October 15, 1971, AB Papers, Index Citation 1/2/3 through 1/2/5.

18. Current, et al., *American History—A Survey*, 911.

19. *CR*, March 24, 1971; P.L. 91-581, *The Geothermal Steam Act of 1970*. See also AB Papers, Box 116.

20. Statement from the office of Senator Bible, November 26, 1971, AB Papers, Index Citation 1/9/1 through 1/9/3 (quote); *Las Vegas Sun*, November 29, 1971.

21. 48 Stat. 1269, amended June 26, 1936 (49 Stat. 1976), July 14, 1939 (53 Stat. 1002), July 30, 1947 (61 Stat. 630), August 6, 1947 (61 Stat. 790), June 19, 1948 (62 Stat. 533), and May 28, 1954 (68 Stat. 151). For a complete explanation of the Taylor Grazing Act and its provisions, see U.S. Department of the Interior, Bureau of Land Management, *The Taylor Grazing Act*.

22. Statements from the office of Senator Bible, February 19, 1962, and January 16, 1963; Alan Bible to Stewart L. Udall, February 11, 1963, and February 13, 1963: AB Papers, Box 94.

23. Department of the Interior News Release, February 15, 1963, AB Papers, Box 94.

24. Wayne Aspinall to Lyndon B. Johnson, November 30, 1965, AB Papers, Index Citation 1/2/3 through 1/2/5.

25. Nevada, "Preliminary Position on Federal Land Laws," March 1, 1966, 4, AB Papers, Index Citation 1/2/3 through 1/2/5.

26. Ibid., 2.

27. Statement of the Nevada State Cattle Association to the Public Land Law Review Commission, November 1, 1967, AB Papers, Index Citation 1/2/3 through 1/2/5.

28. Statement from the office of Senator Bible, December 9, 1968, AB Papers, Box 96. The 1968 proposal was the result of a two-year study by the departments

of Interior and Agriculture to revise the fee schedule for a ten-year period with a base fee as high as $1.23 per AUM. See also George H. Siehl, "A Brief History of Grazing Fees on Federal Land."

29. Statement from the office of Senator Bible, February 27, 1969, AB Papers, Box 96.

30. *One Third of the Nation's Land*, 114, Recommendation 41.

31. U.S. Congress, Senate, *A Bill to Require the Protection, Management, and Control of Wild Free-Roaming Horses and Burros on Public Lands*, S. 1116, 92d Congress, 1st Session, 1971; P.L. 92-195, enacted December 15, 1971.

32. U.S. Congress, Senate, *A Bill Relating to the Administration of Grazing Districts*, S. 2028, 92d Congress, 1st Session, 1971.

33. Roy Whitacre to Alan Bible, June 21, 1967; Department of the Interior News Release, October 3, 1967: AB Papers, Box 118.

34. Timothy G. Haller, "The Legislative Battle over the California-Nevada Interstate Water Compact: A Question of Might versus Native American Right," *Nevada Historical Society Quarterly* 32, no. 3 (Fall 1989): 198–221.

35. *U.S. v. Orr Water Ditch Co. et al.*, U.S. Dist. Ct. D. Nev. Equity No. A3 (1944).

36. *Sierra Club Bulletin*, September 1970, 8–11; *American Heritage* magazine, June 1970.

37. *Pyramid Paiute Tribe of Indians v. Truckee-Carson Irrigation District*, 103 S. CT. 26 09 (1983). See also Chairsell, "The California-Nevada Compact," 107–120. For a passionate and spirited defense of the Paiute Indian of Pyramid Lake, see Martha C. Knack and Omer C. Stewart, *As Long as the River Shall Run: An Ethnohistory of Pyramid Lake Indian Reservation*.

38. *Herminghaus v. Southern California Edison Company*, 200 Cal. 81, 252 PAC 607 (1926).

39. Harrison C. Dunning, "Dam Fights and Water Policy in California," *Journal of the West* 39, no. 3 (July 1990): 14–27.

40. U.S. Congress, Senate, *Water Rights Act of 1967*, S. 2530, 90th Congress, 1st Session, 1967.

41. Clifford P. Hansen to Alan Bible, February 10, 1970, AB Papers, Index Citation 1/2/3 through 1/2/5; *One Third of the Nation's Land*, 146–154, Recommendations 56 through 59.

42. *California v. United States*, 438 US 645 (1978); *Ivanhoe Irrigation District v. MacCracken*, 357 US 275 (1958); *City of Fresno v. California*, 372 US 627 (1963). For a well-written and complete account of recent decisions on federal and state water rights, see Roderick E. Watson, "The Supreme Court's Changed Perspective on Federal-State Water Relations: A Personal Memoir of the New Melones Case," *Journal of the West* 39, no. 3 (July 1990): 28–39.

43. Watson, "The Supreme Court's Changed Perspective," 37.

44. Jack Carpenter to Alan Bible, November 25, 1968, AB Papers, Box 89.

45. Department of the Interior News Release, March 3, 1968, AB Papers, Box 47.

46. Statement from the office of Senator Bible, April 1, 1970; cost estimates and budget proposals by the Department of the Interior, National Park Service, AB Papers, Box 99.

47. Strong, *Tahoe*, 30.

48. Ibid., 46.

49. Douglas H. Strong, "Lake Tahoe Development Concerns," in *Battle Born*, ed. A. Costandina Titus, 45–59. (see 48).

50. Ibid., 50, 51; U.S. Congress, Senate, *A Bill to Establish the Tahoe Regional Planning Compact*, S. 118, 91st Congress, 1st Session, 1971; P.L. 91-148, December 18, 1969.

51. Nevada State Senate Resolution #15, February 26, 1969; *Nevada State Journal*, February 25, 1969.

52. U.S. Congress, Senate, *A Bill to Authorize a Feasibility Study to Establish a National Lakeshore Recreation Area at Lake Tahoe, Nevada*, 2208, 91st Congress, 1st Session, 1971; *CR*, May 20, 1969; S. 5408; P.L. 91-425, enacted September 26, 1970.

53. Alan Bible to Joseph F. McDonald, Sr., September 25, 1969, AB Papers, Box 75; statement from the office of Senator Bible, April 7, 1970, AB Papers, Box 248.

54. U.S. Congress, Senate, *A Bill to Extend the Boundaries of the Toiyabe National Forest*, S. 3279, 91st Congress, 2d Session 1971; Senate Report No. 91-780, 91st Congress, 2d Session, April 23, 1970; P.L. 91-372, *The Land and Water Conservation Fund Act*, 78 Stat 903, section 6; *Sacramento Bee*, April 11, 1970.

55. Strong, "Lake Tahoe Development Concerns," 158–162.

56. Covill and Weinberg, "Alan Bible: Democratic Senator from Nevada," 14–15.

57. Ibid., 15.

58. Strong, "Lake Tahoe Development Concerns," 187.

59. Covill and Weinberg, "Alan Bible: Democratic Senator from Nevada," 1.

60. Ibid., 15; Viola Scott Thomas to Dwight Dyer, February 4, 1971, AB Papers, Box 99.

61. Hartzog, *Battling for the National Parks*, 203, 204.

62. Roderick Nash, *Wilderness and the American Mind*, 290.

63. Hays, *Beauty, Health, and Permanence*, 411.

64. Hartzog, *Battling for the National Parks*, 211.

65. Ibid., 212.

66. Ibid., 213; Loucile Bible interview by author, August 15, 1989; Dr. Fred Anderson interview by author, August 22, 1989; Bob McDonald interview by author, August 22, 1989. In August 1989 the author spent two weeks in Alaska to get some idea of Bible's experience while visiting the state.

67. Hartzog, *Battling for the National Parks*, 213.

68. Ibid., 214.

69. Ibid., 215.

70. Ibid., 216.

71. Ibid., 219, 220.

72. Ibid., 220.

73. Ibid., 221.

74. *CR*, August 28, 1970, 30364.

75. Statement from the office of Senator Jackson, June 12, 1973, AB Papers, Box 292.

CHAPTER TWELVE. CONCLUSION

1. Bible interview by author, September 6, 1986.

2. Chester Smith interview by author, September 17, 1988. Smith and Bible remained friends, but over the years their relationship became strained, especially during election campaigns. Still, Smith believes that Bible did a great deal for Nevada and the nation through expansion of the national park system (Smith to author, October 19, 1993).

3. Bible interview by author, October 3, 1987.

4. Philip L. Fradkin, *Sagebrush Country: Land and the American West*, 231–248. See also Wallace Stegner, *The Uneasy Chair: A Biography of Bernard DeVoto*; and Wallace Stegner, ed., *The Letters of Bernard DeVoto*.

5. Loucile Bible interview by author, August 29, 1990.

6. Bible interview by author, October 4, 1987.

7. Henry P. Canfield, "The Conservation and Environmental Movements," in *Environmental Politics and Policy: Theories and Evidence*, ed. James P. Lester, 2–55.

8. Ibid., 34.

9. Nash, *Wilderness and the American Mind*, 272, 273.

10. Patricia Nelson Limerick, *Desert Passages: Encounters with the American Desert*, 75.

11. Grant Sawyer interview by author, May 4, 1988; Mike O'Callaghan interview by author, September 14, 1988.

12. Nevada, *Political History of Nevada*, 290.

13. U.S. Congress, Senate, *Manual of Rules, Regulations, and Procedures* (Washington, D.C.: GPO, 1975), 853. Bible resigned on December 17, 1974.

14. *Nevada State Journal*, August 29, 1973; *Nevada Appeal*, August 26, 1973, and August 29, 1973; *Las Vegas Review-Journal*, February 15, 1974; *Reno Evening Gazette*, December 17, 1974; Jack McCloskey, "Alan Bible—A Tribute," *Mineral County Independent*, October 1965.

15. Hank Greenspun, "Where I Stand," *Las Vegas Sun*, September 14, 1988.

Bibliography

INTERVIEWS

Anderson, Fred. August 22, 1989.
Bible, Alan. September 5, 1986, September 6, 1986, November 1, 1986, January 9, 1987, January 22, 1987, October 3, 1987, October 4, 1987, February 20, 1988.
Bible, Bill. August 21, 1989.
Bible, Loucile. August 15, 1989, August 22, 1989, August 29, 1990.
Cannon, Howard. October 25, 1988, November 3, 1988, December 28, 1988.
Carnahan, Tom. September 14, 1987.
Carpenter, Jack. October 27, 1987, August 22, 1989.
Gragson, Oran. October 27, 1987.
Hannifan, Laurada. November 8, 1989.
Hartzog, George B., Jr. July 30, 1990.
McDonald, Bob. August 23, 1989, June 11, 1991.
O'Callaghan, Mike. September 8, 1988, September 14, 1988.
Overton, Allen J., Jr. May 2, 1989.
Rice, Gordon. August 22, 1989.
Sawyer, Grant. May 4, 1988, May 22, 1991.
Smith, Chester. September 17, 1988, October 3, 1988, August 18, 1989, August 30, 1989, October 19, 1993.
Wallen, Michael. October 10, 1988.

ORAL HISTORY TRANSCRIPTS

Adams, Eva. "Windows of Washington: Nevada Education, the United States Senate, the U.S. Mint." Reno: University of Nevada Oral History Project, 1968.
Bible, Alan. "Recollections of a Nevada Native Son: The Law, Politics, the Nevada Attorney General's Office, and the United States Senate." Reno: University of Nevada Oral History Project, 1981.
Biltz, Norman. "Memoirs of the Duke of Nevada: Development of Lake Tahoe, California and Nevada: Reminiscences of Nevada Political and Financial Life." Reno: University of Nevada Oral History Project, 1967.
Cahill, Robbins. "Recollections of Work in State Politics, Government, Taxa-

tion, Gaming Control, Clark County Administrator and Nevada Resort Association." Reno: University of Nevada Oral History Project, 1977.

Cahlan, John F. "Reminiscences of a Reno and Las Vegas Newspaperman, University Regent and Public Spirited Citizen." Reno: University of Nevada Oral History Project, 1968.

McCloskey, John R. "Seventy Years of Griping: Newspapers, Politics, Government." Reno: University of Nevada Oral History Project, 1982.

McDonald, Joseph F. "The Life of a Newsboy in Nevada." Reno: University of Nevada Oral History Project, 1971.

MANUSCRIPT COLLECTIONS

Dwight D. Eisenhower Library, Abilene, Kansas
    White House Central File
John F. Kennedy Library, Dorecester, Massachusetts
    White House Name File
Lyndon Baines Johnson Library, Austin, Texas
    Congressional File
    Diary Cards
    John Macey Papers
    Senate Master File
    White House Central File, Name Index
Nevada, State Division of Archives and Records, Carson City
    Attorney General Case and Client Files
Getchell Library, University of Nevada, Reno
    Alan Bible Papers
    Richard C. Sill Papers
    Vertical File for Correspondence of the Great Basin Range National Park Association

THESES AND DISSERTATIONS

Elliott, Gary E. "Land, Water, and Power: The Politics of Nevada Senator Alan Bible, 1934–1974." Ph.D. dissertation, Northern Arizona University, 1990.

Kaufman, Perry Bruce. "The Best City of Them All: A History of Las Vegas." Ph.D. dissertation, University of California, Santa Barbara, 1974.

Oulman, Steve. "Copper, Cows, and Crown Jewels." Master's thesis, University of Oregon, 1987.

CONGRESSIONAL DOCUMENTS

U.S. Congress. House. Banking and Currency Committee. *Hearings on the Coinage Act.* H.R. 8926, June 1965.

U.S. Congress. House. *Report of the Banking and Currency Committee on the Coinage Act*. Report 509, 1965.

————. *Report of the Banking and Currency Committee on the Repeal of the Purchase of Silver*. Report 183, 1963.

————. *Report of the Interior and Insular Affairs Committee by the Government Accounting Office on the 1982 Reclamation Reform Act*. GAO/RCED-90-6, 1989.

————. *Report of the Interior and Insular Affairs Committee by the Government Accounting Office on Rangeland Management*. 1988.

————. *Report of the Interior and Insular Affairs Committee to Preserve the Domestic Gold Mining Industry*. Report 1923, 1966.

U.S. Congress. Senate. Banking and Currency Committee. *Hearings on the Coinage Act*. S. 2036, June 1965.

————. *Hearings on Repeal of the 1934 Silver Purchase Act*. April 29, 1963.

U.S. Congress. Senate. Committee on Interior and Insular Affairs. *Hearings on the Cape Cod National Seashore Park*. S. 857, March 9, 1961.

————. *Hearings on the Great Basin National Park*. S. 2664, December 5, 1959.

————. *Hearings on the Great Basin National Park*. S. 1760, August 3, 1961.

————. *Hearings on the Indiana Dunes National Park*. S. 2249, March 5–7, 1964.

————. *Hearings on the Ozark Rivers National Monument Bill*. S. 1381, July 6, 1961.

————. *Hearings on the Point Reyes National Seashore*. S. 476, March 28–31, 1961.

————. *Hearings on the Sleeping Bear Dunes National Recreation Area*. S. 2153, November 13, 1961.

————. *Hearings on the Southern Nevada Water Project*. S. 32, May 1965.

U.S. Congress. Senate. *Report of the Banking and Currency Committee on the Coinage Act*. Report 317, 1965.

————. *Report of the Interior and Insular Affairs Committee on Extension of the Toiyabe National Forest*. Report 91-780, 1971.

————. *Report of the Interior and Insular Affairs Committee on the National Water Resources Act*. Report 1212, 1966.

————. *Report of the Senate Select Committee on National Water Resources*. Report 29, 1961.

————. *Third Interim Report of the Special Committee to Investigate Organized Crime in Interstate Commerce*. Report 307, 1951.

EXECUTIVE BRANCH DOCUMENTS

U.S. Army Corps of Engineers. *Water Resource Development in Nevada*. Washington, D.C.: GPO, 1959.

U.S. Department of Commerce. Bureau of the Census. *Population, Thirteenth Census of the United States*. Vol. 3. Washington, D.C.: GPO, 1910.

U.S. Department of the Interior. Bureau of Land Management. *Effects of Livestock Grazing on Wildlife Watershed, Recreation and Other Resource Values in Nevada*. Washington, D.C.: GPO, 1975.

————. *The Taylor Grazing Act.* Washington, D.C.: GPO, 1955.

————. *White Pine Power Project: Draft Environmental Impact Statement, Summary.* Washington, D.C.: GPO, 1983.

U.S. Department of the Interior. Bureau of Mines. *Silver.* Bulletin 630. Washington, D.C.: GPO, 1963.

————. *Silver: Facts, Estimates and Projections.* Information Circular 8257. Washington, D.C.: GPO, 1965.

U.S. Department of the Interior. Bureau of Reclamation. *Action Program for Resource Development, Truckee and Carson River Basins, California and Nevada.* Washington, D.C.: GPO, 1964.

U.S. Final Report to the President and to Congress by the National Water Commission. *Water Policies for the Future.* Washington, D.C.: GPO, 1973.

U.S. *President's Water Resources Policy Commission.* Vol. 1. Washington, D.C.: GPO, 1950.

U.S. Report to the President and the Congress by the Public Land Law Review Commission. *One Third of the Nation's Land.* Washington, D.C.: GPO, 1970.

DOCUMENTS: NEVADA

Nevada. *Official Returns of the General Election.* Carson City: State Printing Office, 1954–1974.

————. *Political History of Nevada.* Carson City: State Printing Office, 1986.

————. "Preliminary Position on Federal Land Laws." 1966.

————. *Reports of the Attorney General.* Carson City: State Printing Office, 1938–1956.

Nevada. Director of Conservation and Natural Resources. *Report on Water Supply for the Las Vegas Valley.* Carson City: State Printing Office, 1961.

Nevada. Division of Water and Planning. *Water Supply Report: Water for Southern Nevada.* Carson City: State Printing Office, 1982.

Nevada. State Planning Coordinator's Office. *Nevada Statistical Abstract.* Carson City: State Printing Office, 1981.

ARTICLES

Abbott, Carl. "The Metropolitan Region: Western Cities in the New Urban Era." In *The Twentieth Century West: Historical Interpretations,* edited by Gerald D. Nash and Richard W. Etulain, 71–98. Albuquerque: University of New Mexico Press, 1989.

Athearn, Robert G. "Colonialism: The Enduring Dilemma." In *Major Problems in the History of the American West,* edited by Clyde A. Milner II, 573–588. Lexington: D. C. Heath, 1989.

August, Jack L. "Carl Hayden, Arizona, and the Politics of Water Development in the Southwest, 1923–1928." *Pacific Historical Review* 58, no. 2 (May 1989): 195–216.

Bird, John W. "The End of the Monster of Riparianism in Nevada." *Nevada Historical Society Quarterly* 22 (Winter 1979): 271–277.

———. "A History of Water Rights in Nevada." *Nevada Historical Society Quarterly* 18 (Spring 1975): 27–32.

———. "A History of Water Rights in Nevada—Part II." *Nevada Historical Society Quarterly* 19 (Spring 1976): 27–32.

Bostick, Vernon. "Can We Stop Polluting Lake Mead Now." *Nevadan, Las Vegas Review-Journal,* June 23, 1968, 4–6.

Bowers, Michael W. "Federalism and Gaming Regulation in Nevada: The Case of Spilotro v. State." In *Battle Born,* edited by A. Costandina Titus, 183–195.

Canfield, Henry P. "The Conservation and Environmental Movements." In *Environmental Politics and Policy: Theories and Evidence,* edited by James P. Lester, 2–55. Durham: Duke University Press, 1989.

Carstensen, Vernon. "The Development and Application of Regional-Sectional Concepts, 1900–1950." In *Regionalism in America,* edited by Merrill Jensen, 112–115. Madison: University of Wisconsin Press, 1965.

Chairsell, Christine. "The California-Nevada Compact: Battling for Water in the North." In *Battle Born,* edited by A. Costandina Titus, 107–120.

Chase, Alston. "How to Save Our National Parks." *Atlantic* (July 1987): 35–44.

DeSantis, Hugh. "The Imperialist and American Innocence, 1865–1900." In *American Foreign Relations: A Historiographical Review,* edited by Gerald K. Haines and Samuel J. Walker, 67–78. Westport: Greenwood Press, 1986.

Drucker, Peter. "The Changed World Economy." *Foreign Affairs* 64 (Spring 1986): 768–770.

Dunning, Harrison C. "Dam Fights and Water Policy in California." *Journal of the West* 39, no. 3 (July 1990): 14–27.

Edwards, Jerome E. "Nevada: Gambling and the Federal-State Relationship." *Halcyon: Journal of the Humanities* (1989): 237–254.

Elliott, Gary E. "Arizona v. California: Nevada's Intervenor Role in the Struggle for Colorado River Water." In *Battle Born,* edited by A. Costandina Titus, 97–106.

———. "A Legacy of Support: Senator Alan Bible and the Nevada Mining Industry." *Nevada Historical Society Quarterly* 31, no. 3 (Fall 1988): 183–197.

———. "Senator Alan Bible and the Southern Nevada Water Project, 1954–1971." *Nevada Historical Society Quarterly* 32, no. 3 (Fall 1989): 181–197.

———. "Whose Land Is It: The Battle for the Great Basin National Park, 1957–1967." *Nevada Historical Society Quarterly* 34, no. 1 (Spring 1991): 241–256.

Elliott, Gary E., and Candace C. Kant. "Hank Greenspun Meets Joe McCarthy: The *Las Vegas Sun* Challenges First Amendment Violations." In *Battle Born,* edited by A. Costandina Titus, 196–205.

Findlay, John M. "Suckers and Escapists: Interpreting Las Vegas and Post-War America." *Nevada Historical Society Quarterly* 33, no. 1 (Spring 1990): 1–15.

Firor, John. "The Heating Up of the Climate." *Colorado Journal of International Environmental Law and Policy* 1, no. 1 (Summer 1990): 29–40.

Fritchey, Clayton. "Who Belongs to the Senate Inner Club." *Harper's* 234 (May 1967): 104–110.

Graves, Aubrey. "Fights on to Save Shore Areas." *Washington Post,* June 27, 1961.

Green, Michael S. "The Las Vegas Newspaper War of the 1950s." *Nevada Historical Society Quarterly* 31, no. 3 (Fall 1988): 155–182.

Haller, Timothy G. "The Legislative Battle over the California-Nevada Interstate Water Compact: A Question of Might versus Native American Right." *Nevada Historical Society Quarterly* 32, no. 3 (Fall 1989): 198–221.

Huitt, Ralph K. "Democratic Party Leadership in the Senate." *American Political Science Review* 55 (June 1961): 331–344.

Hundley, Norris, Jr. "The Dark and Bloody Ground of Indian Water Rights: Confusion Elevated to Principle." *Western Historical Quarterly* (October 1978): 455–481.

Hutchenson, Austin E., and Don W. Driggs. "The 1956 Election in Nevada." *Western Political Quarterly* (November 1956): 132–134.

Jensen, Richard. "On Modernizing Frederick Jackson Turner: The Historiography of Regionalism." *Western Historical Quarterly* (July 1980): 307–322.

Kleppner, Paul. "Politics without Parties: The Western States, 1900–1984." In *The Twentieth Century West,* edited by Gerald D. Nash and Richard W. Etulain, 295–338.

Knack, Martha C. "Federal Jurisdiction over Indian Water Rights in Nevada." In *Battle Born,* edited by A. Costandina Titus, 121–135.

Koenig, Louis W. "Reassessing the Imperial Presidency." In *The American Presidency: A Policy Perspective from Readings and Documents,* edited by David C. Kozak and Kenneth N. Ciboski, 568–577. Chicago: Nelson-Hall, 1985.

Kolko, Gabriel. "To Master the Third World." In *Major Problems in American Foreign Policy since 1914,* Vol. 2. edited by Thomas G. Paterson, 620–624. Boston: D. C. Heath, 1986.

Koppes, Clayton R. "Efficiency, Equity, Esthetics: Shifting Themes in American Conservation." In *The Ends of the Earth: Perspectives on Modern Environmental History,* edited by Donald Worster, 230–251. New York: Cambridge University Press, 1988.

Large, Arlen J. "Coin's Silver Content Sparks a New Debate in Congress, Industry." *Wall Street Journal,* April 2, 1964.

Lawson, Steven F. "Civil Rights." In *Exploring the Lyndon Johnson Years,* edited by Robert A. Divine, 93–125. Austin: University of Texas Press, 1981.

Lee, Lawrence B. "100 Years of Reclamation Historiography." *Pacific Historical Review,* 47, no. 4 (November 1978): 507–563.

Malone, Michael P. "Beyond the Last Frontier: Toward a New Approach to Western American History." *Western Historical Quarterly* 20, no. 4 (November 1989): 409–427.

———. "The Collapse of Western Metal Mining: An Historical Epitaph." *Pacific Historical Review* 55 (August 1986): 455–464.

Maxwell, Neal A. "The Conference of Western Senators." *Western Political Quarterly* (December 1957): 902–910.

———. "The West on Capitol Hill." In *Western Politics,* edited by Frank H. Jonas, 357–359.

McCloskey, Michael. "The Wilderness Act of 1964: Its Background and Meaning." *Oregon Law Review* 45 (June 1966): 288–321.

McMahon, Robert J. "The Cold War in Asia: Toward a New Synthesis." *Diplomatic History* 12, no. 3 (Summer 1988): 307–327.

Miller, Catherine M. "Water Rights and the Bankruptcy of Judicial Action: The Case of Herminghaus v. Southern California Edison." *Pacific Historical Review* 68, no. 1 (February 1989): 83–107.

Moehring, Eugene P. "Las Vegas and the Second World War." *Nevada Historical Society Quarterly* 29, no. 1 (Spring 1986): 1–30.

———. "Public Works and the New Deal in Las Vegas, 1933–1940." *Nevada Historical Society Quarterly* 24, no. 2 (Summer 1981): 107–129.

Mood, Fulmer. "The Origin, Evolution, and Application of the Sectional Conflict, 1750–1900." In *Regionalism in America,* edited by Merrill Jensen, 5–98.

Pickens, Donald K. "Westward Expansion and the End of American Exceptionalism: Sumner, Turner, and Webb." *Western Historical Quarterly* (October 1981): 409–418.

Pisani, Donald J. "Conflict over Conservation: The Reclamation Service and the Tahoe Contract." *Western Historical Quarterly* 10, no. 2 (April 1979): 167–190.

———. "Enterprise and Equity: A Critique of Western Water Law in the Nineteenth Century." *Western Historical Quarterly* 23, no. 1 (January 1978): 15–37.

———. "Federal Reclamation and Water Rights in Nevada." *Agricultural History* (July 1977): 540–558.

———. "The Irrigation District and the Federal Relationship: Neglected Aspects of Water History in the Twentieth Century." In *The Twentieth Century West,* edited by Gerald D. Nash and Richard W. Etulain, 257–292.

———. "The Polluted Truckee: A Study in Interstate Water Quality." *Nevada Historical Society Quarterly* 20, no. 3 (Fall 1977): 151–166.

———. "State v. Nation: Federal Reclamation and Water Rights in the Progressive Era." *Pacific Historical Review* (August 1981): 265–282.

———. "The Strange Death of the California-Nevada Compact: A Study in Interstate Water Negotiations." *Pacific Historical Review* (November 1978): 637–658.

———. "Western Nevada's Water Crisis, 1915–1935." *Nevada Historical Society Quarterly* 22, no. 1 (Spring 1979): 3–20.

Rourke, John T. "Congress and the Cold War." *World Affairs* 139, no. 4 (Spring 1977): 260–273.

Rowley, William D. "Francis G. Newlands and the Promises of American Life." *Nevada Historical Society Quarterly* 32, no. 3 (Fall 1989): 169–180.

Salaman, Lester M. "The Presidency and Domestic Policy Formulation." In

Analyzing the Presidency, edited by Robert E. DiClerico, 208–229. Guilford: Dushkin Publishing Group, 1985.

Shafer, Michael. "Mineral Myths." *Foreign Affairs* 47 (Summer 1982): 154–171.

Siehl, George H. *A Brief History of Grazing Fees on Federal Land*. Washington, D.C.: Legislative Reference Service no. NR111, 1969.

Smith, Claude C. "The 1952 Election in Nevada." *Western Political Quarterly* 6, no. 1 (March 1953): 117–120.

———. "The 1954 Election in Nevada." *Western Political Quarterly* 7, no. 4 (December 1954): 614–616.

Smith, Harold T. "Pittman, Creel, and New Deal Politics." *Nevada Historical Society Quarterly* 22, no. 4 (Winter 1979): 254–270.

Steiner, Michael C. "The Significance of Turner's Sectional Thesis." *Western Historical Quarterly* (October 1979): 437–466.

Stoler, Mark A. "World War II Diplomacy in Historical Writing: Prelude to Cold War." In *American Foreign Relations*, edited by Gerald K. Haines and Samuel J. Walker, 187–206.

Strong, Douglas H. "Lake Tahoe Development Concerns." In *Battle Born*, edited by A. Costandina Titus, 45–59.

Titus, A. Costandina. "Senator Howard Cannon and Civil Rights Legislation, 1959–1968." *Nevada Historical Society Quarterly* 4 (Winter 1990): 13–29.

Walker, Samuel J. "Historians and the Cold War." In *American Foreign Relations*, edited by Gerald K. Haines and Samuel J. Walker, 207–236.

Watson, Roderick E. "The Supreme Court's Changed Perspective on Federal-State Water Relations: A Personal Memoir of the New Melones Case." *Journal of the West* 39, no. 3 (July 1990): 28–39.

Wier, Jeanne Elizabeth. "The Mystery of Nevada." In *Rocky Mountain Politics*, edited by Thomas C. Donnelly, 88–114. Albuquerque: University of New Mexico Press, 1940.

Worster, Donald. "New West, True West: Interpreting the Region's History." *Western Historical Quarterly* (April 1987): 141–156.

BOOKS

Abbey, Edward. *Desert Solitaire*. New York: Ballantine Books, 1968.

Abbott, Carl. *The New Urban America: Growth and Politics in Sunbelt Cities*. Chapel Hill: University of North Carolina Press, 1981.

Ackerman, Bruce. *We the People: Foundations*. Cambridge: Belknap Press of the Harvard University Press, 1991.

Agnew, John. *The United States and the World Economy: A Regional Biography*. New York: Cambridge University Press, 1987.

Albright, Horace M. *The Birth of the National Park System: The Founding Years, 1913–1933*. Salt Lake City: Institute of the American West Book, 1985.

Ambrose, Stephen E. *Nixon: The Education of a Politician, 1913–1962*. New York: Simon and Schuster, 1987.

———. *Nixon: The Triumph of a Politician, 1962–1972*. New York: Simon and Schuster, 1987.

Bailey, Stephen Kemp. *Congress in the Seventies*. New York: St. Martin's Press, 1970.

———. *Congress Makes a Law: The Story behind the Employment Act of 1946*. Westport: Greenwood Press, 1950.

Baker, Richard Allan. *Conservation Politics: The Senate Career of Clinton P. Anderson*. Albuquerque: University of New Mexico Press, 1985.

Burt, Robert A. *The Constitution in Conflict*. Cambridge: Belknap Press of the Harvard University Press, 1992.

Caro, Robert A. *The Years of Lyndon Johnson*, vol. 1, *The Path to Power*. New York: Random House, 1981.

———. *The Years of Lyndon Johnson*, vol. 2, *Means of Ascent*. New York: Alfred A. Knopf, 1990.

Chan, Loren B. *Sagebrush Statesman: Tasker L. Oddie of Nevada*. Reno: University of Nevada Press, 1973.

Clark, Joseph S. *The Senate Establishment*. New York: Hill and Wang, 1963.

Clausen, Aage R. *How Congressmen Decide: A Policy Focus*. New York: St. Martin's Press, 1973.

Cronon, William. *Changes in the Land: Indians, Colonists, and Ecology of New England*. New York: Hill and Wang, 1983.

———. *Nature's Metropolis: Chicago and the Great West*. New York: W. W. Norton, 1991.

Current, Richard, T. Harry Williams, Frank Freidel, and Alan Brinkley. *American History—A Survey*. 7th ed. New York: Alfred A. Knopf, 1987.

Dahl, Robert A. *Pluralist Democracy in the United States: Conflict and Consent*. Chicago: Rand McNally, 1967.

DiClerico, Robert E. *The American Presidency*. Englewood Cliffs: Prentice-Hall, 1979.

Diggins, John Patrick. *The Proud Decades: America in War and Peace, 1941–1960*. New York: W. W. Norton, 1988.

Dodd, Lawrence C., and Bruce I. Oppenheimer. *Congress Reconsidered*. New York: Praeger Publishers, 1977.

Dodd, Lawrence C., and Richard L. Schott. *Congress and the Administrative State*. New York: St. Martin's Press, 1970.

Douglas, Paul H. *In the Fullness of Time: The Memoirs of Paul H. Douglas*. New York: Harcourt, Brace, Jovanovich, 1971.

Dunbar, Robert G. *Forging New Rights in Western Waters*. Lincoln: University of Nebraska Press, 1983.

Edwards, Jerome E. *Pat McCarran: Political Boss of Nevada*. Reno: University of Nevada Press, 1982.

Elliott, Russell R. *Nevada's Twentieth-Century Mining Boom: Tonopah, Goldfield, Ely*. Reno: University of Nevada Press, 1966.

——— . *Servant of Power: A Political Biography of Senator William M. Stewart*. Reno: University of Nevada Press, 1983.

Elliott, Russell R., and William D. Rowley. *History of Nevada*. 2d ed. Lincoln: University of Nebraska Press, 1987.

Engel, Ronald J. *Sacred Sands: The Struggle for Community in the Indiana Dunes*. Middletown: Wesleyan University Press, 1983.

Feinberg, Richard E. *The Intemperate Zone: The Third World Challenge to U.S. Foreign Policy*. New York: W. W. Norton, 1983.

Fenno, Richard F., Jr. *Homestyle: House Members in Their Districts*. Glenview: Scott, Foresman, 1978.

——— . *The Making of a Senator: Dan Quayle*. Washington, D.C.: Congressional Quarterly Press, 1989.

Findley, John M. *People of Chance: Gambling in American Society from Jamestown to Las Vegas*. New York: Oxford University Press, 1986.

Foley, Michael. *The New Senate: Liberal Influence on a Conservative Institution, 1959–1972*. New Haven: Yale University Press, 1980.

Foss, Phillip O. *Politics and Grass: The Administration of Grazing on the Public Domain*. Seattle: University of Washington Press, 1960.

Fradkin, Philip L. *A River No More: The Colorado River and the West*. New York: Alfred A. Knopf, 1981.

——— . *Sagebrush Country: Land and the American West*. New York: Alfred A. Knopf, 1989.

Franklin, Kay, and Norma Schaeffer. *Duel for the Dunes: Land Use Conflict on the Shores of Lake Michigan*. Urbana: University of Illinois Press, 1983.

Froman, Lewis A., Jr. *The Congressional Process: Strategies, Rules, and Procedures*. Boston: Little, Brown, Co., 1967.

Gates, Paul W., and Robert W. Swenson. *History of Public Land Law Development*. Washington, D.C.: Zenger Publishing, 1968.

Gilbert, James. *Another Chance: Postwar America, 1945–1985*. Chicago: Dorsey Press, 1986.

Glad, Betty. *Key Pittman: The Tragedy of a Senate Insider*. New York: Columbia University Press, 1986.

Glass, Mary Ellen. *Nevada's Turbulent '50s: Decade of Political and Economic Change*. Reno: University of Nevada Press, 1981.

——— . *Silver and Politics in Nevada, 1892–1902*. Reno: University of Nevada Press, 1969.

Goldman, Eric F. *The Crucial Decade and After: America 1945–1960*. New York: Alfred A. Knopf, 1973.

——— . *The Tragedy of Lyndon Johnson*. New York: Dell Publishing, 1968.

Graebner, Norman A. *Empire on the Pacific: A Study in American Continental Expansion*. Santa Barbara: ABC-CLIO, 1955.

Greenspun, Hank, and Alex Pelle. *Where I Stand: The Record of a Reckless Man*. New York: David McKay, 1966.

Hardeman, D. B., and Donald C. Bacon. *Rayburn: A Biography*. New York: Madison Books, 1987.

Hartzog, George B., Jr. *Battling for the National Parks*. Mt. Kisco: Moyer Bell Limited, 1988.

Hays, Samuel P. *Beauty, Health, and Permanence: Environmental Politics in the United States, 1955–1985*. New York: Cambridge University Press, 1987.

———. *Conservation and the Gospel of Efficiency: The Progressive Conservation Movement, 1890–1920*. Cambridge: Harvard University Press, 1959.

Holcombe, Alan N. *Our More Perfect Union*. Cambridge: Harvard University Press, 1958.

Horn, Stephen. *Unused Power: The Work of the Senate Committee on Appropriations*. Washington, D.C.: Brookings Institution, 1970.

Hulse, James W. *Forty Years in the Wilderness: Impressions of Nevada, 1940–1980*. Reno: University of Nevada Press, 1986.

Hundley, Norris, Jr. *Water and the West: The Colorado River Compact and the Politics of Water in the American West*. Berkeley: University of California Press, 1975.

Ingram, Helen. *Water Politics: Continuity and Change*. Albuquerque: University of New Mexico Press, 1990.

Ise, John. *Our National Park Policy: A Critical History*. Baltimore: Johns Hopkins University Press, 1961.

Israel, Fred L. *Nevada's Key Pittman*. Lincoln: University of Nebraska Press, 1963.

Jackson, Gregory. *Regional Diversity: Growth in the United States, 1960–1990*. Boston: Auburn House Publishing, 1981.

Jensen, Merrill. *Regionalism in America*. Madison: University of Wisconsin Press, 1965.

Jonas, Frank H. *Western Politics*. Salt Lake City: University of Utah Press, 1961.

Jones, Florence Lee, and John F. Cahlan. *Water: A History of Las Vegas*. 2 vols. Las Vegas: Las Vegas Valley Water District, 1975.

Kahrl, William. *Water and Power*. Berkeley: University of California Press, 1982.

Kaiser, Charles. *1968 in America*. New York: Weidenfeld and Nicolson, 1988.

Kerr, Robert S. *Land, Water, and Wood*. New York: Fleet Publishing, 1960.

Knack, Martha C., and Omer C. Stewart. *As Long as the River Shall Run: An Ethnohistory of Pyramid Lake Indian Reservation*. Berkeley: University of California Press, 1984.

Koenig, Louis W. *The American Presidency: A Policy Perspective from Readings and Documents*. Chicago: Nelson-Hall, 1985.

———. *The Chief Executive*. New York: Harcourt, Brace, and World, 1968.

Lawson, Steven F. *Exploring the Lyndon Johnson Years*. Austin: University of Texas Press, 1981.

Leuchtenburg, William E. *In the Shadow of FDR: From Harry Truman to Ronald Reagan*. Ithaca: Cornell University Press, 1983.

Leydet, François. *The Last Redwoods and the Parkland of Redwood Creek*. San Francisco: Sierra Club–Ballantine Books, 1969.

Lillard, Richard. *Desert Challenge: An Interpretation of Nevada*. Lincoln: University of Nebraska Press, 1966.

Limerick, Patricia Nelson. *Desert Passages: Encounters with the American Desert*. Niwot: University Press of Colorado, 1989.

———. *The Legacy of Conquest: The Unbroken Past of the American West*. New York: W. W. Norton, 1987.

Lowitt, Richard. *The New Deal and the West*. Bloomington: Indiana University Press, 1984.

Luckingham, Bradford. *The Urban Southwest: A Profile History of Albuquerque–El Paso–Phoenix–Tucson*. El Paso: Texas Western Press, 1982.

Magdoff, Harry. *The Age of Imperialism: The Economics of U.S. Foreign Policy*. New York: Monthly Review Press, 1969.

Malone, Michael, and Richard Etulain. *The American West: A Twentieth Century History*. Lincoln: University of Nebraska Press, 1989.

Matthews, Donald R. *U.S. Senators and Their World*. Chapel Hill: University of North Carolina Press, 1960.

Maxwell, Neal A. *Regionalism in the United States Senate*. Research Monograph No. 5. Salt Lake City: Institute of Government, University of Utah, 1961.

Mayers, David. *George Kennan and the Dilemmas of U.S. Foreign Policy*. New York: Oxford University Press, 1988.

McConnell, Grant. *Private Power and American Democracy*. New York: Alfred A. Knopf, 1966.

Milner, Clyde A., III, ed. *Major Problems in the History of the American West*. Lexington: D. C. Heath, 1989.

Mitchell, Lee Clark. *Witness to a Vanishing America: The Nineteenth-Century Response*. Princeton: Princeton University Press, 1981.

Moehring, Eugene P. *Resort City in the Sunbelt: Las Vegas, 1930–1970*. Reno: University of Nevada Press, 1989.

Moody, Eric N. *Southern Gentleman of Nevada Politics: Vail M. Pittman*. Reno: University of Nevada Press, 1974.

Morgan, Anne Hodges. *Robert S. Kerr: The Senate Years*. Norman: University of Oklahoma Press, 1977.

Nash, Gerald D. *The American West Transformed: The Impact of the Second World War*. Bloomington: Indiana University Press, 1985.

Nash, Gerald D., and Richard W. Etulain, eds. *The Twentieth Century West: Historical Interpretations*. Albuquerque: University of New Mexico Press, 1989.

Nash, Roderick. *Wilderness and the American Mind*. New Haven: Yale University Press, 1967.

Neustadt, Richard E. *Presidential Power: The Politics of Leadership*. New York: John Wiley and Sons, 1960.

Ognibene, Peter J. *Scoop: The Life and Politics of Henry M. Jackson*. New York: Stein and Day Publishers, 1975.

O'Neill, Tip, and William Novak. *Man of the House: The Life and Political Memoirs of Speaker Tip O'Neill*. New York: Random House, 1987.

Palmer, Tim. *Endangered Rivers and the Conservation Movement.* Berkeley: University of California Press, 1986.

Pastor, Robert A. *Congress and the Politics of U.S. Foreign Economic Policy, 1929–1976.* Berkeley: University of California Press, 1980.

Pepper, Claude Denson, and Hays Gorey. *Pepper: Eyewitness to a Century.* New York: Harcourt Brace Jovanovich, Publishers, 1987.

Pomeroy, Earl. *The Pacific Slope: A History of California, Oregon, Washington, Idaho, Utah, and Nevada.* New York: Alfred A. Knopf, 1966.

Powledge, Fred. *Water: The Nature, Uses, and Future of Our Most Precious and Abused Resource.* New York: Farrar, Straus and Giroux, 1982.

Reedy, George E. *The U.S. Senate.* New York: Mentor, 1986.

Reisner, Marc. *Cadillac Desert: The American West and Its Disappearing Water.* New York: Viking Press, 1986.

Richardson, Elmo. *Dams, Parks, and Politics: Resource Development and Preservation in the Truman-Eisenhower Era.* Lexington: University Press of Kentucky, 1973.

Ripley, Randall B. *Power in the Senate.* New York: St. Martin's Press, 1969.

Rohrbough, Malcolm J. *Aspen: The History of a Silver Mining Town, 1879–1893.* New York: Oxford University Press, 1986.

Rosenthal, Alan. *Toward a Majority Rule in the United States Senate.* New York: McGraw-Hill, 1962.

Rowley, William D. *U.S. Forest Service Grazing and Rangelands: A History.* College Station: Texas A & M University Press, 1985.

Runte, Alfred. *National Parks: The American Experience.* Lincoln: University of Nebraska Press, 1979.

Rusco, Elmer R. *Voting Behavior in Nevada.* Reno: University of Nevada Press, 1966.

Schlesinger, Arthur M., Jr. *The Cycles of American History.* Boston: Houghton Mifflin, 1973.

———. *The Imperial Presidency.* Boston: Houghton Mifflin, 1973.

Smith, Duane A. *Mining America: The Industry and the Environment, 1800–1980.* Lawrence: University Press of Kansas, 1987.

Smith, Hedrick. *The Power Game: How Washington Works.* New York: Ballantine Books, 1988.

Smith, Henry Nash. *The Virgin Land: The American West as Symbol and Myth.* Cambridge: Harvard University Press, 1950.

Sorensen, Theodore C. *Kennedy.* New York: Harper and Row Publishers, 1965.

Stegner, Wallace. *Beyond the Hundredth Meridian: John Wesley Powell and the Opening of the West.* Lincoln: University of Nebraska Press, 1953.

———. *The Uneasy Chair: A Biography of Bernard DeVoto.* New York: Doubleday, 1974.

———, ed. *The Letters of Bernard DeVoto.* New York: Doubleday, 1975.

Strong, Douglas H. *Tahoe: An Environmental History.* Lincoln: University of Nebraska Press, 1984.

Sundquist, James L. *Politics and Policy: The Eisenhower, Kennedy, and Johnson Years.* Washington, D.C.: Brookings Institution, 1968.

Titus, A. Costandina. *Bombs in the Backyard: Atomic Testing and American Politics.* Reno: University of Nevada Press, 1986.

————, ed. *Battle Born: Federal-State Conflict in Nevada during the Twentieth Century.* Dubuque: Kendall Hunt Publishing, 1989.

Townley, John M. *Turn This Water into Gold: The Story of the Newlands Project.* Reno: Nevada Historical Society, 1977.

Udall, Stewart L. *The Quiet Crisis.* New York: Holt, Rinehart and Winston, 1963.

Watson, Denton L. *Lion in the Lobby: Clarence Mitchell, Jr.'s Struggle for the Passage of Civil Rights Laws.* New York: William Morrow, 1990.

Weatherford, Gary D., and F. Lee Brown. *New Courses for the Colorado River: Major Issues for the Next Century.* Albuquerque: University of New Mexico Press, 1986.

White, William S. *Citadel: The Story of the U.S. Senate.* New York: Harper and Brothers Publishers, 1956.

Wild, Peter. *Pioneer Conservationists of Western America.* Missoula: Mountain Press Publishing, 1979.

Wiley, Peter, and Robert Gottlieb. *Empires in the Sun: The Rise of the New American West.* New York: G. P. Putnam's Sons, 1982.

Wirth, Conrad L. *Parks, Politics, and the People.* Norman: University of Oklahoma Press, 1980.

Williams, Michael. *Americans and Their Forests: A Historical Geography.* New York: Cambridge University Press, 1989.

Worster, Donald. *Dust Bowl: The Southern Plains in the 1930s.* New York: Oxford University Press, 1979.

————. *Nature's Economy: A History of Ecological Ideas.* New York: Cambridge University Press, 1977.

————. *Rivers of Empire: Water, Aridity and the Growth of the American West.* New York: Pantheon Books, 1985.

————. *Under Western Skies: Nature and History in the American West.* New York: Oxford University Press, 1992.

————, ed. *The Ends of the Earth: Perspectives on Modern Environmental History.* Cambridge: Cambridge University Press, 1988.

Wyant, William K. *Westward in Eden: The Public Conservation Movement.* Berkeley: University of California Press, 1982.

UNPUBLISHED MANUSCRIPTS

Covill, Bruce, and Beverly Wexler Weinberg. "Alan Bible: Democratic Senator from Nevada." Ralph Nader's Congress Project, Citizens Look at Congress, 1972.

Eadington, William R., ed. "The Evolution of Corporate Gambling in Nevada."

Proceedings of the Fifth National Conference on Gambling and Risk Taking, Reno, 1982.

LEGAL CASES

Anderson et al. v. *Kearney*
Arizona v. *California*
Baker v. *Carr*
Brown v. *Board of Education of Topeka, Kansas*
Brown v. *Georgetta*
California v. *United States*
City of Fresno v. *California*
City of Reno v. *McGowan*
Federal Power Commission v. *Oregon et al.*
Herminghaus v. *Southern California Edison Company*
Ivanhoe Irrigation District v. *MacCracken*
Kansas v. *California*
Pyramid Paiute Tribe of Indians v. *Truckee-Carson Irrigation District*
Reynolds v. *Sims*
State v. *Lincoln County Power District*
U.S. v. *Nevada*
U.S. v. *Orr Water Ditch Co., et al.*
U.S. v. *Rio Grande Dam and Irrigation Company*
Winters v. *United States*

Index

Adams, Eva, 39, 81–83, 84, 119–20
agricultural industry in Nevada, 1, 3
Alaska: acreage protected from
  development, 198; Alan Bible and,
  195–97; development of natural
  resources and, 195, 206; efforts to
  preserve wilderness of, xviii,
  195–98
Alaska National Interest Lands
  Conservation Act of 1980, 197–98
Alaska Native Claims Settlement Act
  (1971), 195
Albright, Horace M., 50
Aldo, Leopold, 99
Allott, Gordon (R-Colo.), 85, 136, 179
American Mining Congress, 102, 180,
  181
Anderson, Clinton P. (D-N.Mex.), 86,
  138, 144; Alan Bible and, 47–49, 96,
  134; Colorado River water allot-
  ments and, 47–49; desalinization
  legislation, 96; environmental
  advocacy of, xviii; progovernment
  activist, 85; public lands for parks
  and recreation, 108, 140; Upper
  Colorado River Storage Project and,
  49–51; Water Resources Planning
  Act of 1965, 130
Andrus, Cecil D., 197
Appropriations Committee (Senate
  Congressional), 77, 85
Arizona: Central Arizona Project
  (CAP), 47, 49, 132, 153; Colorado
  River water allotment of, 35, 37,
  131; conflict with California over
  Colorado River allotment, 131, 132,

153; Gila River water and, 37, 131,
  153; population growth of, 27;
  water rights of, 131, 133
Arizona v. California, 31, 57, 131, 151,
  153, 186; Nevada's interest in, 35–37
Asian markets and U.S. economy, 90
Aspinall, Wayne (D-Colo.), 95, 96,
  104, 136, 179, 184
Assateague Island National Seashore,
  141–42
atomic energy as alternative energy
  source, 181–82

Baring, Walter (D-Nev.): election of,
  72; Great Basin National Park plan,
  102, 103–4, 161–66; LBJ's dislike of,
  117, 154–55, 163; popularity with
  Nevada voters of, 117; reputation
  of, 122, 154; Southern Nevada
  Water Project and, 97, 154–56;
  unpopularity with fellow Democrats, 117, 154, 156, 162–63
Barrett, Frank A. (R-Wyo.), 45, 58
Barrett-D'Ewart bills, 44–45
Basic Magnesium Plant, 18, 21, 24, 35
Bayh, Birch (D-Ind.), 141
Bender, Edwin, 26
Bennett, Wallace F. (D-Utah), 126
Bible, Alan (D-Nev.): accolades and
  honors for, 1, 193; Alaska and, 195–
  97; birth and early life of, 1–4; Bob
  McDonald and, 26, 27, 30–31;
  children of, 27; civil rights issues
  and, 201; Clinton P. Anderson and,
  47–49, 96, 134; college years, 4–5;
  Colorado River Commission and,

Library of Congress

Cataloging-in-Publication Data

Elliott, Gary, 1941–

Senator Alan Bible and the politics of

the new West / Gary E. Elliott.

p.   cm. – (Wilbur S. Shepperson series

in history and humanities ; no. 36)

Includes bibliographical references

and index.

ISBN 0-87417-240-3 (alk. paper)

1. Bible, Alan, 1909–   .   2. Nevada–

Politics and government.

3. Legislators–United States–Biography.

4. United States. Congress.

Senate–Biography.   I. Title.   II. Series.

E840.8B53E45   1994

328.73'092–dc20

[B]   94-9701

                                        CIP

Wilbur S. Shepperson Series in History and Humanities

Temples of Justice: County
Courthouses of Nevada
Ronald M. James

Senator Alan Bible and the Politics of
the New West
Gary E. Elliott